Date Due

~~MAY 8 1987~~			
~~OCT 2 3 1987~~			
~~FEB 1 6 1990~~			
~~NOV 2 3 1990~~			
DEC 1 4 1990			
MAY 0 8 1992			
May 18 '98			
APR 1 5 2008			

Preface

Over the past several years, U.S. business people, concerned with problems of declining productivity in their own industries, have been impressed with Japan's phenomenal success in various sectors of its economy. This has led to a proliferation of literature on why Japanese management styles and practices are conducive to higher productivity, and how U.S. businesses can emulate the Japanese success story.

One aspect of U.S.-Japan trade relations has remained largely unresearched, however—namely, business negotiations between entities from the two countries. A desire to share in the Japanese economic miracle, coupled with Japan's attempts to ease its remaining restrictions on foreign imports and investment, has made more and more U.S. firms eager to enter into cooperative arrangements, such as joint ventures, with Japanese entities. To secure favorable terms in such joint ventures and to benefit fully from them, U.S. business people must become familiar with the Japanese approach to business negotiations. Given the vast sociocultural differences between the two nations, a U.S. businessman could not approach a business negotiation with a Japanese partner with the same attitude and perspective he would assume for a domestic or West European counterpart. The Japanese businessman benefits from being better versed in U.S. business practices than vice versa. This familiarity has been acquired through assiduous study of U.S. industry by the Japanese since World War II. U.S. businessmen, on the other hand, have only recently discovered the Japanese way of doing business.

This book will examine Japanese attitudes and values with respect to business negotiations, and will provide guidelines for practitioners preparing for business negotiations with the Japanese. The information presented has application also for firms in other countries that trade with Japan. Even companies that have had previous business relationships with the Japanese will benefit from the information presented here. This is important in light of the dismal finding of a 1981 survey conducted by the Japanese Ministry of International Trade and Industry—namely, that one out of every seven foreign companies "retrenched and eventually pulled out of Japan" (*Foreign Companies*, 1982, p. 8).

This book should also be of interest to researchers in international business. Little research has been done on factors that could affect the success or failure of international business negotiations. This book does not develop a theoretical model of international business negotiations, but its analysis of the dynamics of the relationships between certain variables may be useful in such a theoretical effort. Such a theoretical model in turn can help improve the quality of future international business negotiations.

The book examines the processes involved in U.S.-Japan business negotiations and the general problems of doing business in Japan. Specifically, the book studies and identifies: (1) the mechanics of such business negotiations; (2) how U.S. companies prepare for the negotiations; (3) the factors that contribute to success or failure of such negotiations; (4) how U.S. companies organize for trade with Japan; and (5) how a select number of U.S. firms from different industries have negotiated with Japanese companies to establish joint-venture arrangements or other forms of economic cooperation. The information provided is based on a survey of 114 U.S. firms that have entered into various types of business negotiations with the Japanese: for import and export agreements; to establish manufacturing facilities in Japan; to establish manufacturing facilities in the United States; for cooperative contracts such as joint ventures, licensing agreements, and commercial and service contractual arrangements; for change of equity position in existing joint ventures; and to terminate joint-venture agreements. In addition, in-depth interviews were conducted with a select sample of U.S. firms on their preparation for such negotiations, their experiences, and the outcomes. These are presented as case studies. They include firms that have entered into negotiations on such matters as joint ventures for the manufacture of mainframe computers, production and distribution of ethical drugs in both the United States and Japan; production of automotive chemicals; the dissolution of a joint venture producing industrial equipment and instruments as a result of irreconcilable differences between the parties; and a joint program to manufacture components used in the production of commercial aircraft.

I would like to thank all those individuals who have given their time willingly and generously toward the successful completion of this project. Because respondents to the questionnaire survey were not required to disclose the names of their organizations, I cannot cite them here by name.

I am particularly grateful to those individuals who gave their time generously by taking part in the interviews to provide a more comprehensive picture of their companies' business negotiations with the Japanese. Specifically, I would like to thank Mr. Thomas Bacher, director, International Business, Boeing Commercial Airplane Company; Mr. Louis J. Casanova, vice-president, joint ventures-Japan, Sperry Univac; Mr. William M. Kinch, executive vice-president-operations, Pacific-Interamerican Division, W.R. Grace and Company; Mr. P. Reed Maurer, vice-president, Merck, Sharp and Dohme International; Mr. Shiro Omata, former president of Nippon Univac Kaisha, Ltd., who is now retired; Mr. Peter Sears, vice-president, corporate development, SmithKline Beckman Corporation; Mr. Gary L. Snable, vice-president and chief operating officer, Fujisawa Smith-Kline Corporation; and Mr. Quincy N. Williams, vice-president, planning and development, Smith Kline & French Laboratories. Interviews for the book were also conducted with Mr. W.F. Corkran, vice-president, international operations, Preformed Line Products Co.; and Mr. Stanley Epstein, president, Anglo American Aviation Company.

I would like to thank the Office of the Dean at The Wharton School and the Wharton Center for International Management Studies for providing partial funding for the research project. I would also like to thank Linda Mitchell, a M.B.A. candidate at The Wharton School, for assisting with statistical analysis of portions of the data.

Last, but not least, I would like to thank my husband, Byron, for his moral support and understanding, and my daughter, Michele, for keeping my spirits up throughout the project.

1 An Overview of U.S.-Japan Trade

Ever since July 8, 1853, when four warships under the command of Commodore Perry of the U.S. Navy steamed into the bay at Uraga, Japan, the issue of trade has been an important subject of contention and hence of bilateral negotiations between the United States and Japan.

In 1853 Commodore Perry hand-delivered a letter from the president of the United States to the governor of Uraga, requesting the opening of certain Japanese ports to U.S. trade. In February 1854 Commodore Perry again entered Edo Bay, accompanied by a larger and more formidable squadron to demonstrate U.S. might and determination (Sadler, 1963). After a month of negotiations, a treaty was signed at Kanagawa with vague provisions for limited trading activities (Gubbins, 1911). Nothing substantive relating to the actual conduct of trade was achieved until a later mission headed by Townsend Harris. Under Harris, the United States finally obtained a treaty of commerce with the Bakufu government, one provision being the opening of Yokohama to trade in 1858. After that trade between the two nations flourished and expanded.

December 1982 represented another milestone in U.S.-Japan trade relations. A high-ranking official of the U.S. government stated that trade between the two countries had become a "political issue" (*Wall Street Journal,* 3 December 1982, p. 36).

What prompted this U.S. official to remark that "for the first time" trade tensions between the two countries have taken on political dimensions? (This statement should actually read "for the first time since 1853.") This chapter examines trade between the United States and Japan since the late 1950s, and discusses the problems and prospects of future trade relations between the two countries. This review will provide a backdrop for discussion of the specific issues of U.S.-Japan business negotiations in subsequent chapters.

Table 1-1 presents statistics on two-way trade between the United States and Japan for selected years prior to 1956 and for the period from 1956 to the first eight months of 1982. Specifically, the statistics for three selected years prior to 1956 were included: 1938, shortly before the outbreak of hostilities between the two countries in World War II; 1948, during the U.S. Occupation; and 1953, the first year after the formal ending of Allied Occupation. Tables 1-2 and 1-3 provide a breakdown of the composition of Japanese exports to and imports from the United States between 1972 and 1980.

1

Table 1-1
Japan's Exports to and Imports from the United States, 1938-1982
(In millions of U.S. dollars)

Year	Japan's Exports to United States	Percentage Change	Japan's Imports from United States	Percentage Change	Balance of Trade in Japan's Favor[a]
1938	124	—	261.1	—	-137.1
1948	65.7	-47.0	441.4	69.1	-375.7
1953	233.9	256.0	757.5	71.6	-523.6
1956	511.4	118.6	1,067.3	40.9	-555.9
1957	606.5	18.59	1,626.2	52.4	-1,019.7
1958	692.5	14.0	1,057.7	-34.9	-365.2
1959	1,051.3	51.8	1,116.1	5.5	-64.8
1960	1,107.0	5.3	1,554.2	39.3	-447.2
1961	1,073.0	-3.1	2,096.7	34.9	-1,023.7
1962	1,410.6	31.5	1,809.1	-13.7	-389.5
1963	1,522.4	7.9	2,078.7	14.9	-556.3
1964	1,866.3	22.6	2,336.9	12.4	-470.6
1965	2,517.1	34.9	2,364.3	1.0	+152.8
1966	3,009.8	19.6	2,658.1	12.4	+351.7
1967	3,048.8	1.3	3,212.7	20.9	-163.9
1968	4,132.7	35.6	3,526.6	9.8	+606.1
1969	5,017.1	21.4	4,094.1	16.1	+923.0
1970	6,015.0	19.9	5,564.3	35.9	+450.7
1971	7,616.0	26.6	4,983.0	-10.5	+2,633
1972	8,847.7	16.2	5,851.6	17.4	+2,996.1
1973	9,448.7	6.8	9,269.5	58.4	+179.1
1974	12,799.5	35.6	12,682.2	36.8	+117.3
1975	11,148.6	-12.8	11,608.0	-8.4	-459.4
1976	15,689.6	40.0	11,809.3	1.7	+3,880.3
1977	19,716.9	26.4	12,396.1	4.9	+7,320.8
1978	24,914.7	26.4	14,790.4	19.3	+10,124.3
1979	26,402.5	6.0	20,430.8	38.1	+5,971.7
1980	31,367.3	18.8	24,408.0	19.5	+6,959.3
1981	37,922.0	20.9	25,057.0	2.7	+12,865.0
1982[b]	24,521.0		16,535.0		7,986.0

Sources: (1938-1971, 1981): Statistics Bureau, International Monetary Fund and International Bank for Reconstruction and Development, *Direction of Trade*; (1972-1980): Japan External Trade Organization (JETRO), 2-5, Toranomon 2-Chome, Minato-Ku, Tokyo 105, Japan, *White Paper on International Trade, Japan, 1972-1981.*

[a]Due to differences in accounting for shipping costs, the trade-balance figures reported by U.S. and Japanese sources may vary.
[b]Only the 8-month trade figures for 1982 were available.

On the basis of two-way trade statistics over the years, several observations could be made about trade between the United States and Japan:

1. Before 1968—except for two years, 1965 and 1966—the United States enjoyed a balance-of-trade surplus over Japan. The specter of a chronic U.S. balance-of-trade deficit with Japan did not emerge until the 1970s. The gloomy picture of huge trade deficits has sometimes been exacerbated by the different standards employed by the two nations in accounting for shipping costs. For example, U.S. sources of information are generally measured on a *fast-along-ship* (f.a.s.) basis for both imports and exports, whereas Japanese sources are generally based on a customs-clearance basis (*White Paper,* 1981). Thus for 1980 Japanese sources recorded a trade surplus of approximately $6.96 billion over the United States, but the latter reported a $9.9-billion trade deficit with Japan—a difference of nearly $2.94 billion. Furthermore, the size of the trade imbalances may have been dramatized through inconsistent accounting practices on the part of the United States. Although U.S. sources of information are generally measured on a f.a.s. basis for both imports and exports, this practice was abandoned in 1981. In that year U.S. sources measured exports on a f.a.s. basis, but imports were calculated on a *cost-insurance-freight* (c.i.f.) basis. Based on these different standards, the balance-of-trade deficit with Japan was calculated at $18.0 billion. Had the usual f.a.s. basis been applied to both imports and exports, the balance-of-trade deficit would have been only $15.8 billion (Lincoln 1982, p. 29).

2. Trade tensions between the two nations may have been exacerbated by an undue focus on import and export statistics, with insufficient attention to those areas in which the United States excels. A study conducted by the U.S.-Japan Trade Study Group, which includes representatives of government agencies and the private sectors of both countries, found that the goods and services sold by subsidiaries of U.S. multinationals in Japan were valued at $20 billion a year, compared with $5 billion in sales of goods and services by subsidiaries of Japanese multinationals in the United States. Furthermore, oil produced by U.S. petroleum firms outside the United States and sold to Japan was not reflected in the merchandise trade statistics. In 1980, for instance, it was estimated that U.S. petroleum companies sold $21 billion worth of crude oil to Japan via third countries (*Wall Street Journal,* 16 February 1983, p. 35). These statistics were nowhere reflected in the balance-of-payments figures. Consequently, the performance of the United States vis-à-vis Japan may not be as dismal as the balance-of-payments figures suggest.

3. The volume of two-way trade between the United States and Japan has grown dramatically since the formal end of the Allied Occupation in April 1952. Except for five years—1958, 1961, 1962, 1971, and 1975—in which Japanese exports to and imports from the United States declined by

Table 1-2
Japan's Exports to the United States
(in millions of U.S. dollars)

	1972	1973	Percentage Change	1974	Percentage Change	1975	Percentage Change	1976	Percentage Change	1977	Percentage Change	1978	Percentage Change	1979	Percentage Change	1980	Percentage Change
Foodstuffs	222	254	14	242	-0.4	165	-32	236	43	200	-15	218	9	119	-45	245	30
Raw materials and fuels	38	51	34	54	6.0	30	-44	30	0	48	60	68	42	137	101	78	-43
Light industrial products	1,580	1,424	-10	1,344	-6	1,161	-14	1,639	41	2,095	28	2,343	12	2,201	-6	2,664	21
Textile products	618	605	-2	523	-14	489	-7	576	18	669	16	710	6	522	-26	593	14
Textile fabrics	235	188	-20	189	0	191	1	237	24	254	7	289	14	229	-21	256	12
Synthetic fabrics	N/A	83	N/A	86	3.6	122	42	156	28	168	8	202	20	152	-25	161	6
Polyester fabrics	N/A	75	N/A	66	-12.0	N/A	N/A	N/A	NA	107	N/A	154	44	N/A	N/A	N/A	N/A
Textile secondary products	337	291	-13	228	-22	204	-11	288	41	325	13	354	9	242	-32	292	21
Clothing	N/A	234	N/A	180	-23	157	-13	218	39	246	13	274	11	165	-40	209	27
Knits and attachment	N/A	97	N/A	82	-16	N/A	N/A	N/A	N/A	109	N/A	101	-7	55	453	70	26
Nonmetallic mineral products	186	206	11	202	-2	180	-11	257	42	337	31	403	20	437	9	464	6
Pottery	116	131	13	131	0	126	-4	177	41	234	32	247	6	239	-4	282	18
Other light industrial products	776	695	-10	653	-6	548	-16	806	47	1,088	35	1,230	13	1,240	.8	1,606	30
Tire and tubes	N/A	65	N/A	67	3	58	-14	118	103	142	20	171	21	173	1	237	37
Wood products and cork products	N/A	79	N/A	69	-12	54	-22	77	43	98	27	88	-11	73	-16	54	26
Musical instruments	N/A	60	N/A	64	7	52	-19	65	25	87	34	103	18	77	-25	83	.8
Heavy industrial and chemical products	6,099	7,585	24	10,898	44	9,508	-13	13,524	42	17,146	27	22,054	28	23,601	7	27,956	19
Chemicals	246	239	-3	574	140	346	-40	413	20	488	18	592	21	653	10	767	18
Organic compounds	N/A	110	N/A	326	198	181	-45	194	8	218	12	263	21	270	2	299	11
Metal products	1,568	1,572	.2	1,572	0	3,240	106	3,618	12	4,155	15	4,397	6	4,850	10	4,950	2
Plastic materials and resins	–	50	–	113	126	N/A	N/A	N/A	N/A	105	N/A	139	33	147	5	170	16
Machinery and equipment	5,100	5,773	13	7,084	23	6,663	-6	10,212	53	13,353	31	17,955	35	19,008	6	23,021	21
General machinery	603	829	37	957	15	953	-0.4	1,273	34	1,776	40	2,695	52	2,993	11	3,369	13
Electrical machinery	1,903	2,053	8	2,089	2	1,992	-5	3,739	88	4,048	8	4,721	17	4,393	-7	5,135	17
Television	298	265	-11	212	-20	256	20	617	141	506	-18	465	-8	232	-50	196	-16
Radio	556	577	3	485	-16	389	-20	700	80	821	17	1,005	23	786	-22	783	-1
Tape recorders	351	567	61	827	46	465	-44	518	-11	822	59	1,144	39	924	-19	1,142	24
Household electrical appliances	N/A	120	N/A	138	15	133	-4	209	57	289	38	324	12	265	-18	290	9
Cameras	N/A	100	N/A	111	11	98	-12	141	44	217	54	356	64	296	-17	339	-4

Table 1-2 *(continued)*

	1972	1973	Percentage Change	1974	Percentage Change	1975	Percentage Change	1976	Percentage Change	1977	Percentage Change	1978	Percentage Change	1979	Percentage Change	1980	Percentage Change
Precision instruments	322	383	19	441	15	494	12	725	47	1,069	47	1,486	39	1,516	2	1,698	12
Watches and clocks	N/A	100	N/A	111	10	N/A	N/A	N/A	N/A	169	N/A	231	37	188	-18	254	35
Railway vehicles	N/A	74	N/A	108	46	77	-29	89	16	186	106	330	77	257	-22	402	156
Telecommunication equipment	N/A	1,166	N/A	1,141	-3	1,168	2	2,496	114	2,285	-.04	2,415	6	1,906	-21	2,035	8
Transportation	2,247	2,508	12	3,544	41	3,239	-7	4,474	38	6,461	44	9,053	40	10,107	12	12,821	27
Buses and trucks	227	289	27	460	59	N/A	N/A	N/A	N/A	N/A	N/A	N/A	N/A	N/A	N/A	N/A	N/A
Motorcycles	589	488	-17	840	72	577	-31	435	-25	650	49	785	21	N/A	N/A	N/A	N/A
Motor vehicles (excluding parts)	N/A	N/A	N/A	N/A	N/A	N/A	N/A	3,530	N/A	4,935	31	7,030	43	8,245	17	10,118	23
Passenger cars (including chassis)	N/A	1,315	N/A	1,713	30	1,918	12	2,890	49	4,123	72	5,737	39	6,722	17	8,271	23
Passenger cars (1,000cc-2,000cc)	N/A	1,090	N/A	1,379	27	N/A	N/A	N/A	N/A	2,724	N/A	3,812	40	4,793	25	6,525	36
Passenger cars (2,000cc)	N/A	222	N/A	333	50	N/A	N/A	N/A	N/A	1,391	N/A	1,911	38	1,927	0.8	1,742	-0.5
Motor-vehicle parts	N/A	120	N/A	169	40	167	-1	231	38	339	47	471	39	472	0.2	484	3
Reexports, commodity and transaction not classified according to kind	98	136	39	262	93	286	9	261	-8	229	-12	232	1	425	83	425	54
Total	8,848	9,449	7	12,800	36	11,149	-13	15,690	40	19,717	25	24,915	27	26,403	6	31,367	19

Source: *White Paper on International Trade Japan*, 1972-1980, Japan External Trade Organization.

Table 1-3
Japan's Imports from the United States
(in millions of U.S. dollars)

	1972	1973	Percentage Change	1974	Percentage Change	1975	Percentage Change	1976	Percentage Change	1977	Percentage Change	1978	Percentage Change	1979	Percentage Change	1980	Percentage Change
Foodstuffs	868	1,979	128	2,606	32	2,489	-5	2,684	8	3,430	28	4,357	27	4,423	2	5,171	17
Meats	N/A	132	N/A	57	-57	155	171	246	58	201	-18	331	65	432	31	432	0
Wheat (excl. feeds)	156	380	144	594	56	544	-8	524	-4	428	-18	481	13	613	27	701	15
Maize (for feeds)	190	501	164	725	45	727	-0.3	676	-7	706	4	844	20	1,019	21	1,470	45
Kauliang (feeds)	114	218	91	325	49	263	-19	256	-2	246	-4	220	-11	259	18	539	108
Wheat (feeds)	N/A	63	N/A	71	13	N/A	N/A	N/A	N/A	120	N/A	105	-13	N/A	N/A	N/A	N/A
Cereals (excellent feeds)	N/A	534	N/A	867	62	698	-20	704	0.8	N/A	N/A	N/A	N/A	N/A	N/A	N/A	N/A
Grains and grain preparations	N/A	20	N/A	N/A	N/A	N/A	N/A	N/A	N/A	1,293	N/A	1,746	35	2,184	25	3,135	44
Fruits	107	132	23	170	28	159	-7	185	16	211	14	300	42	N/A	N/A	N/A	N/A
Raw materials	1,712	2,977	74	3,992	34	3,144	-21	3,150	0.2	3,600	14	4,185	16	6,012	44	6,383	6
Leaf tobacco	N/A	90	N/A	123	37	185	50	217	18	187	-14	254	36	315	24	267	-15
Textile materials	124	217	75	330	52	282	-15	268	-5	357	33	389	9	540	39	601	11
Raw cotton	111	197	78	N/A	N/A	N/A	N/A	N/A	N/A	N/A	N/A	N/A	N/A	509	N/A	583	15
Ginned cotton	N/A	N/A	N/A	N/A	N/A	270	N/A	254	-6	347	36	363	5	501	38	572	15
Soybeans	434	667	54	793	19	854	8	770	-10	1,040	35	1,103	6	1,169	6	1,250	7
Iron and steel scrap	81	302	273	352	16	278	-21	114	-59	80	-31	272	242	385	41	415	8
Wood and lumber	634	1,140	80	1,040	-9	1,061	2	1,170	10.3	1,503	28	1,641	10	1,979	21	1,843	-7
Mineral fuels	570	621	8.9	1,815	192	1,909	5	1,447	-24	2,034	41	1,588	-23	1,357	-15	2,098	55
Coal	470	509	8.	1,635	221	1,687	3	1,218	-28	1,737	43	1,279	-27	1,031	-20	1,581	53
Manufactured products	2,658	3,648	37	4,821	32	4,011	-17	4,466	11	4,889	10	6,431	32	8,506	32	10,607	25
Chemical products	411	716	74	1,017	42	775	-24	1,084	40	1,226	13	1,499	22	2,053	37	2,536	24
General machinery	663	929	41	1,103	19	986	-11	1,051	7	1,160	10	1,261	9	1,617	32	2,031	26
Machinery and equipment	1,499	1,866	25	2,550	37	2,195	-14	2,252	2	2,406	7	3,100	29	4,310	39	5,015	16
Transportation equipment	430	323	-25	649	101	500	-23	358	-28	348	-3	610	75	986	62	1,091	11
Aircraft	373	228	-39	524	129	964	84	232	-76	134	-42	309	131	716	132	890	24
Precision instruments	94.9	127	34	174	37	158	-9	176	12	200	14	253	26	358	42	405	13
Passenger cars	27.9	65	133	84.2	29	N/A	N/A	N/A	N/A	N/A	N/A	N/A	N/A	170	N/A	98	-42
Other products	749	1,070	43	1,253	18	1,041	-17	1,130	9	1,118	-1	1,552	39	2,142	38	3,056	43
Reimports, commodity and transaction not classified according to kind.	43	44	2	48	9	55	15	62	13	78	26	119	53	133	12	149	12
Total	5,852	9,270	58	12,682	37	11,608	-8.4	11,809	2	12,396	5	14,790	19	20,431	38	24,408	20

Source: *White Paper on International Trade Japan*, 1972-1980, Japan External Trade Organization.

several percentage points, the volume of trade between the two countries has expanded steadily, from a mere $233.9 million in Japanese exports in 1953 to a staggering $31.367 billion in 1980. Japanese imports from the United States increased from $757.5 million in 1953 to $24.408 billion in 1980.

4. Over the years the value of Japanese exports of textile products has declined, and that of its exports of automobiles and sophisticated electronic goods and equipments has increased. In 1980 the United States was the largest importer of Japanese products and services, accounting for 24.2 percent of Japan's total exports (*Nippon,* 1982, p. 111). This shift in export patterns has accompanied the changing focus of Japanese industrial policy. Immediately after World War II Japan relied on the export of textiles and other light-industrial products that used a fairly low level of technology. In the 1980s the government's emphasis is on the export of high-quality products with a higher added value per unit that would use Japan's own "original technology" (*White Paper,* 1981, p. 40). In the coming decades Japanese exports will compete more directly with U.S. products both in the United States and elsewhere.

5. Conversely, Japanese imports of manufactured products and machinery from the United States have declined over the years, and its imports of foodstuffs and other raw materials have increased. This reflects Japan's continued dependence on raw materials from abroad to fuel its industrial growth, and the need to import foodstuffs and other agricultural products to feed its 117 million people. The latter area offers prospects for U.S. exporters. In 1980 the United States was the major supplier of products and services to Japan, accounting for 17.3 percent of total Japanese imports for the year (*Nippon,* 1982, p. 111).

Problems and Prospects for U.S.-Japan Trade

This cursory review of trade between the United States and Japan indicates that since the early 1970s Japan has enjoyed a growing balance-of-trade surplus with the United States at a time the latter's economy has been faltering in various sectors. This has led to trade tensions between the two nations, centered around two broad categories. First, the United States alleges that the Japanese market is closed to U.S. imports and foreign investment because of high tariffs and restrictive nontariff barriers. Second, Japan's policy of industrial targeting (government protection and incentives to Japanese exporters and manufacturers) places their U.S. counterparts at a distinct disadvantage in both the Japanese and the world markets.

These allegations will be examined through discussion of the following subjects: (1) Japan's efforts to liberalize trade since the 1950s—what has been accomplished and what remains to be done? (2) nontariff barriers—what are they and how have they hurt U.S. exporters and investors? (3) government protection of Japanese manufacturers and exporters; (4) the role of foreign firms in Japan.

Efforts toward Trade Liberalization

Before 1949 Japan had no unified set of regulations governing its foreign trade and foreign exchange. After Japan's defeat in World War II, with its industries destroyed, the postwar government decided to take immediate action to rebuild the country's industrial infrastructure. To facilitate economic reconstruction, the Japanese government protected domestic industries from excessive foreign competition through legislation regulating imports and foreign investment in Japan. After several years of deliberation, the Foreign Exchange and Foreign Trade Control Law (FEFTCL) was promulgated on December 1, 1949. The government contended that, given the urgency of the task of economic reconstruction, Japan could not afford the luxury of free trade. Rather, circumstances dictated the "use of direct control in the sphere of external trade" (Ozaki 1972, p. 23). Under the provisions of the FEFTCL, all imports were subjected to close government scrutiny, designed to conserve scarce foreign exchange and protect domestic industries from excessive foreign competition. The government decided what categories of items could be imported and in what quantities. Certain industries, such as steel, shipbuilding, automobiles, fertilizer, coal, and power were designated as strategic industries. Computers were added to this list in the 1960s. These were given priority in terms of unrestricted raw-material quotas, duty-free imports, accelerated depreciation, government bank loans, and access to foreign technology and equipment that would foster domestic growth of these industries. Furthermore, the FEFTCL stipulated that foreign direct investment would be permitted only under two circumstances: (1) if the investment had a positive impact on Japan's balance of payments; (2) if it could lead to "self-sufficiency and sound development of the Japanese economy" (Yoshino 1975, p. 275).

The Pre-1965 Phase. Under government protection, the Japanese economy recovered rapidly from the war's devastation. By the mid- to late 1950s Japan sought to become a major actor in the world trade system. To assume this new role, however, Japan had to relax its stringent regulations on foreign trade and foreign exchange. As Nukazawa (1980, p. 40) aptly described it, "trade and capital liberalization served as a kind of initiation fee into the GATT, IMF-OECD club." Consequently, from the mid-1950s on, Japan adopted its first measures designed to liberalize foreign trade and capital investment. In 1955 Japan acquired membership in the General Agreement on Tariffs and Trade (GATT). The tariff system was revised, and extremely high duties on consumer goods were reduced. In April 1962 quota restrictions on imports were replaced by a list of items that could be imported "only with explicit authorization." Previously, the quota restrictions had listed only those items that *were* permitted into the country (Krause and Sekiguichi 1976, p. 454).

At the same time, strict provisions governing foreign investment were gradually relaxed. In 1956 revisions to the Law Concerning Foreign Investment permitted the establishment of so-called yen-based companies. Foreign firms could acquire full ownership of Japanese firms, provided they "forgo the right to repatriate profits and principal" (Krause and Sekiguichi 1976, p. 453). Between 1956 and 1963 a total of 316 such yen-based companies were established. The stipulation preventing the repatriation of profits and principal was repealed in 1963, when Japan accepted Article 8 of the International Monetary Fund (IMF), which prohibited the imposition of restrictions on repatriation of profits and principals of transnational corporations (Yoshino 1975).

In June 1960 the Fundamental Policy to Liberalize Foreign Trade and Exchanges was promulgated. Its provisions liberalized the import of 257 items listed under the Brussels Tariff Nomenclature (BTN). These 257 items represented 44 percent of the value of Japanese imports. At the same time, foreigners were allowed to acquire equity shares in Japanese companies within certain prescribed limits (Krause and Sekiguichi 1976). By the early 1960s the conditions governing foreign direct investment were further relaxed. Foreign investment was allowed if the following two conditions were met: (1) the foreign investment would not seriously disrupt the operations of small domestic enterprises or "impede the domestic development of industrial techniques"; (2) the foreign investment would not negatively affect the existing industrial order in Japan (Yoshino 1975, p. 276). At first foreign equity participation was limited to a maximum of 49 percent. This was later changed to allow for the establishment of 50-50 joint ventures between Japanese and foreign entities. Such ventures, however, were still subject to close government scrutiny and required the approval of the Foreign Investment Council (FIC). Until the mid-1960s the criteria for approving joint-venture applications were deliberately left vague so that the FIC could exercise considerable discretion in excluding foreign investment in industries that were officially open to foreign participation. Nippon Univac Kaisha and Nippon Merck Banyu were two of the earliest joint ventures between U.S. and Japanese entities in the late 1950s.

To demonstrate its willingness to become a responsible partner in the world trade system, Japan also began to regulate its own exports to prevent undue disruptions to its balance-of-payments position with other countries.

In 1957, for instance, Japan imposed voluntary restraints on its export of cotton textiles to the United States. In 1963 Japan stopped providing direct subsidies to its own exporters in the form of tax credits and discontinued its foreign-exchange budget allocations. The government still allowed preferential access to credit for exporting, however. In 1964 Japan became a member of the Organization for Economic Cooperation and Development (OECD), but it was allowed to retain its restrictions on inward capital investment (Krause and Sekiguichi 1976).

The First Round of Liberalization. By the mid-1960s Japan was a wealthy nation, and pressures began to mount from the other industrialized nations for Japan to relax its restrictive foreign-investment policies. In response to these external pressures, the FIC was commissioned to review existing laws and develop recommendations on capital liberalization. In June 1967 the FIC suggested that foreign investment should be allowed as long as it had a positive impact on Japan's balance of payments and did not cause material injury to domestic industries (Krause and Sekiguichi 1976, p. 455). Henceforth, foreign-investment applications would be classified into one of three categories:

1. One-hundred-percent foreign equity ownership would be permitted in seventeen industries, including ordinary steel, motorcycles, hotels, and cement.
2. Fifty-percent foreign equity ownership would be allowed in thirty-three other industries, including pharmaceuticals, cameras, and household appliances.
3. In the remaining industries, foreign investment would be reviewed and permitted on a case-by-case basis (Krause and Sekiguichi 1976; Yoshino 1975).

The FIC report contained specific guidelines for the conduct of foreign firms, including provisions for articles of incorporation of joint ventures in Japan. For example, there must be more Japanese representation on the board of directors of joint ventures in proportion to Japanese equity ownership in the venture (Yoshino 1975, p. 280). The FIC's recommendations on inward direct investment were approved and went into effect on July 1, 1967. In June 1968 the Ministry of International Trade and Industry (MITI) liberalized imports of technology in all but seven manufacturing industries. Among the industries excluded were computers and military defense (Yoshino 1975).

In 1968 the Kennedy Round of multilateral trade negotiations was concluded and implemented. Tariffs on manufactured products of the industrialized nations were decreased by an average of 35 percent. Since many Japanese exports fell into this category, Japan benefited substantially from these tariff reductions. Besides tariff reductions, the Kennedy Round of negotiations resulted in an agreement among the industrialized nations to broaden the list of voluntary export quotas. Consequently, in January 1969 Japan imposed voluntary restraints on its export of steel to the United States. In October 1971 these voluntary restrictions were extended to non-cotton textile exports to the United States.

The Second, Third, Fourth, and Fifth Rounds of Liberalization. By the late 1960s Japan was one of the world's economic giants. In 1967, for instance, Japan became the second largest manufacturer of motor vehicles in the world, outstripping Great Britain in 1966 and West Germany in 1967 (Tung 1982b). By this time Japan had come under increasing attack from the other industrialized nations to open its market further to foreign imports and inward investment. In March 1969 Japan embarked on the second phase of liberalization of inward direct investment. The number of industries that allow 50-percent foreign equity ownership was increased from 33 to 160; and the category of industries permitting 100-percent foreign equity ownership was expanded from 17 to 44 (Yoshino 1975; Krause and Sekiguichi 1976). In June 1971 the government promulgated "eight items of urgent policy measures to avoid yen revaluation." Under this policy provisions were made for reducing tariffs and nontariff barriers, and establishing a General Scheme of Preferential Tariffs for import of manufactured products from the developing nations.

Under the third round of liberalization, in April 1971, the number of industries that allowed 50-percent foreign equity ownership was expanded to 453; the category of industries permitting 100-percent foreign equity ownership was increased to 77. In 1971, for the first time, the Japanese government allowed foreign equity participation in the automobile industry.

In the fourth round of liberalization, which went into effect in August 1971, the list of industries allowing foreign equity participation was further expanded. Only seven industries continued to require review on a case-by-case basis. These seven industries were agriculture, computers, information processing, retailing, oil refining, leather manufacture, and real estate (Yoshino 1975, p. 287). Fifty-percent foreign equity ownership would be automatically allowed in 228 industries (Krause and Sekiguichi 1976).

In May 1972 the Japanese government enacted an International Economic Countermeasures Emergency Program. The program expanded quotas on imports and called for the promotion of orderly exports under the supervision of MITI (Krause and Sekiguichi 1976). In late 1972 measures were adopted to improve international cooperation. These included an overall 20-percent reduction in tariffs on industrial and processed agricultural products, and a 30-percent expansion on existing import quotas. At the same time, the government discontinued its Japan-only pur-chase policy (Krause and Sekiguichi 1976, p. 457).

In the fifth round of liberalization of inward capital investment, which went into effect on May 1, 1973, the list of industries requiring review on a case-by-case basis was further reduced to five: agriculture, oil refining, retailing, mining, and leather manufacture. Except for these industries, 100-percent foreign equity ownership was automatically allowed. The schedule for liberalizing seventeen other industries was accelerated, and the stringent regulations governing acquisition of existing enterprises in Japan were also relaxed. Henceforth foreign acquisition would be permitted as long as the Japanese interests to be acquired did not object (Yoshino 1975; Krause and Sekiguichi 1976).

The Tokyo Round, 1979.   In the Tokyo Round of multilateral trade nego-tiations, which ended in April 1979, Japan agreed to reduce tariffs on 2,600 industrial products by an average of 50 percent by 1987. This compared with a promised reduction of 30 percent by the United States and of 25 per-cent by the European Economic Community (EEC) nations. When im-plemented, the average tariff rate in Japan will be 3 percent globally, com-pared with 4.3 percent for the United States (Abegglen et al. 1980, p. 15). At the Tokyo Round, Japan also agreed to implement an open tender system pertaining to procurements by its government agencies, and to simplify pro-cedures for processing applications for import licenses. Based on the efforts toward liberalization in the Tokyo Round, many close observers believed that Japan "is now as open to industrial imports as any in the world" (Abegglen et al. 1980, p. vii). Although residual import restrictions remain for twenty-two kinds of agricultural and aquatic products (ranging from beef to citrus fruits) and for five categories of industrial products, these statistics compared favorably with those for other industrialized nations. For example, as of February 1979, the United States had residual import restrictions on six categories of industrial products and one agricultural and aquatic product; West Germany had import restrictions on eleven categor-ies of industrial products and three agricultural and aquatic products; and France had residual import restrictions on twenty-seven categories of in-dustrial products and nineteen agricultural and aquatic products (*Japan,* 1980, pp. 2-3).

Post-1979.   Despite impressive efforts toward liberalization, the United States and the EEC countries feel that major obstacles to penetrating the Japanese market still remain. According to the *London Times,* Japan has emerged as the "world's leading industrialized nation" (Johnson 1982, p. 304). This enviable status has made the country the subject of vehement at-tack. The competitiveness of Japanese exports, coupled with the lackluster performance of the U.S. and West European economies have resulted in increasing trade tensions between Japan, on the one hand, and the United States and the EEC countries on the other. In early 1982, for instance, the United States lodged an official complaint against Japan by citing the existence of fifty-one separate tariffs and nontariff barriers, which in their opinion restricted the import of U.S. automobiles, tobacco, semiconductors, and other high-technology products (*Wall Street Journal*, 26 January 1982, p. 1). The issue of nontariff barriers to trade will be addressed later.

To ease these trade tensions, the Japanese have agreed to make concessions in several areas. In late 1982-early 1983 tariffs were reduced on a number of products, most significantly on tobacco products (from 35 to 20 percent) and on chocolate and biscuits (from 30 to 20 percent). The government also promised to strengthen the role of the Office of Trade Ombudsman, which was created in the summer of 1982. This office was established to deal with complaints by foreign investors. At first, foreign investors were disappointed with the inertia of the office. Many claimed it merely rerouted complaints back to the government agency against which the foreign investor had a grievance. One high-ranking U.S. official compared it to a "dead-letter drop" (*Wall Street Journal*, 12 January 1983, p. 33). In addition, the Japanese government promised to expedite plans to assist foreign tobacco manufacturers to gain wider access to the Japanese market and to repeal approximately 40 laws pertaining to import-inspections procedures (*Wall Street Journal*, 12 January 1983, p. 33). In May 1983 the Japanese Parliament enacted legislations designed to ease import procedures for a variety of foreign products ranging from automobiles, medical instruments, pharmaceuticals, and cosmetics to farm machinery (*Wall Street Journal*, 19 May 1983, p. 38). In the sensitive area of automobile exports to the United States, the Japanese government had asked its major manufacturers voluntarily to restrict their exports to 1,680,000 units per annum for the two years ending March 1, 1983. This voluntary restraint was extended for another year, although the United States requested a two-year extension. In 1982 the Japanese government reportedly spent $8 billion to keep the yen from depreciating too sharply against the dollar. A weaker yen, of course, would boost Japanese exports (Seil 1983, p. 3). In February 1983 the United States and Japan concluded a work-program arrangement whereby Japan will, first, seek to eliminate investment and trade barriers in high-technology industries; and, second, ameliorate its industrial-targeting practices, whereby manufacturers in a given industry work in concert to achieve dominance in certain export markets. The work-program arrangement, together with the measures announced in May 1982 to liberalize the import of high-technology products, should give U.S. manufacturers and exporters wider access to the Japanese market (*Wall Street Journal*, 11 February 1983, p. 6).

No provisions, however, were made for easing restrictions on the import of citrus fruits and beef, two items the United States wants to sell to Japan. Although Japan has little arable land, the country's rate of food self-sufficiency is approximately 70 percent (Naitoh 1980, p. 64). Consequently, although Japan is dependent on foreign sources of food supply, increased beef and citrus fruit exports from the United States may never be great enough to affect the balance-of-payments position between the two countries significantly.

During his January 1983 visit to Washington, only two months after his election, Prime Minister Nakasone left the impression that he was a "staunchly pro-American leader" (*Wall Street Journal,* 20 January 1983). Nakasone reaffirmed his intentions "to discharge Japan's responsibilities more than in the past, and in line with Japan's strengthened importance" (*Wall Street Journal,* 19 January 1983, p. 3). As evidence of his commitment to this principle, he cited the example of how he had to intervene personally and "defy powerful members of his party and cabinet" in order to obtain the passage of the tariff reduction on tobacco products (*Wall Street Journal,* 7 January 1983, p. 20). Despite his commitment to freer trade, there are obstacles to Nakasone's efforts to bring about such changes in Japan effectively and rapidly. These obstacles to change will now be discussed.

First, the redistribution of seats in the Japanese Diet after World War II has forced the ruling party to rely on political support from its constituencies in the agricultural communities. Thus by definition the political base of the Liberal Democratic party is agrarian. Any concessions regarding residual import restrictions on the remaining twenty-two agricultural and aquatic products could cause the Liberal Democratic party to lose its mandate in the country. In January 1983 some ten thousand farmers demonstrated in Tokyo to protest possible liberalization in the area of citrus and beef imports, even before the government had made a formal liberalization proposal. Tadashi Kuranari, an influential member of the Liberal Democratic party, compared the magnitude of U.S. agriculture vis-à-vis that of Japan to the parable of the elephant and the ant: "We cannot let the elephant crush the ant—even if Japan becomes very, very poor as a result of other nations' retaliation" (*Wall Street Journal,* 14 January 1983, p. 14). If the Liberal Democratic party, which has traditionally been probusiness, were ousted from power, Japan might well have a government with a stronger "nationalist tilt," one "more prone to protectionism" (Nukazawa 1980, p. 41). Furthermore, removing the residual import restrictions on beef and citrus fruits, which at present are covered by an agreement until March 1984, will not significantly improve the U.S. balance-of-payments position with Japan.

Second, because of cultural factors, the Japanese do not make decisions or changes as rapidly as people do in some other countries. In Japan the most senior officials are often described as "men of inaction" because "an individual's advancement depends largely upon the ability to avoid making mistakes" (Kojima 1980, pp. 54-55). Because of the highly competitive nature of all aspects of Japanese society—from kindergarten to industrial organizations and government agencies—a person cannot afford to do anything that will arouse the hostility or resentment of his or her peers, subordinates, or superiors, or that is out of line with the general sentiments of the times. A Japanese proverb, *Deru kugi utareru,* means literally, "The nail that sticks up is hit with the hammer" (Van Zandt 1970, p. 47). This avoidance of mistakes is reinforced by the practice of consensus decision making. As Nakasone indicated during his trip to Washington in January 1983, he could not always override his party and cabinet members on important matters. He added with a smile that he was elected as a leader, not a dictator (*Wall Street Journal,* 7 January 1983, p. 20). Consequently, Nakasone must proceed cautiously, and things may not progress as rapidly as many Americans would like. The sentiments of the majority of Japanese officials about mounting U.S. pressures are perhaps best represented in the statements made by Shintaro Abe, head of the Ministry of International Trade and Industry, in an interview with *Fortune* magazine. In general, Abe felt that Americans have overestimated the strength of the Japanese economy. He pointed to U.S. superiority in aircraft manufacturing, computers, and petroleum technology, and to the softening of the Japanese economy and export sales. Furthermore, the Japanese economy is heavily dependent on foreign sources of raw materials and foodstuffs, an area Abe called "our fatal fragility" (*Fortune,* 4 October 1982, pp. 91-92).

A third factor compounding the problem of further liberalization is the timing of these moves. The demands on Japan to liberalize its market further come at a time when the country is beset by internal problems. In September 1982 Prime Minister Suzuki declared a "state of emergency" over Japan's public finances. Although many viewed this as a political move preceding the upcoming elections, there are indeed weak spots in the Japanese economy. First, there is a growing government deficit. Second, exports are declining: In 1982 Japan's exports declined for the first time since 1952. Japan's current-account surplus fell from $765 million in July 1982 to $632 million in August. In August 1982 the country had an unadjusted long-term capital deficit of $2.29 billion, compared with a surplus of $253 million in 1981 (*Wall Street Journal,* 30 September 1982, p. 3). A third problem is rising unemployment. In January 1983 the unemployment rate rose to 2.7 percent from 2.4 percent in December 1982. Though low by international standards, this was the highest in the past three decades (*Wall Street Journal,* 9 March 1983, p. 32). According to forecasts by Japan's Economic Planning Agency, the projected growth rate for 1983 is a modest 3.1 percent, and 3.4 percent in 1984 (*Wall Street Journal,* 1 February 1983, p. 38; *U.S. News and World Report,*

7 February 1983, p. 39). These are gloomy forecasts compared with Japan's double-digit growth rates in the 1960s and 1970s. From 1966 to 1970, for instance, the Japanese gross national product (GNP) expanded at an average annual rate of 12.3 percent, the highest growth rate for any industrialized nation for the same period (*Japanese Consumer,* 1980, p. 6). Production capacities in several key industries are at an all-time low. For example, Kawasaki Steel Corporation and most other major steel manufacturers were operating at only 60-percent capacity in 1982 (*Wall Street Journal,* 17 February 1983, p. 34).

A fourth factor affecting Japan's ability to accommodate the demands of U.S. exporters and manufacturers is that many of the nontariff barriers to trade are culture-based. These will be discussed in the section on nontariff barriers.

Nontariff Barriers to Trade

Although Japan has lowered its duties on foreign imports considerably, U.S. manufacturers and exporters complain that insurmountable nontariff restrictions to trade and foreign investment remain. Nontariff barriers refer to government policies and procedures designed to discriminate against foreign imports in favor of domestic manufactures. Nontariff barriers in Japan include stringent import-inspections procedures, the complex distribution system, the problems of acquiring Japanese companies, the difficulty of recruiting capable Japanese employees to work for foreign firms, restrictions imposed on U.S. lawyers who wish to practice in Japan, and—to some—the Japanese language.

An often cited example of stringent import-inspections procedures pertains to shipments of metal baseball bats from the United States. Baseball is a favorite sport in Japan; the market for metal baseball bats is approximately $30 million per annum. The lion's share of this market is occupied by Japanese manufacturers. U.S. producers attribute this to the restrictive practice of requiring special markings on baseball bats imported into Japan. Until 1983 all metal baseball bats sold in the Japanese market (regardless of country of origin) had to bear the S mark. Although Japanese manufacturers also had to comply, U.S. manufacturers complained that this imposed an unnecessary hardship because all baseball bats have to be uncrated and inspected individually for the appropriate markings. After a year of negotiations, the Nakasone government finally agreed to discontinue the practice of requiring the S mark, effective January 6, 1983. Other hurdles remain, however. For example, MITI still has to simplify the procedures for foreign manufacturers to obtain the voluntary SG mark, a prerequisite for the voluntary JSBB mark. Without these marks, it would be difficult to sell foreign-made baseball bats in Japan. MITI hoped to resolve this last hurdle by the end of January 1983. U.S. shipments of baseball bats to Japan under the simplified procedures would begin in the spring of 1984, a full four years after the two governments started talks on the issue. Americans use this incident to illustrate the difficulty of obtaining minor concessions from the Japanese government. The Japanese, on the other hand, cite this as an example of how responsive and accommodating their government is with regard to U.S. complaints (*Wall Street Journal,* 19 January 1983, p. 34).

Other complaints pertain to the import of ethical drugs into Japan. In the past the Ministry of Health and Welfare in Japan (whose role is similar to that of the Food and Drug Administration in the United States) seldom accepted foreign laboratory results demonstrating the efficacy and safety of the drugs for humans. Before being introduced into the Japanese market, these drugs had to undergo rigorous testing in Japanese laboratories. This often delayed the introduction of the product by several years. Furthermore, since the Japanese are shorter on average than Westerners, the dosages must be adjusted accordingly. Toxicology studies must be performed. Even when production begins, the Ministry exercises tight supervision over the manufacturing procedures, and "any side effects, anywhere in Japan" have to be reported immediately to the Ministry (*Foreign Companies,* 1982, p. 25). This issue will be addressed in greater detail in the cases of SmithKline Beckman Corporation and Merck and Company. In May 1983 the Japanese Parliament enacted legislation allowing foreign manufacturers to use results of laboratory tests performed in their home countries for certification purposes (*Wall Street Journal,* 19 May 1983, p. 38).

A second alleged form of nontariff barrier is the complex distribution system in Japanese. The press frequently reports the problems of distributing foreign pharmaceutical and tobacco products in the Japanese market. In Japan, because prescription drugs are sold primarily through hospitals and physicians, the distribution system is more complex than in the United States: there are wholesalers, secondary wholesalers, and healthcare professionals. This complex distribution network applies to domestic pharmaceutical companies as well. To penetrate this system, most large Japanese pharmaceutical companies employ as many as a thousand detailmen, far more than most U.S. companies do (*Foreign Companies,* 1982, p. 25).

The distribution system for tobacco products is just as formidable. In 1982 foreign cigarette sales accounted for only 1.4 percent of the Japanese market. U.S. tobacco manufacturers attribute this to the high tariff and the prohibitions on retail distribution of foreign brands. Previously, under the regulations of the Japan Tobacco and Salt Corporation, only 20,035 of Japan's 247,801 licensed retailers were authorized to sell foreign brands of cigarettes. In 1982 proposals were made to double the number of retail outlets authorized to sell foreign brands from 20,035 to 40,041 by March

31, 1983, with further provisions to allow all retailers to sell imported cigarettes by March 31, 1986 (*Wall Street Journal,* 30 September 1983, p. 30). In
early 1983 the Nakasone government reduced the tariffs on imported tobacco
products from 35 to 20 percent. At the same time the government agreed to
accelerate the plan to liberalize the sale of foreign tobacco products in
Japan. Under the 1983 proposal, all retailers in major cities, except Osaka
and Tokyo, were authorized to carry foreign brands by March 31, 1983
(*Wall Street Journal,* 12 January 1983, p. 33).

Although the Japanese distribution system appears formidable to foreign manufacturers and exporters, it is nearly as perplexing for domestic
manufacturers. In a country of 117 million people, there are 250,000 wholesalers and 1.5 million retailers. As Tsurumi (1981b, p. 296) notes, the
nebulous distribution network in Japan is not "the product of antiforeign
conspiracy but the remnant of the old Japanese society and mercantile practice." Until recently, there were no huge retail outlets like those in the
United States. The purchasing habits of Japanese consumers, together with
the fact that private automobiles are still not as widespread in Japan as in
the United States, necessitate the existence of many small retailers dis-
persed throughout the country. Even today, only large, well-established
Japanese firms have ready access to the complex national distribution
system. For example, in the 1950s the Sony Corporation had a difficult time
convincing wholesalers and retailers to carry its products. In the past decade
several large retail outlets have emerged, which are designed to simplify the
distribution system. These include Daiei, Nichii, Seiyu, and Ito-Yokado. In
1979, for example, the volume of retail business at Daiei reached a staggering $5 billion. Approximately half the items sold at Daiei are nonfood prod-
ucts (Abegglen et al. 1980). U.S. manufacturers could use these outlets to
distribute their products in Japan.

Even critics of the Japanese scene concede that Japan is now more open
to foreign imports than ever before. According to a study conducted by the
U.S.-Japan Study Group, which comprises members from government agencies and private industries in both countries, U.S. presence in the Japanese
economy is more prevalent than is generally realized. This finding was based
on a survey of 195 firms in the wholesale, retail, and service sectors and 126
manufacturing companies in Japan. The study pointed out that U.S. exporters and manufacturers may be "needlessly discouraged by misleading
assumptions" about the problems of entry into the Japanese market (*Wall
Street Journal,* 16 February 1983, p. 35). Many experienced traders believe
that the major obstacle to successful market penetration in Japan is not so
much the existence of nontariff barriers as the highly competitive market.
As Michael Emery, head of DuPont Company in North Asia, notes, the key
to success in Japan is to introduce innovative products suited to Japanese
needs and tastes. Foreign manufacturers must realize that "me-too" prod-

ucts do not sell in Japan. At the same time, according to Emery, Japanese consumers are almost "fanatical" about quality, customer service, and technical support (*Wall Street Journal,* 12 May 1982, p. 1). Any foreign firm that hopes to make significant inroads into the Japanese market must be prepared to compete with its Japanese counterparts on these grounds. As N. Kobayashi, a Harvard-educated professor of business at Japan's prestigious Keio University, aptly points out: "It is useless for the foreign investor to decry the [Japanese system]." Foreign manufacturers may be dissatisfied with the Japanese system, and vice versa; but, a foreign manufacturer who wants to be successful in Japan "must do it the Japanese way. . . . He really has no choice" (Yoshino 1972, p. 123).

For example, although duties on U.S. automobiles have declined steadily over the years, Japanese consumers simply do not find U.S. cars appealing or suitable. The consumer has to pay extra to convert a U.S. auto from left- to righthand drive. As Abe, chief of MITI, notes, Japanese consumers prefer Toyotas and Nissans because they are "well built and suit the Japanese better" (*Fortune,* 4 October 1982, p. 92). In 1982 only 3,562 U.S.-made automobiles were sold in Japan, about half the amount sold in 1981 (*Wall Street Journal,* 10 February 1983, p. 35). Although this sharp decline could be attributed in part to the strength of the U.S. dollar, in fact the overall quality, style, and build of U.S. automobiles may not be suited to Japanese tastes and needs. Similarly, when U.S. manufacturers tried to sell bubble bath in Japan, they met with little success because Japanese baths are designed for soaking, not washing (Plimpton 1982).

A third form of alleged nontariff barrier is the difficulty of acquiring Japanese companies. Although the laws on acquisition of existing Japanese concerns have been liberalized, such acquisitions are still very rare. This phenomenon may be largely culture-based. In Japan an acquisition is not viewed as a mere purchase of capital assets, as in the West. The people who work for a company are also "acquired." This trading of human assets is considered unethical because people who join a company make a commitment to the company for life; in return the owner agrees to assume responsibility for their well-being and livelihood. Thus an acquisition constitutes a reneging on this implicit contract between employer and employees. In the words of Abe, "Even among the Japanese, buying another company outright is considered unethical even though there are no legal restraints" (*Fortune,* 4 October 1982, p. 96). As a result of this deep-rooted cultural tradition, the Japanese government under prime ministers Suzuki and Nakasone has encouraged the establishment of joint-venture operations between Japanese companies and foreign entities, rather than the outright acquisition of Japanese interests by foreign firms.

A fourth alleged nontariff barrier is the difficulty of recruiting capable Japanese employees to work for foreign firms. Although there is still some social stigma associated with working for a foreign firm, this attitude has gradually changed over the years. Increasingly, capable Japanese are willing to work for well-established and prestigious foreign companies such as International Business Machines (IBM) (*Wall Street Journal,* 12 May 1983, p. 1). The lingering reluctance to work for foreign firms is primarily culture-based. Japanese employees want the security of lifetime employment. Furthermore, social status is determined largely by the company for which one works. A Japanese child, when asked about the occupation of his or her father, will not respond, "He is an accountant," or "He is an engineer." Rather, the typical response is, "My father works for Mitsubishi Heavy Industries" or for some other company. Every year the *Nikkei Business* lists and rank-orders the fifty most desirable companies to work for based on a comprehensive survey of the graduates of elite universities. None of these top fifty companies are foreign enterprises (Tung 1984). Only IBM Japan had the distinction of being ranked among the top five companies among science graduates (*Wall Street Journal,* 25 April 1983, p. 30).

A fifth nontariff barrier is the restrictions imposed on U.S. lawyers who wish to practice in Japan. There are two major problems. First, there are excessive delays in obtaining visas. Under a Treaty of Friendship, Commerce, and Navigation concluded in 1953, U.S. attorneys who wished to consult with their clients in Japan would routinely be granted multiple-entry visas of up to 180 days over a four-year period. This practice prevailed until the late 1970s. Since then these procedures have tightened considerably. U.S. lawyers are now commonly requested to sign an agreement that they will not object if it takes three months or more to process such visa applications. Second, most foreign attorneys are prohibited from taking the bar exam in Japan because of their nationality. Since 1955 foreign attorneys who wish to pass the bar exam must fulfill the language competency requirement. Given the uniqueness of the Japanese language, it is estimated that there are now only twenty foreign attorneys, mostly U.S. citizens, who are licensed to practice in Japan.

A number of international law firms have tried to circumvent this hurdle by establishing subsidiary operations that hire both Japanese and foreign attorneys, with the latter serving under the guise of law clerks (Upham 1981, pp. 153-154). The present system allows U.S. attorneys to serve as in-house lawyers to specific U.S. companies on various activities, including negotiations. According to the Japan Federation of Bar Association (JFBA), the dispute centers on whether U.S. attorneys could be permitted to establish law offices in Japan to service an "unspecified and indefinite number of clients" (*Japan Times,* 14 July 1982, p. 2). These restrictive procedures may arise in part from the Japanese attitude toward law and litigation, and also from the fact that Japan has only 15,000 lawyers, or one attorney per 10,250 people, compared with one attorney to every 630 people in the United States (Upham 1981, p. 151).

Nontariff barriers have sometimes been considered to include the Japanese language itself. Because Japanese in its oral form differs from every other language in the world, and in its written form resembles only written Chinese, some foreign investors have considered the language a hindrance to successful entry into the Japanese market. Language, however, cannot legitimately be considered a nontariff barrier. Any manufacturer who wishes to penetrate a foreign country must be willing to study the prevailing customs in that market, including language. In response to complaints about the difficulty of the Japanese language, a Tokyo importer remarked that successful Japanese manufacturers and exporters take great pains to learn English and patiently cultivate market share. U.S. exporters and manufacturers are partly to blame for their lack of success if they spend their time complaining rather than trying to learn (*Wall Street Journal*, 26 January 1982, p. 1).

Despite genuine problems with certain of Japan's nontariff barriers, it is evident that some of these alleged barriers are culture-based and not a "product of antiforeign conspiracy" (Tsurumi 1981b, p. 296). Rather, the key to the Japanese market may lie in a willingness to introduce products that meet the tastes and preferences of the Japanese consumer. As Abegglen aptly notes, Japanese barriers to trade were gradually dismantled over the past fifteen years, so that they are now no more formidable than those of other industrialized nations. In his opinion: "the issue is not a particular trade barrier or two, nor one particular government policy or another. The issue is rather the generally held view that Japan is an ungenerous and narrowly self-seeking participant in world affairs" (Abegglen 1981, p. 30).

Attitudes die hard. Although the Japanese government doubtless could take further steps to open the Japanese market to foreign imports and investments, U.S. manufacturers must also consider the appropriateness of their own products for the Japanese market, and must be willing to learn Japanese customs. These will be the subject discussed in chapter 2.

The Role of the Government

A striking characteristic of the Japanese industrial scene appears to be the common objectives and ethos shared by the government, big business, and labor, giving the impression that the three sectors act in unison. James Abegglen, a long-time observer of the Japanese industrial scene, has called this phenomenon "Japan Incorporated." This characteristic has often been described as a form of "enterprise or entrepreneurial nationalism" whereby business and consumer welfare interests are often subjugated to those of the nation-state. Under this form of economic nationalism, consumers often accept the premise that "what is good for Japanese producers is necessarily good for them, whereas what is good for foreign business in Japan is likely to be bad to their welfare" (Ozaki 1972, pp. 125-126).

Although the notion of Japan Incorporated may be somewhat fallacious—big business may not always comply with the wishes of the government—in general business and government share common objectives of economic development. Both parties trust that the other will have the good sense to carry out this common goal. This meeting of the minds between government and big business is rooted in Japanese culture as well as in economic necessity.

We shall first consider the cultural roots. In the traditional Japanese view, the entire nation is a family. Thus "Japanese statism has its roots in familism." Although the postwar constitution defined sovereignty as residing with individuals, many Japanese continued to adhere to the traditional interpretation. From this perspective, government bureaucrats "exercise authority not in the name of the people but in the name of the House of Japan." Instead of viewing the state as meddling in the affairs of private business and consumers, the people welcomed state involvement, as "the productive activities of 'private business' are very much a part of the business of the whole nation-state" (Haitani 1976, p. 39).

Second, the strong government role was perceived as an economic necessity of the times. When Japan first began its modernization in 1868, the government recognized the need to exercise strong administrative guidance since the country's industrial infrastructure and technology were grossly underdeveloped. To avoid the fate of the Qing Dynasty in China, the Japanese government was determined to play a strong role in the country's industrialization. For example, the government imported and established modern textile mills, which were subsequently transferred to the private sector. As the industrial sector developed, the giant *zaibatsu*s assumed responsibility for formulating policies in the economic sphere. With the dissolution of the zaibatsus after World War II, the burden of charting Japan's economic growth again reverted to the government, primarily to the Ministry of International Trade and Industry (MITI), generally credited as the "chief architect of Japan's postwar industrial policy" (Rapp 1975, p. 39). To rebuild Japan's industrial infrastructure, the government designated certain industries as strategic—including steel, shipbuilding, fertilizer, coal, and energy. In the 1960s computers were added to the list. The government fostered the growth of these strategic industries through various means, such as government bank loans, duty-free imports, unrestricted raw-material quotas, accelerated depreciation, and various subsidies and other tax incentives. Although the government's industrial policy has been revised to conform to changing world conditions over the years, in general it "stressed growth, industry sequencing, export promotion, and rapid plant and equipment investment" (Rapp 1975, p. 42). Johnson, author of *MITI and the Japanese Economic Miracle* (1982, p. 241), went further, describing Japan as operating under a siege mentality in the economic sphere. Although the war effort had formally ended with Japan's defeat in 1945, Japan had "remained on a war footing"; the goal had changed from military conquest and victory to economic development. In such an economic war effort, the private sector must cooperate under government leadership. Consequently, the government has the responsibility to "protect and promote industry for the good of the country" (Haitani 1976, p. 134).

The Japanese government has used several tactics in its successful economic warfare against other industrialized nations, including the formation of three-way committees, or *kondankai,* and the reorganization and rationalization of industry. As Japan liberalized imports and inward capital investment, MITI authorized the formation of *kondankai,* three-way committees comprising representatives of government, business, and finance to "establish and carry out 'promotion standards' for each industry." Johnson notes that the meaning of *kondankai* includes more than its usual English translation, "discussion group or committee." He preferred the translation provided in the fourth edition of *Kenkyusha's New Japanese-English Dictionary,* which equates the term with the Italian word *conversazione,* "a verbal agreement between two or more parties, which suggests something less than a contract but considerably more than a conversation" (Johnson 1982, p. 258). In his opinion this translation more adequately captures the essence of the term, which describes the collaborative arrangements among the government, industry, and the financial sector.

The Japanese government also began the rationalization and reorganization of industry. *Rationalization* refers to the overall improvement of "production technology and facilities"; *reorganization* refers to the procedures designed to bring about greater economies of scale in production through specialization and consolidation, resulting in an optimal number of firms in each industry (Haitani 1976). There are two primary mechanisms for achieving rationalization and reorganization in industry: through mergers and the formation of cartels, and through the granting of various tax incentives, subsidies, and loans to protect domestic industries. In short, MITI "pursues an implicit policy of protection of the existing industries" (Haitani 1976, p. 135), often referred to as *industrial targeting,* which has become the latest buzzword in Washington.

Under the Japanese Antimonopoly Law, the formation of cartels is permitted for certain economic reasons. Cartels are classified into one of four categories: recession, rationalization, special-law, and guidance.

Recession cartels are permitted when there is an oversupply of a certain commodity; the manufacturers in a given industry are then allowed to fix prices and place a ceiling on capacity expansion, thus limiting the volume of production or sales. Between 1964 and 1973 an average of 3.2 recession cartels existed in any one year. In 1966 the number peaked at sixteen. As of the end of March 1974, all recession cartels had been disbanded.

Rationalization cartels are established to raise technical efficiency, improve the quality of products, and reduce costs (Haitani 1976). Under such cartel arrangements, collective activities to restrain the volume of output or price are prohibited. Rather, these cartels are designed to limit product lines or restrict the "competitive use of new technology." Between 1964 and 1973 the number of rationalization cartels per annum ranged from ten to fourteen. Nine remained at the end of March 1974. The formation of both recession and rationalization cartels requires the prior approval of the Fair Trade Commission.

The third category is *special-law cartels,* which are established under special legislation and do not require the approval of the Fair Trade Commission. They are formed with the approval of the respective minister, who has the obligation to notify the Fair Trade Commission. At the end of March 1974 there were 899 special-law cartels.

The final category is *guidance cartels*, which are organized under the leadership of MITI itself. MITI uses them as a mechanism for regulating the volume of output, prices of commodities, and investment programs of specific industries and enterprises. These objectives are generally accomplished through guidelines for increases in price, cutbacks in production, and designation of certain industries and firms as targets for investment. These broad directives provide the basis for consultation among the various firms and trade associations. Although such guidelines are generally incorporated into the decisions made by the big corporations, sometimes the latter could strongly resist the administrative guidance offered by MITI, although they may have to pay a heavy price for noncompliance. In 1965, for instance, when there was an oversupply of steel in Japan, MITI urged the major steel manufacturers to reduce production by at least 10 percent. When Sumitomo Metal Industries refused to comply, MITI retaliated by suspending Sumitomo's license to import coal, a prime ingredient in steel manufacture. After lengthy negotiations, a compromise was finally reached. In 1982 there were 489 cartels in Japan that were designed to protect depressed industries in the country (*Fortune,* 4 October 1982, p. 96).

Under guidance cartels, certain industries are designated as strategic sectors. Resources are funneled into these industries so as to achieve maximum development. In the 1960s development in heavy industry was encouraged. In the 1970s attention was diverted to the knowledge-intensive industries. In the 1980s telecommunication equipments and aerospace/armaments have been targeted as growth industries. Although the Japanese government has denied any intentions to increase Japan's share of telecommunication gears in the world market, the industry has expanded rapidly with government support and encouragement. In 1970, for example, Japan supplied only 5 percent of the world's market in telecommunication gears. By 1980 Japan's market share has doubled. It is estimated that Nippon Electric Corporation (the leading producer of communication gears in Japan), which is now the seventh-largest manufacturer in the world, will most likely displace Europe as the number-two producer in the world in the next several years (*Wall Street Journal,* 13 January 1983, p. 1). After American Telephone & Telegraph (AT&T) allows its local telephone operating companies to procure their equipment from independent suppliers, the Japanese will undoubtedly compete more vigorously in the U.S. market. By 1979 Japan had overtaken both West Germany and Sweden to become the world's major exporter of telephone and telegraph equipment. The United States is now the fourth-largest exporter.

Similarly, Japan's arms industry has expanded rapidly under the protective auspices of the government to become the seventh largest in the world (*Wall Street Journal,* 26 November 1982, p. 1). Expansion in the arms industry is accompanied by Japan's commitment to developing its aerospace and commercial-aircraft industry. The country's sales of aerospace products and equipments have increased 17 percent over the twelve-month period ending March 1982. Sales are projected to increase by another 29 percent in the year ending March 1983, to reach $1.94 billion (*Wall Street Journal,* 18 May 1982, p. 35). The case of Boeing Commercial Airplane Company presented in chapter 5 discusses the formation of a joint program between Boeing and the Civil Transport Development Corporation (a Japanese quasi-government organization) for the production of parts used in the manufacture of 767s, Boeing's latest line of commercial airplanes. Encouraged by the results of the first joint program, Boeing has recently concluded a second agreement to allow greater Japanese participation in the development of its YXX series of planes (*Japan Economic Journal,* 25 January 1983).

This policy of targeting certain industries for domestic development has enabled the designated sectors to expand rapidly. Although industry targeting is intended primarily for domestic development, it also leads to greater export sales and hence to increased competitiveness in the international market. U.S. manufacturers and exporters view these activities as giving their Japanese counterparts an unfair advantage in the world market. In U.S. Trade Representative Brock's talks with Japanese trade ministers in February 1983, the issue of industrial targeting was raised for the first time (*Wall Street Journal,* 8 February 1983, p. 37).

Besides forming cartels for economic reasons, MITI has also encouraged mergers to achieve greater rationalization in a given industry. This policy was vigorously pursued in the 1960s. In 1964, for instance, ninety-seven shipping companies were consolidated into six major groupings. In the same year a new Mitsubishi Heavy Industries was formed as a result of the merger of three former Mitsubishi Heavy Industries firms. In 1965

Prince Motors, Japan's fourth-largest automobile manufacturer, was combined with Nissan Motors, the second-largest automobile manufacture (Haitani 1976).

Although Japanese industries have expanded rapidly under government protection, it may be unfair for U.S. manufacturers and exporters to blame Japan for all the problems plaguing the U.S. economy. In the automobile industry, for instance, shortsightedness kept U.S. manufacturers from developing a compact car. In the steel industry, high wages and lack of capital investment are responsible in large part for the industry's decline. In 1982, for instance, the average U.S. steel worker received $26 per hour in wages and benefits compared with $12 in Japan. In general, the level of fixed investment in U.S. industries declined drastically since the end of World War II. This has resulted in a lag in adapting new technology. An insightful article, "Who Killed the Steel Industry—the Unions, the Company, the Government, or All of the Above?" which appeared in the March 1979 issue of *The Washington Monthly,* reported that Inland Steel, the fifth largest steel manufacturer in the United States, had not installed a new blast furnace since World War II (Kojima 1980, pp. 53-62). Furthermore, Japan's increasing competitiveness among industrialized nations could be attributed in large part to its higher labor-productivity rates over the years. Between 1970 and 1977, for instance, the labor-productivity rate in Japan's automobile industry increased 44 percent, compared with 29 percent for the United States. For the same period, labor productivity in the steel industry increased 27 percent in Japan, compared with 10 percent in the United States. In electrical machinery, labor productivity in Japan increased by an astounding 90 percent between 1970 and 1979, compared with 27 percent in the United States. According to statistics presented in the *Bentsen Report* prepared by the U.S. comptroller-general, labor-productivity increases in the United States were less than one-third of Japan's for the eighteen-year period from 1960 to 1977 (Abegglen et al. 1980, p. 17). These concur with statistics from Japanese sources. For the twenty-year period from 1960 to 1979, the Japanese estimated that their labor productivity increased at an average annual rate of 8.2 percent, approximately 2.5 times higher than that in the United States (*White Paper,* 1981, p. 50).

Besides government protection and higher productivity rates, a host of other factors have contributed to the phenomenal growth in the Japanese economy. First, Japan has a highly skilled and educated labor force. Today the literacy rate in Japan is almost 100 percent, compared with 96 percent in the United States (Cole 1981). Second, the Japanese have a strong work ethic. Although the Labor Standards Law restricts the number of working hours, many employees voluntarily put in extra hours to meet company deadlines. Third, Japan has peaceful labor-management relations, with an absence of prolonged work stoppages. Fourth, the Japanese are frugal. Despite rising per capita income, the Japanese remain among the most frugal people in the world. Throughout the 1960s and the 1970s the savings rate averaged 20-23 percent, compared with 7 percent for the United States, 5 percent for the United Kingdom, and 10 percent for France (Bartholomew 1981a, p. 247). This higher savings rate provided capital for further domestic expansion (Tung 1982c).

The Role of Foreign Firms in Japan

In light of the Japanese government's efforts to liberalize inward capital investment, its removal of tariff and nontariff barriers to trade, and its role in industrial development, it is interesting to examine some statistics on foreign firms in Japan. Here, *foreign participation* refers to non-Japanese firms that own 25 percent or more equity interest in companies incorporated in Japan.

The foreign firms that established operations in Japan in the late 1950s and early 1960s were mostly the giant multinationals. Since the liberalization of inward capital investment in the late 1960s and early 1970s, more smaller firms have entered the Japanese market. For example, between 1973 and 1979 more than half the foreign firms that began operations in Japan were capitalized at less than 30 million yen ($133,000 at the conversion rate at that time). This represented a substantial increase over the previous two decades. Prior to 1967, for instance, less than one-quarter of the foreign firms in Japan were capitalized at 30 million yen or less (*Foreign Companies*, 1982, p. 4). Although smaller foreign firms have entered the Japanese market, the giant multinationals still account for the lion's share of sales by non-Japanese companies in Japan. In 1979, for instance, the giant multinationals listed in *Fortune's* top 200 U.S. firms and top 100 non-U.S. enterprises accounted for 82.6 percent of total sales by foreign companies in Japan (*Foreign Companies*, 1982, p. 6).

With the liberalization of inward capital investment, more foreign firms were encouraged to establish operations in Japan. In 1979 the average sales for 155 foreign firms with capitalization of 1 billion yen ($4.4 million) were 74 billion yen ($328 million), compared with average sales of 352 billion yen ($1.56 billion) for the major 521 Japanese corporations. The number of foreign firms starting operations in Japan peaked in 1972 and 1973. Then the number of new starts declined, to approximately 260-270 per annum, until 1977. In fiscal 1978 the pace of foreign investment increased again, reaching 337 new starts in 1980. A number of factors have contributed to this resurgence: (1) the liberalization of the late 1970s, which provided a more favorable investment climate; (2) the growing strength of the Japanese economy; and (3) the increased value of the yen (*Foreign Companies*, 1982, p. 8).

Since 1967 MITI has conducted annual surveys of the performance of foreign firms in Japan. The 1977-1978 survey included 1,260 foreign firms, accounting for 90.2 percent of total foreign equity investment in Japan. For that year U.S. firms made up more than half of the foreign investment in Japan (50.4 percent), compared with 30.7 percent for all of Europe (*Keys to Success,* 1980). According to statistics compiled by the U.S. Department of Commerce, the net book value of U.S. foreign direct investment in Japan increased 14.8 percent in 1979, to a total of $197.2 billion (*Yearbook of U.S.-Japan Economic Relations in 1980,* p. 66). This lends support to the findings by the U.S.-Japan Study Group in early 1983 that the U.S. presence in the Japanese market may be greater than generally assumed. Although the United States still accounts for a substantial share of the total foreign equity investment in Japan, European companies have expanded more rapidly than their U.S. counterparts. For example, between 1975 and 1979 the number of European firms that established subsidiary operations in Japan increased from 30 to 41.2 percent, while the percentage of U.S. equity participation has declined. In 1979 the total sales of foreign firms amounted to 14 trillion yen ($62.1 billion), representing 2 percent of total corporate sales in Japan (*Foreign Companies,* 1982, pp. 5-7).

In the same MITI study two trends appeared to be emerging. First, the number of foreign wholly owned subsidiaries or firms with greater than 50-percent foreign equity increased in fiscal 1978. This may reflect increasing efforts by the Japanese government to liberalize inward capital investment. Second, more foreign firms have entered the commercial sector as opposed to manufacturing activities. The percentage of new foreign operations in the commercial sector increased from 43.5 in 1973 to 53.4 in 1979 (*Foreign Companies,* 1982, p. 8; *Keys to Success,* 1980, p. 29ff.).

It has been estimated that one out of every seven foreign firms eventually fails and divests from the Japanese market. Between 1975 and 1977, 169 foreign firms divested from Japan. The rate has declined slightly since then. Between 1978 and 1980 only 134 foreign firms withdrew from the Japanese market. Although specific statistics were not available, it was estimated that for those enterprises that pulled out of the Japanese market in 1980, for instance, the average firm had been in Japan for eight or more years (*Foreign Companies,* 1982, p. 8).

Prospects for Cooperation

Although trade tensions between the United States and Japan reached an unprecedented high in 1982, there are signs that they may be abating for now. As was discussed earlier, the Japanese government has further liberalized trade and inward capital investment, to the point where many observers agree that the existing barriers to trade in Japan are no more formidable than those of any other industrialized nation. Second, when Nakasone became prime minister in late 1982, he demonstrated a greater willingness than had any of his predecessors in accommodating U.S. interests. Nakasone has been described as a "self-styled bold leader" who is prepared to undertake any measures necessary to maintain "economic peace" with the United States and the other European Economic Community (EEC) nations (*Wall Street Journal,* 14 January 1983, p. 14). After Nakasone's first official visit to Washington in January 1983, U.S. President Reagan announced that "first significant steps" toward the resolution of trade disputes had been made (*Wall Street Journal,* 20 January 1983, p. 3). This increased willingness is manifested in at least three areas: (1) in lower tariffs and further removal of nontariff barriers to trade; (2) in the promotion of cooperative efforts between industrial concerns from the two nations; and (3) in military defense.

Attempts to lower tariffs and remove nontariff barriers were discussed in the previous section. As for the promotion of joint cooperative efforts in various industries, the overall climate appears to be more supportive of collaborative agreements between U.S. and Japanese entities. The agreement signed between General Motors and Toyota in mid-February 1983, to establish a 50-50 joint venture for the manufacture of compact cars in Fremont, California, is an indication in this direction. U.S. Trade Representative William Brock lauded the agreement as an indication that the Japanese are "finally doing what we've been asking" (*Wall Street Journal,* 16 February 1983, p. 28). About the same time, the world's largest manufacturer of computers, IBM, concluded a memorandum of agreement to discuss a possible joint venture with Japan's Matsushita Electric Industrial Company to manufacture low-cost data-processing products (*Wall Street Journal,* 17 February 1983, p. 2). This agreement was signed at a time when relations between U.S. and Japanese electronic manufacturers were strained because of the so-called Japanscam scandal, in which several employees of Mitsubishi Electric Corporation and Hitachi Electric Corporation (two of the largest electronic firms in Japan) were charged with stealing IBM secrets.

Such joint ventures, will help promote better relations between industrial concerns from the two countries. Nevertheless, objections to the formation of such joint ventures have been raised from several quarters. For example, with respect to the General Motors-Toyota joint venture, Lee Iacocca, chairman of the board of Chrysler (the third-largest auto manufacturer in the United States), denounced the agreement as "fundamentally bad" because the cars to be produced by the joint venture will compete directly with models now built by other U.S. manufacturers, such as General Motors' own Chevette and Ford's Escort. Others decried the pact because they believed that Toyota has more to gain from such a joint venture than does General Motors. Such critics point to major gains for Toyota, such as minimal risk and lessening of "hostile sentiments." Still others have ascribed sinister motives to Toyota's decision to enter into the joint-venture arrangement. As one market researcher described it, by agreeing to the joint venture, General Motors is conceding that the company has to seek assistance from Toyota to build small cars. This will give Toyota a "halo effect" in the market (*Wall Street Journal,* 15 February 1983, p. 3; 16 February 1983, p. 28). These criticisms aside, the conclusion of the joint-venture agreement between General Motors and Toyota does point to a fundamental reversal in strategies between the two automobile giants from an adversarial position to one of collaboration and cooperation. Such changes will tend to lessen animosity between the two countries and strengthen the economic bonds between them.

In the area of military defense, for some time now the U.S. government has protested against Japan's reluctance to assume greater responsibility for the military defense of Southeast Asia. According to statistics compiled by the International Institute for Strategic Studies (IISS), it was estimated that the military-defense budget for the United States accounted for a full 6.1 percent of the country's GNP in 1981. This compared with a meager outlay by the Japanese, whose military budget accounted for only 0.9 percent of the country's GNP, lower than that of any NATO nation. It should be noted, however, that Japan is not a member of NATO (*Wall Street Journal,* 1 December 1982, p. 26).

This meant that Japan could allocate more of its GNP to other types of industrial production, which in turn meant more exports and increased competitiveness in the world market, thus posing greater hardship for the U.S. balance-of-payments position. The United States has accused the Japanese of dragging their feet on the issue. The Japanese, for their part, allude to the difficulties of increasing military spending because of general antimilitarist sentiments since the bombing of Hiroshima and Nagasaki, the suspicion harbored by Japan's Asian neighbors of any apparent resurgence of Japanese militarism, and the softening of the Japanese economy. At his first news conference after taking office as prime minister, Nakasone, formerly head of the Japan Defense Agency, conceded that Japan's defense efforts "have not been adequate," and promised to address the problem through increasing defense spending and expanding the sea lanes of communication and skies (SLOCs) (*Wall Street Journal,* 1 December 1982, p. 26). For example, in 1981 Japan agreed to expand the SLOCs above it out to 1,000 miles. For the fiscal year beginning April 1, 1983, Japan plans to boost its defense budget by 6.5 percent, a full percentage point below U.S. expectations but well above the 5.1-percent increase originally designated by the Ministry of Finance. Though disappointed with the actual amount, the United States acknowledges that this increased expenditure represents an "important step in the direction of meaningful self-defense capability" (*Wall Street Journal,* 31 December 1982, p. 9).

Increased defense spending may lessen the burden borne by the United States, but it may also have serious political and economic repercussions. Although antimilitarist sentiments are still strong in Japan, a militarily strong Japanese Empire might again harbor expansionist ambitions in Asia. Economically, increased defense spending will strengthen the military and arms industry in Japan. As pointed out previously, Japan is at present the world's seventh-largest arms producer. Charles Mraz, McDonnell-Douglas's representative in Japan, noted that, given Japan's technical capabilities, Japanese-made tanks and fighters may come to dominate the world market just as its cameras and televisions do.

Even if Japan does not become an international arms merchant, increased defense spending could help it become a major manufacturer of commercial aircraft, one of the last strongholds of U.S. industry. The Japanese claim that their technology in this area is ten years behind that of Europe and fifteen to twenty years behind that of the United States, but their potential challenge must not be underestimated: The Japanese made similar statements about their automobile industry in the 1960s. In only two decades Japan became the world's largest auto manufacturer. A major difference between the auto industry and the aircraft industry is that in the latter the Japanese government has encouraged joint-development programs with foreign firms. The case of the Boeing Commercial Airplane Company is an instance of this. In March 1983 a $2-billion consortium was formed among seven U.S., European, and Japanese firms to build jet engines (*Wall Street Journal,* 9 March 1983, p. 6). Even with this developmental strategy, products manufactured by the joint-development programs may ultimately erode the U.S. share of international market (*Wall Street Journal,* 18 May 1982, p. 35; 26 January 1983, p. 1).

Besides joint development in commercial-aircraft production, the United States and Japan have agreed to engage in other joint research activities. In late 1982 an agreement was reached for providing assistance to high-technology firms of either country. Reciprocal arrangements would permit tax incentives and government-sponsored research programs now available to domestic firms to be extended to the other country's foreign subsidiary firms. If implemented, this would enable Japanese subsidiaries of U.S. multinationals to participate in the Japanese government-funded program to build a so-called fifth-generation computer with artificial intelligence. In January 1983 Japan lifted its restrictions to permit transfers of purely military technology to the United States. While this may not have any significant short-run impact, but it could have important ramifications in the future (*Wall Street Journal,* 17 January 1983, p. 26).

The Japanese government under Nakasone has demonstrated an increased willingness to cooperate with U.S. interests in various sectors and to accommodate U.S. complaints. Perhaps there is some truth beyond mere political rhetoric in Reagan's statement at the end of Nakasone's official visit to Washington in January 1983, in which Reagan described the relationship between the United States and Japan as a "happy marriage," albeit periodically marred by disputes (*Wall Street Journal,* 18 January 1983). The Japanese foreign minister declared that he had always been optimistic about U.S.-Japan relations "because we cannot fail—we're both too big" (*Wall Street Journal,* 14 January 1983, p. 14). Perhaps the political and economic destinies of the two nations are so closely intertwined that both have too much to lose in an adversarial relationship. Rather than emphasizing discord and friction between the two nations, the United States and Japan should focus on areas of common interest and seek joint economic development.

2 Adapting to the Japanese Way

In chapter 1 it was noted that Japan has lowered import duties and liberalized inward capital investment to the point where its present tariff barriers to trade are no more formidable than those of any other advanced industrialized nation. The remaining nontariff barriers to trade have been eased under the Nakasone administration. One major obstacle to the removal of these remaining barriers is that many such restrictions are deeply ingrained in Japanese society. They do not represent xenophobia on the part of the Japanese government, but may be viewed as an integral part of doing business in Japan. As Kobayashi cautioned, a foreign investor who hopes to make inroads into the Japanese market "must do it the Japanese way. . . . He really has no choice" (Yoshino 1972, p. 123). A study published by the U.S.-Japan Study Group found that U.S. presence in the Japanese economy may be more prevalent than is generally thought (*Wall Street Journal*, 16 February 1983, p. 35). Those foreign firms that have successfully established a foothold in Japan have demonstrated a genuine willingness to adapt to Japanese customs. This is not to minimize the importance of product line to successful penetration of the Japanese market. Given the competitiveness of Japanese manufacturers and consumers' obsession with quality and service, a foreign firm will not succeed if the products it introduces into the Japanese market are not somehow unique, or if they do not meet the exacting standards of the Japanese clients. An outstanding product, however, must be accompanied by an ability to adapt to the Japanese way of doing business. Product characteristic will not be discussed in this book. Rather, the emphasis will be on the unique attributes of the Japanese system as they pertain to the operations of foreign firms. This chapter will examine the "Japanese way"—what it is and how it affects the operations of a firm.

A firm that wishes to operate successfully in Japan must adapt to several unique characteristics of the Japanese environment: (1) the distribution system; (2) the recruitment of employees and personnel policies, including the paternalistic relation between employer and employee and the familial obligations emanating from it; (3) the role of the Japanese government as it affects the foreign firm; (4) the role of litigation in Japanese society; and (5) cultural characteristics that affect management styles, employee and consumer attitudes, and the overall operations of the company. Each of these characteristics will be examined in some detail in this chapter.

The Distribution System

As noted earlier, Japan's complex distribution system has often been cited as a nontariff barrier to trade. The complexities of the distribution system, however, are not the result of a xenophobic conspiracy. Rather, this system is a "remnant of the old Japanese society and mercantile practice"; domestic industries also must operate within the constraints of this framework (Tsurumi 1981b, p. 296). Because of the size and experience of the well-established domestic firms, however, they are better able to deal with the system. The small or newly established Japanese firm may find the distribution system as formidable as does the neophyte foreign firm. This section will examine the characteristics of the Japanese distribution system and why they pose a barrier to marketing products in Japan.

Characteristics of the Distribution System

One of the principal characteristics of the Japanese distribution system is the "high degree of fragmentation and specialization" with respect to end sales (Ratcliffe 1975, p. 101). According to a 1979 Japanese government survey, 77 percent of total retail sales went through neighborhood retail outlets rather than department stores and chain stores. The number of retailers in Japan is staggering in relation to the size of its economy. In 1980, for instance, the GNP and population in Japan was slightly under one-half those of the United States. The number of retail stores, however, was comparable. In 1979 there were 1.67 million retail stores in Japan, compared with 1.86 million in the United States. There are two primary reasons for the large number of retail outlets in Japan: First, the average Japanese housewife shops daily because of a preference for fresh food, the smaller size of home refrigerators, and the fact that fewer households in Japan than in the United States own a family car. Second, most shoppers enjoy the convenience and services provided by the neighborhood retail stores, which offer home deliveries and provide a meeting place where neighbors can socialize (*Planning for Distribution*, 1982).

A second distinguishing feature of the Japanese distribution system is the existence of several intermediary layers between the manufacturer and the end user. Besides the large number of retail units in Japan, there are several added layers in the distribution system. In 1979, for example, the ratio of all wholesale outlets to retailers was 3.7:1, compared with 1.7:1 in the United States. Most of these retail and wholesale operations are relatively small. In 1979 approximately 96 percent of the retailers and 75 percent of the wholesalers employed fewer than ten people. There are several reasons for the large number of intermediary layers. The first is financing.

Since most retailers have limited access to capital, sales are generally made on a consignment basis with credits extending to several months. Second, storage facilities are limited. Because most retail outlets are small, wholesalers generally have to provide storage facilities for inventories. Third, there is the phenomenon of detailing. Wholesalers in Japan are expected to maintain close, friendly relations with the retailers through periodic visits to the latter to assist with display, advertising, feedback, and other matters relating to product sales.

Implications for Foreign Firms

The large number of retail outlets in Japan and the existence of several intermediary layers in the distribution system create greater problems of adjustment for a foreign manufacturer or exporter who is used to dealing with a smaller number of retailers and wholesale outlets. These problems, however, are by no means insurmountable.

First, the length of the distribution channel varies according to industry. In general the length is determined by the size of the manufacturer and of the retailers. (*Size* is defined here in terms of volume of sales and market share.) The length of the distribution channel is in turn related to the degree of concentration in distribution. The extent of concentration in distribution varies according to industry along a continuum. At the high-concentration end of the continuum there is little need for assembly of the items made by various manufacturers. Products in this category include automobiles, musical instruments, and electrical appliances. In this category the manufacturer generally plays the major role in distribution.

In the second category the manufacturer takes some initiative. Products included in this category are film, cosmetics, detergents, and cameras. In the third category the wholesaler takes the initiative. Products included in this category are mayonnaise, butter, cheese, seasonings, chewing gum, chocolate, whisky, toothpaste, and over-the-counter drugs.

The fourth category of products requires both the wholesaler and retailer to take the initiative. Products include furniture, men's and women's apparel, eyeglasses, and shoes. At the bottom of the continuum distribution is highly decentralized. Products included in this category are local food supplies and miscellaneous household items (*Planning for Distribution*, 1982, pp. 22-23).

There are, of course, exceptions to each category. For instance, Levi Strauss (which is in the apparel industry) sells directly to the chain stores and boutiques. Because most Japanese stores are small, however, there is usually insufficient space for storage of inventory. Consequently, Levi Strauss must make weekly deliveries of jeans to the stores, compared with monthly deliveries in the United States (*Foreign Companies*, 1982, p. 44).

Second, there have been trends toward greater concentration in the past several years. As pointed out in the previous chapter, a number of large retail outlets have been established in the past decade, such as Daiei, Nichii, Seiyu, and Ito-Yokado. Although small retailers still controlled 77.4 percent of the retail business in 1979, their share had declined from 79.7 percent in 1976 and 80.6 percent in 1974. Besides the establishment of large retail outlets, many of the small retail units are now organized into a franchise system of convenience stores (*Planning for Distribution*, 1982). Greater concentration in distribution will tend to disentangle the maze of marketing products in Japan.

Besides the large retail outlets, general trading companies and other well-established firms in the industry could assist the foreign manufacturer. In 1979, for instance, 66.8 percent of imports into Japan were handled by the general trading companies (*Role of Trading Companies*, 1982, p. 6). Foreign manufacturers that have used the existing wholesale facilities rather than establishing their own distribution networks include Nestlé, whose instant coffee is sold through 100,000 or more stores, and United Fruit, whose bananas are sold through 66,000 stores (Ratcliffe 1975, pp. 107, 117).

Besides using the services of the Japanese general trading companies, U.S. manufacturers have two other alternatives. First, foreign manufacturers in various industries could join together to form their own trading companies. Since the passage of the U.S. Export Trading Act in October 1982, U.S. firms have been permitted to form joint ventures for the purpose of selling goods in foreign markets without violating antitrust laws in the United States. This would help U.S. manufacturers combine resources to present a more formidable challenge in the Japanese market. Second, a number of Japanese manufacturers have offered to market complementary lines of foreign products, referred to as *tie-ups* with Japanese manufacturers. For example, Sony markets a more specialized line of products than Matsushita does. Consequently, Sony is less aggressive than Matsushita in establishing chain stores around Japan. To correct the situation, Sony has offered to import and market U.S. products that complement its own product line. A tie-up of this nature represents an opportunity for foreign manufacturers because using Sony's existing network is definitely more economical than establishing their own distribution systems (Ratcliffe 1975). The Japan External Trade Organization (JETRO) has offered some guidelines on screening prospective candidates for possible tie-ups. These procedures include an evaluation of the distribution capabilities of the tie-up company—the number and types of outlets and the size of its detail force; its compatibility with one's own product lines; an assessment of the sales volume; and an evaluation of the tie-up company's past performance. JETRO cautions foreign manufacturers about timing press releases to the news media about such tie-ups, warning that these should not be publicized before the prospective candidate is "virtually decided." Otherwise, publicity could lead to misunderstanding and complicate the negotiations (*Planning for Distribution*, 1982, p. 57). In general, Japanese firms are very sensitive about press releases. This issue will be discussed in greater detail in chapter 4.

For U.S. manufacturers and exporters that choose to establish their own distribution networks in Japan, the following three conditions must be met. First, the U.S. manufacturer must be prepared to invest time, money, and sufficient resources to developing a network extensive enough to market its products effectively. Such costs could be prohibitive. The firm should engage in a feasibility study to determine whether the benefits of developing its own distribution network would far outweigh the cost.

Second, the U.S. manufacturer must understand and adapt to the differences in advertising in Japan. In Japan, in-channel promotions targeted at wholesalers and retailers are often used in conjunction with media advertising. Such promotions include margins, rebates, assistance to retailers, and in-store promotion. In general, the margin for the primary wholesaler is approximately 15 percent of the retail price, and 10 percent for the secondary wholesaler (*Planning for Distribution*, 1982, pp. 24-25). Rebates are similar to those given in the United States, ranging from 3 to 6 percent. In Japan, antitrust legislation does not restrict the levels of rebates that can be granted, although other aspects of pricing are subject to regulations (*Sales Promotion*, 1981, pp. 6-7).

Media advertising in Japan is similar to that in the West. Total expenditures on media advertising in Japan doubled over a five-year period to reach $9.6 billion in 1981. According to a survey conducted by *Advertising Age*, the largest promotional agency in Japan ranked highest in the world in terms of total volume of advertising fees (*Sales Promotion*, 1981, pp. 11, 27).

A third prerequisite to successful establishment of one's own distribution system involves the careful selection of distributors and agents, and/or employment of competent Japanese personnel. The president of Emerson Japan emphatically stated that this latter factor was crucial to the success of his firm. To ensure good service, Emerson Japan offers a generous incentive program to its distributors, including high commissions, free trips to the United States, and so on (*Keys to Success*, 1981). Employment of Japanese nationals will be discussed in the next section.

Recruitment and Personnel Policies

Those foreign manufacturers that choose to establish operations, either on a wholly owned or a joint-venture basis, must be familiar with employment and personnel practices in Japan, which are very different from those in the

United States. This section examines the distinguishing characteristics of the Japanese recruitment system and personnel policies, as they bear on the operations of the foreign firm. These are: (1) the system of lifetime employment, (2) the loyalty of employees, (3) the company's concern for all aspects of the employee's welfare, and (4) the general reluctance to work for foreign firms. Each of these will be discussed in some detail.

The System of Lifetime Employment

The practice of lifetime employment has no legal basis. Rather, it is a moral or psychological contract entered into between employer and employee at the time of recruitment, usually immediately after graduation from college. This psychological contract is generally extended until the mandatory retirement age of 55 (Ouchi 1981). Approximately one-third of Japan's labor force is covered by this system of lifetime employment (Cole 1981). This protection, however, is usually provided by large, well-established Japanese companies only to career staff—generally male college graduates.

The system of lifetime employment makes it difficult for foreign firms to recruit capable Japanese employees. Since most career employees of major Japanese firms are hired on graduation from college, the company invests considerable time, money, and resources in educating and training them. Consequently, promotion is invariably from within the ranks of the firm. Therefore, a person who changes jobs over the course of his career will likely give up all seniority and have to start over in a new organization (*Japanese Corporate Personnel Management*, 1982). Understandably, most employees are reluctant to follow this path. As Mr. Yoshio Terasawa, the chairman and chief executive officer of Nomura Securities International Incorporated (the largest Japanese investment banker) described it, the decision to work for a particular firm on graduation is one of the most crucial decisions in one's life. It may be even more crucial than selecting one's spouse; in the latter case one could always seek a divorce, but this alternative is not available in the case of one's employer. It is "very difficult to leave the company and join another, unless one sacrifices himself, both financially and status-wise" (Tung 1984). This explains to a large extent the low turnover rate in Japan. In a comparative study of turnover rates in the U.S. and in Japan, it was found that approximately 60 percent of Japanese employees never changed employers, compared with 23 percent in the United States (Cole 1981, p. 34). This makes it very difficult for foreign firms to attract experienced employees from well-established indigenous companies.

Furthermore, as pointed out in chapter 1, social status is determined largely by the company to which one belongs. Every year the *Nikkei Business* lists and rank-orders the fifty most desirable companies to work for based on a comprehensive survey of the graduates of elite universities. None of these top fifty companies are foreign firms. Thus most foreign firms (except those as prestigious as say, IBM Japan) have a difficult time competing with indigenous Japanese firms for the recruitment of capable college graduates. This difficulty is evident in the cases presented in this book.

Loyalty to Company

A second distinguishing feature of the Japanese employment system is the employee's loyalty to the employer. This stems from the strong group tradition that pervades Japanese society; it explains why the Japanese identify so closely with the achievements of their company and work section (Haitani 1976). Because of the internalization of organizational goals, a Japanese employee will voluntarily work extra hours without pay to meet company deadlines. This loyalty is perhaps best exhibited in a news article that appeared in the July 1978 issue of *Chuo Koron*, a leading monthly magazine. The news article recounted the death of the wife of an official of MITI. The official's wife died *alone* of pneumonia because her sickness coincided with budgetary time at the ministry. Since her husband's first loyalty was to MITI, he could not be with her. The article, noting that such incidents were not uncommon, ended with a quote from the vice-minister of MITI saying that the woman died a "tragic death on the battlefield as the wife of a government bureaucrat" (Bartholomew 1981b, p. 331).

Although this attitude may be changing among younger people, it is widely believed that, given the extremely competitive environment in Japanese organizations, as these younger people take on positions of responsibility, their attitudes will more closely resemble that of their elders (Tung 1984). For this reason an employer will often evaluate the performance of an employee on the basis of the individual's "dedication to the company and ability to cooperate with co-workers," rather than on the typical Western attributes of initiative and self motivation (*Keys to Success,* 1980, p. 22).

This unquestioning loyalty to the company has both positive and negative implications for the foreign firm. On the positive side, a Japanese who chooses to work for a foreign firm will usually be completely loyal and "will go to great lengths to defeat competitors" (Van Zandt 1970, p. 47). On the negative side, it is difficult for foreign firms to acquire existing Japanese enterprises. As noted in chapter 1, any acquisition of human beings is considered unethical and hence is uncommon even among Japanese firms.

A second negative implication for the foreign firm pertains to the operation of joint-venture concerns with Japanese entities. Because of the difficulty of recruiting competent Japanese graduates for foreign firms, the Japanese partner often provides the employees for the joint venture. Because the

employees come from the Japanese partner, however, there may be problems of divided loyalty. Most of these employees will continue to perceive
themselves as working for the Japanese partner, not for the joint venture.
The foreign partner may be shortchanged under this kind of arrangement.
Chapter 8 discusses problems of this nature. Acquisitions and joint ventures
are problematic even among Japanese firms. Employees do not easily for-
sake their loyalties to their previous company; hence they tend to form cliques
in the newly established venture. The employees of the acquired company or
the lesser partner in a joint venture are generally assigned an inferior status
and discriminated against by employees of the acquiring company or the
major partner in the joint venture (Haitani 1976, p. 139).

Employer's Concern for the Total Person

The Japanese employee identifies closely with his company. In turn, the
employer, as head of the corporate household, is obliged to assume responsibility for the employee's well-being. This phenomenon, called *amaeru* in
Japanese, is alien to the Western mentality. Many foreign firms do not understand the peculiar relationship that prevails between employer and
employee in Japan, and thus are unable to meet the obligations arising from
it (Van Zandt 1970).

A Japanese employer is concerned not only with all aspects of employees'
work life, but also with their private and family life. An employer is expected to arrange social events for the employees and their families on
weekends and major holidays throughout the year. Many companies provide low-cost housing for employees. For example, Nippon Steel Corporation, the largest steel manufacturer in Japan, provides dormitories for
single employees and company housing for approximately 35 percent of its
married employees. Those firms that do not offer similar facilities may provide financing for the purchase or construction of employees' homes (*Nippon*, 1982, pp. 239-241). To attract competent Japanese workers, a foreign
firm should be prepared to fulfill many of these obligations. On the positive
side, this relationship between employer and employee often leads to more
harmonious labor-management relations (Ishikawa 1963).

General Reluctance to Work for Foreign Firms

There is a general reluctance among graduates of elite Japanese universities
to work for foreign firms for two primary reasons: (1) a strong sense of nationalism means that a stigma is associated with working for a foreign firm;
(2) the practice of lifetime employment and the employer's concern for the
total person make many Japanese fear that foreign firms will not fulfill such

obligations. Foreign firms have a bad reputation for periodic firing and layoffs of employees (*Keys to Success*, 1980). Although the situation is slightly different in the electronics industry (*Wall Street Journal*, 25 April 1983, p. 30), because of these two factors, many foreign firms experience difficulty in recruiting capable Japanese to work for them, as is evident in almost all the cases presented in this book.

One might ask why foreign firms do not simply hire parent-country nationals? The use of parent-country nationals is difficult not only because of the prohibitive cost of sending expatriates overseas, but more specifically because of the tremendous differences in cultural environment and management styles between the two countries. In general, U.S. employees (and their families in particular) are less adept than their European and Japanese counterparts at living and working in a foreign country, particularly Japan. This maladjustment often causes lower productivity and poor performance (Tung 1981). Further, given the unique characteristics of the Japanese distribution system and other institutional settings, local nationals may simply be more suitable for the job. They tend to have a greater understanding of the Japanese business environment and can interact more effectively with their fellow employees. Consequently, the use of parent-country nationals may not be a viable alternative.

Many foreign subsidiaries do have at least one or two parent-country nationals for purposes of liaison with the parent headquarters. As one foreign firm puts it, since people from different cultures think differently, their perceptions—and hence their reporting—also differ. The foreign firm needs someone "who thinks the way we think to report back home" (*Keys to Success*, 1981, p. 14).

Foreign firms often err, however, in rotating their expatriate staff too often. This may be inappropriate for at least two reasons. First, the Japanese take time to develop relationships with other people. Frequent rotation interrupts the development of such relationships and may lead to misunderstanding and cause Japanese employees to lose their sense of belonging to the company. Second, given the vast cultural differences between the two countries, it generally takes a number of years for a foreigner "to begin to understand some of the idiosyncrasies" of the Japanese market and hence to become an asset to the Japanese subsidiary and the parent company (*Keys to Success*, 1981, p. 14). If a foreign firm rotates its expatriates too often, however, employees may be recalled just as they have acquired some expertise. Foreign firms may need a longer-term perspective with respect to expatriate assignments to Japan.

The Role of the Government

In the previous chapter the role of the Japanese government with respect to inward capital investment and development of the industrial sector was discussed. Although the government influences the functioning of various industries through administrative guidance, most foreign firms acknowledge that the government does not play an active role in actual business negotiations. Foreign firms do have to apply to the respective government agencies for approval to establish local subsidiaries or joint ventures with Japanese entities, but these procedures are generally perfunctory. Except in strategic sectors, such applications are usually approved as a matter of course.

This section examines the role of the Japanese government in the operation of foreign firms. This influence is felt in three general areas. The first is the strong support provided by the government for the development of key industries, or the policy of industrial targeting. This practice has been alleged to place foreign firms at a disadvantage in competing with local enterprises. This was examined in the previous chapter. Second, although government participation in the formation of specific joint ventures is virtually nonexistent in most cases, a number of foreign firms indicated that their Japanese partners may refer to *they* (meaning the government) when stalling or demanding concessions in certain areas—that *they* may not agree, or that the Japanese partner has to consult with the government before reaching agreement on a certain issue. Third, the camaraderie that often prevails between government personnel and indigenous Japanese firms can be traced to two sources: (1) the phenomenon of *amakudari* and (2) the strong alumni ties that persist through life. Each of these phenomena will be examined briefly.

Amakudari translates as "descent from heaven" and refers to the process whereby government bureaucrats resign their positions to assume high-ranking, well-paid positions in the private sector. This phenomenon can be attributed to the fact that whenever a bureaucrat is promoted to minister or vice-minister of a specific ministry or agency, his colleagues who entered the government at the same time that he did have to resign because it is inappropriate for two people from the same incoming year to assume a superior-subordinate relationship. This would mean that most bureaucrats would be weeded out of government before the official retirement age. Because in Japan it is considered very prestigious to work for the government, many of the brightest graduates of the elite universities are willing to assume relatively low-paying government positions. To prepare for their eventual "descent from heaven," most would cultivate good relationships with large corporations (Johnson 1982). As Haitani (1976, p. 44) described it, the bureaucrat's first career in the government is viewed as a "stepping stone" to a financially more lucrative second career in the private sector. Private industry, on the other hand, is very happy to take in these retired government officials for a variety of reasons: one, many of these are extremely capable individuals; two, they have access to their former colleagues in the government;

and three, they are thoroughly familiar with the operations of the government pertaining to approvals and licensing procedures.

A second reason for the close relationship between personnel in government and industry is that many of them are graduates of the same university or belonged to the same graduating class. This is the phenomenon of *gakubatsu*, or the old boys' network, which is very pervasive in Japan. Some Japanese prefer to use the term *daibatsu* to refer to the cliques of Tokyo University graduates. Tokyo University (*Todai* for short) is Japan's elite university, whose top graduates often work for the government on graduation. For example, 11 of the 12 highest ranking officials at MITI in 1974 were graduates of Todai (Haitani 1976, p. 44). The remaining Todai graduates generally choose a career with the large, well-established Japanese companies such as those listed among the 50 most desirable companies in the annual survey of *Nikkei Business*. The alumni of Todai, both in government and in industry, maintain strong ties among themselves. Johnson (1982, pp. 59-62) noted that the private sector is very desirous of employing Todai graduates (and, for that matter, the graduates of other elite universities) not only for purposes of liaison with the government but also, more important, because it means that "both government offices and board rooms are staffed by men who share a common outlook." Since foreign firms can seldom recruit the top graduates of the elite universities for the reasons mentioned earlier, they may not have as much access and lobbying power as the large, well-established indigenous companies do.

The Role of Litigation

In the previous chapter it was noted that the restrictions imposed on U.S. lawyers who wish to practice in Japan have often been cited as a nontariff barrier to foreign investment. These include the difficulty of obtaining multiple-entry visas to consult with clients in Japan, and the restrictive requirements for taking the bar exam. As a result, it is believed that there are only approximately twenty foreign attorneys (primarily U.S. citizens) licensed to practice in Japan (Upham 1981). Foreign firms that wish to enter into business relations with the Japanese must also be aware of several factors pertaining to litigation in Japanese society: (1) the role of lawyers; (2) the Japanese attitude toward contracts; and (3) conflict resolution in the case of disputes. Each of these will be examined in some detail.

The Role of Lawyers

In Japan there is a general distrust of lawyers. Hahn (1982, p. 22) ascribed this attitude to two primary factors. First, there is a general belief that lawyers tend to destroy the harmony or *wa* that is paramount in Japanese society, by focusing on the positions of their clients and hence "ignoring compromises that benefit society as a whole." It is widely believed that since lawyers are hired to represent one side, they may hinder compromise by pitting one party against the other. Second, a business relationship between a Japanese and a foreign partner is built on the principles of mutual trust, friendship, and cooperation rather than on legalistic grounds. The Japanese generally believe that lawyers obstruct the development of such cooperative business relationships. Even in business meetings among Japanese firms, introducing a lawyer into the situation is often considered an "unfriendly act, an implied threat of litigation," since lawyers are traditionally used for that specific purpose (Upham 1981, p. 152).

In Japan lawyers and litigation are simply not as widely used as in the United States. The U.S. attitude toward negotiations is very legalistic. It is generally assumed that nothing is binding until the final legal documents are signed. Japanese negotiators often view this attitude as constituting a revocation of agreements supposedly reached earlier in the negotiating process. Given the Japanese distrust of lawyers, it may be advisable for foreign firms to exclude attorneys from the actual negotiations altogether and to seek legal advice outside the negotiations (Tsurumi 1981c, p. 308). If a U.S. firm has to bring its lawyer, Hahn (1982) cautioned that U.S. attorneys who are present in the negotiations should emphasize their roles as "facilitators of negotiations" rather than arbitrators or representatives of a particular interest group.

The traditional Japanese distaste for lawyers and litigation may account for the presence of significantly fewer lawyers in Japan, where there is one attorney for every 10,250 people, compared with one per 630 people in the United States. Since the end of World War II the annual rate of litigation in Japan has stood at approximately 140-180 formal trials per 100,000 persons. In 1970, for example, approximately 175,000 trials were begun in Japan, with a population at the time of 113 million. This compared with 138,643 cases (excluding juvenile and probate cases) in the state of Ohio alone, with a population of only 10.6 million. The incidence of litigation in Japan is perhaps the lowest for any industrialized nations. The Danes, for instance, tend to sue about four times as frequently as the Japanese, the British three times as often, and the West Germans twice as often (Upham 1981, p. 149).

Another reason for the relative scarcity of lawyers in Japan may be the difficulty of the bar entrance requirements. To qualify as a lawyer in Japan, a candidate must attend two years of training at the officially designated Legal Training and Research Institute. The prerequisites for entry to the institute are obtaining a degree from a law school plus passing the tough entrance exam to the institute. In 1975 the admission rate was only 1.7 percent—472 out of 27,791 candidates. This rate declined to 1.6 percent in

1977. In fact, it was estimated that in 1975 the number per capita of Japanese writing the bar exam was slightly above that of the United States. The major difference lay in the passing rate: Only 1.7 percent passed in Japan, compared with 74 percent in the United States (Upham 1981, p. 151). Consequently, those who are licensed to practice law in Japan can command very high fees. This has implications for foreign firms that attempt to obtain legal services in Japan.

The Japanese Attitude toward Contracts

The Japanese attitude toward contracts is very different from that of U.S. residents. The typical U.S. view is that a contract defines the rights and responsibilities of the parties and seeks to cover all possible contingencies, such as dissolution. An example is the marriage contract in the United States, whereby some people enter into prior arrangements on how to divide communal properties between man and wife should the marriage end in a divorce. The traditional Japanese view, on the other hand, is that a contract is secondary in a business transaction, which should be premised on an "ongoing, harmonious relationship" between two parties who are committed to the pursuit of similar objectives (Hahn 1982, p. 22). Consequently, relationships, not contracts, are negotiated.

Details of a contract are seldom haggled over, and legal documents are usually kept as brief and flexible as possible to accommodate the evolving relationship between the parties. Long legal agreements drafted by one side are viewed with suspicion by the Japanese and would almost immediately portray the foreign firm as an adversary (Van Zandt 1970). In Japan contracts can be as brief as one page and may be couched in vague language, stipulating, for example, that should a dispute arise between the parties, it will be negotiated in good faith. The Japanese believe that "warm subjective relationship" should take precedence over "formal rights and obligations," and that all practical problems could be resolved through "mutual compromise and accommodation" (Stevens 1972, p. 1272). The desire to establish mutual trust as a basis for business relationship may account for the longer time it takes to negotiate an agreement with the Japanese, and is related to the issue of conflict resolution discussed in the following section.

There are, of course, exceptions to this general Japanese attitude toward law and litigation. For example, Stanley Epstein, president of Anglo American Aviation Company, used the services of several smaller Japanese general trading companies. He described the relationship with one of these as highly unsatisfactory because the latter abrogated the terms of the contract by declaring that the agreement was not valid in the first place because it had not been "ratified by the proper people on their board of directors."

Later, however, the same trading company hired some U.S. lawyers to sue Anglo American for owing commissions in accordance with the schedule of the contract they had earlier declared null and void.

Conflict Resolution

Given these observations on the Japanese attitude toward contracts, it follows that the preferred methods of conflict resolution in Japan would be different from those in the United States. The Japanese prefer conciliation and mediation over litigation in business matters, for several reasons: (1) reduced costs; (2) the limited number of attorneys in Japan (some cases drag on for 10 years before a final decision is reached); (3) the Japanese emphasis on harmony or reconciliation. In the prewar Japanese Constitution, Article 17 stated that "Japan, unlike other countries where rights and duties prevail, must strive to resolve interpersonal cases by harmony and compromise" (Kawashima 1963, p. 53 ff.). This is the principle of *chotei*, which was officially reinstated after the war. Under *chotei*, disputes should be "washed away" (*mizu ni nagasu*) through compromise and conciliation. Given the Japanese emphasis on harmony (*wa*) and face-saving, relationships could be preserved through a conciliatory process without undue loss of face to either party. As Kawashima (1963) notes, litigation presupposes that there is a right and a wrong, which is contrary to the traditional Japanese view. Furthermore, through compromise, the chances of "an all or nothing decision" are minimized (Upham 1981, p. 152).

This preference for conciliation and mediation is evident in other aspects of Japanese society as well. For example, very few claims pertaining to traffic accidents are brought to the law courts every year. Specific provisions for arbitration exist but are seldom used. For example, there were only 2 applications for arbitration with the Ministry of Construction between October 1956 and April 1961, compared with 14 applications for mediation.

Even in disputes between labor and management, arbitration is seldom used. Statistics show that the number of arbitration cases over the years has been extremely low. Furthermore, 3 out of every 5 arbitration cases were actually withdrawn before proceedings began because they had been settled through some other conciliatory process (Kawashima 1963). Most of these cases are settled through extrajudicial procedures.

John Owen Haley, a professor of law at the University of Washington and a former member of a Tokyo legal firm, notes that there is some myth about the Japanese reluctance to sue. In the February 1982 crash of one of the planes of Japan Air Lines (JAL) where 24 passengers were killed and 142 injured, none of the victims sued the carrier. It was understood by the aggrieved parties that the airlines would resolve the matter outside the litigation framework, and that they would be compensated for their losses. The president of JAL personally visited the family of each victim and bowed low as a symbol of atonement. Furthermore, each family received monetary indemnities ranging from $168,000 to $280,000. Haley indicates that one reason the victims did not sue in this incident could be that they knew that JAL would be able to offer financial settlements as large as what they would have obtained through legal means. He contrasted this case to the hotel fire that broke out in Tokyo the same week as the air crash, killing 33 people. In the latter incident, 8 suits had been filed thus far against the hotel operators. The latter, of course, did not have as great financial assets as JAL (*Wall Street Journal*, 14 April 1983, p. 32).

Cultural Characteristics

As noted earlier, some alleged nontariff barriers may be culture-based. Hence there may be obstacles to the removal of such so-called barriers. Furthermore, given the vast cultural differences between the United States and Japan, an American could not approach a business transaction with a Japanese partner in the same manner as he would in the United States. Business practices in any given nation generally represent the culmination of centuries of social, economic, and cultural evolution. To operate successfully in Japan, the foreign businessman must adapt to its unique cultural characteristics. Otherwise, he may inadvertently antagonize his Japanese partner by transgressing against strong cultural traditions and values (Hahn 1982). Consequently, it is imperative that the foreign firm devote sufficient time to studying such cultural differences.

This section examines the most salient cultural characteristics pertaining to the conduct of business in Japan. This discussion does not claim to be all-encompassing. For more detailed discussions of the Japanese culture, see, for example, Ruth Benedict's *The Chrysanthemum and the Sword* (1964) and Chie Nakane's *Japanese Society* (1970).

Consensus Decision Making

One salient characteristic of the Japanese industrial system is the inordinate amount of time it takes to reach a decision. This stems primarily from the consensus decision-making process, referred to as the *ringi-sho*. Under this system a proposal must be endorsed by all concerned individuals. Although some decisions are made through the edict of top management, which in the Japanese context is referred to as *tsuru no hitoke* or "one screech of the crane," most decisions at the lower- or middle-management levels of Japanese companies are made through consensus. The so-called one-screech-of-the-crane method is most widely used where the chief executive officer is also the founder of the company (*Japanese Corporate Decision Making*, 1982).

This style of decision making has several implications for foreign firms. First, given that an agreement can be arrived at only with the approval of all concerned individuals, the foreign firm should remember that in a negotiation it is not enough merely to convince the representative of the other party; rather, "the whole group must be won over" (Van Zandt 1970, p. 47). This often takes time because the proposal must be discussed and endorsed by all concerned individuals. Patience on the part of the foreign firm is required. As is evident in the findings of the questionnaire survey presented in chapter 3 and in the cases provided in this book, patience is a key ingredient in successful negotiation and operations in Japan.

A number of factors may further increase the time it takes to arrive at a decision. First, given the Japanese emphasis on long-term relationships, the first meeting between two partners seldom goes beyond an exchange of formalities. A foreign firm should not try to discuss the specifics of a proposed business transaction during the first meeting. Second, as pointed out in chapter 1, the Ministry of International Trade and Industry has authorized the establishment of *kondankai*, or three-way committees, comprising representatives from government, industry, and finance, to provide a forum for the discussion of important issues pertaining to a particular industry. Consequently, in negotiations involving significant business transactions, the Japanese partner may have to consult with the government or other firms in the industry through the *kondankai*. This will, of course, delay the time it takes to arrive at a decision. Third, since most negotiations involve the use of interpreters, it generally takes at least twice as long to ensure that the two parties adequately understand each other on all the specific issues covered in a business transaction.

Given these peculiarities of the Japanese system, it often takes a long time to reach a decision. Inability to comprehend this phenomenon may lead to misunderstanding. Van Zandt (1970), for instance, recounts the incident of a U.S. company that insisted that the Japanese partner undertake a certain course of action as prescribed in the contract. When two months had elapsed and no action had been taken by the Japanese partner, the U.S. side interpreted the delay as constituting a revocation of the terms of the contract, which was not the case. Although the Japanese might sometimes stall or hedge on a particular issue, in general a lack of immediate action on the Japanese side should not be interpreted as a disinterest or revocation of terms agreed to earlier.

Considerable patience is required in dealing with the Japanese. In Japan it is believed that patience was one of the attributes that differentiated the elite, or samurai class, from the peasants during the warring feudal period. A

Japanese proverb says that "the samurai is skilled at broiling fish, while the poor man is only capable of toasting rice cakes." The former "waits patiently, until the proper moment when, with lightning precision, he flips the fish." The poor man, on the other hand, "nervously pokes away at his rice cake, flipping it over and over again until it is crisp and puffy on all sides." Similarly, foreign businessmen are often compared to the poor man who has not mastered the skill of waiting patiently for the most opportune time (Plimpton 1982, p. 3).

A concomitant virtue that is indispensable in dealing with the Japanese is persistence. According to the findings of the Japan External Trade Organization on the performance of foreign firms, a common denominator for successful operation in Japan is the ability to persevere despite hardships (*Foreign Companies*, 1982). Because of the inordinate amount of patience and persistence that may be required in doing business in Japan, Howard Van Zandt, a former senior officer at ITT Japan who spent 25 years in the country, has cautioned that it may take 6 times as long and be 3 times as hard to arrive at an agreement with a Japanese partner, compared with a typical U.S. negotiation (Van Zandt 1970).

Emphasis on Harmony

As noted previously, in Japan the emphasis on harmony or *wa* is institutionalized under the principle of *chotei*. This overriding concern for harmony is exhibited in several forms. One was discussed previously—the concept of *ringi-sho*, whereby all concerned individuals have to approve a proposal before a decision is reached. Second, because of the desire for harmony, the Japanese generally avoid extremes and tend to take the middle ground. This national trait will be discussed further subsequently. Third, because of the desire to maintain harmony, the Japanese often avoid confrontation by disguising their true feelings (Graham 1981). Fourth, because of the Japanese emphasis on saving face, it may be necessary to cloak discord rather than confront the issue directly. Direct confrontations may not only result in a loss of face for one or both parties but, more important, may represent a breakdown of the much cherished principle of *chotei*. The issue of face will be examined in greater detail subsequently.

Nationalism

One underlying theme of international business is nationalism. To operate successfully in the international environment, a multinational must understand the nationalistic sentiments that may prevail in foreign markets, and how to cope with them effectively. This need to cope with the ramifications of nationalism is great in the case of Japan. As noted earlier the Japanese identify very closely with the achievements of their country, their company, and their work section. This stems from the strong group tradition that pervades Japanese society, and explains why individuals continue to subjugate themselves and their interests to that of the nation-state even though the postwar constitution defined sovereignty as residing with the individual. Most Japanese continue to view the nation as the family-state and hence willingly subordinate themselves to government bureaucrats, who are believed to "exercise authority not in the name of the people but in the name of the House of Japan." Consequently, the people welcome active state intervention in the private sector (Haitani 1976, p. 39).

Nationalism is expressed in several forms in Japan. During World War II, for instance, kamikaze pilots demonstrated their allegiance to their country by plunging their bomb-laden aircrafts into their targets to ensure a no-miss situation. In times of peace there is no need for such an extreme demonstration of nationalism. Nationalism is, however, manifested in practically all facets of Japanese society. In this section I shall examine the ways nationalism could affect the operations of the foreign firms.

One way nationalism could affect the operations of foreign firms relates to the difficulty of recruiting capable Japanese college graduates to work for them. Although reluctance to work for a foreign enterprise may stem in part from a desire for security through the system of lifetime employment and the generous welfare benefits traditionally granted by the large, well-established Japanese enterprises, much of the unwillingness could be attributed to the social stigma still attached to working for a foreign firm.

A second way in which nationalism may affect the operations of foreign firms is the problem of divided loyalty among employees in joint ventures established between Japanese and foreign entities. Most of the workers in a joint venture usually come from the Japanese partner, and many of them maintain their allegiance to the former rather than to the joint venture. Although this may be described as a form of loyalty to one's employer given the psychological contract entered into between employer and employee at the time of employment, the phenomenon might be less dominant were it not for the strong nationalistic sentiments of the Japanese.

A third way in which nationalism could influence the operations of foreign firms is in terms of the purchase policies of manufacturers and consumers. In general, "Japanese like Japanese things unless they are consumer items" (*Keys to Success*, 1981, pp. 6-7). This explains why expensive French designer clothes sell so well and why U.S.-style restaurants, with Western decor and food and employing "West-coast, out-doorsy American waiters" are flourishing in Japan (*Wall Street Journal*, 8 March 1983, p. 40).

Beyond consumer items, however, the Japanese are generally unwilling to purchase foreign products if comparable items are available from a domestic manufacturer. This explains why the chief executive officer of DuPont Company in North Asia noted that me-too products do not sell in Japan, and that in order to make significant inroads into the Japanese market a foreign manufacturer must introduce truly innovative products (*Wall Street Journal*, 12 May 1982, p. 1). The Japanese are almost fanatical about innovative products. Any new item that serves a useful function will be in demand, regardless of country of origin. Beyond consumer products and items in which a foreign manufacturer has a competitive edge, however, the Japanese prefer to purchase homemade goods. This preference may be strengthened by the strong friendship ties that develop among alumni of elite universities and schools. The phenomenon of *gakubatsu* was noted earlier as a powerful force in Japanese industrial society. Consequently, the decision to purchase from certain suppliers may not be dictated by pure economic factors, but affected by strong sentimental ties such as the section chief (*kacho*) of the purchasing company having graduated from the same university as the kacho of the supplying company (*Foreign Companies*, 1982).

A fourth way nationalism could affect the operations of a foreign firm is in the prohibitions placed on foreign attorneys to practice law or consult with their clients in Japan. Japan is one of the most homogeneous societies in the world. The number of ethnic minorities in the country is minimal; there are only 800,000 alien residents in a country of 117 million, of whom 650,000 are the progeny of Korean workers brought to Japan during World War II to engage in forced labor. The laws that apply to nonnationals are often discriminatory. For example, Japan's alien-registration legislation requires that all foreigners who reside in Japan for more than one year must be fingerprinted, and such documents must be carried by aliens at all times. Foreign residents have condemned these requirements as "denigrating and demeaning." Other discriminatory measures include the denial of most social-welfare benefits to aliens until recently, and strict naturalization laws that prevent the children of aliens born in Japan from becoming naturalized citizens unless they adopted a Japanese name (*Philadelphia Inquirer*, 20 February 1983, p. 6-D). Given Japan's strong nationalistic sentiments, it is definitely to a foreign firm's advantage to establish an image as a local corporation. Local manufacturing, as opposed to pure importing, may be one way to improve the local image of the corporation. This may mitigate some of the xenophobic sentiments.

Quality and Service

A fourth distinguishing feature of Japanese industrial society is the emphasis on quality of product and after-sale service. Japanese manufacturers and consumers place a high premium on zero defect. Although the concept of quality-control circles (QCC) was first introduced by Denning, a U.S.

statistician, it was not well received in the United States. The Japanese, however, welcomed this innovative idea and made Denning a sort of industrial folk hero. The annual Denning award remains one of the most coveted prizes of Japanese industrial firms. As an extension of quality-control circles, there evolved a zero-defect movement that has been implemented in many large Japanese companies. The movement emphasizes the need to identify the causes of various defects (including the human factor) and to devise methods for minimizing these errors, with the ultimate goal of reaching zero defect (*Productivity*, 1981). Whereas most U.S. manufacturers accept a certain level of defect in their end products, these standards are generally unacceptable in Japan. Foreign firms that hope to succeed in the Japanese market must conform to the exacting local requirements.

Besides emphasizing quality, "the Japanese are notorious sticklers for punctuality" (*Keys to Success*, 1981, p. 7). Because of the tight production schedules of most manufacturing plants and the just-in-time inventory systems maintained at the factories, the Japanese demand prompt delivery of machineries and parts. Firms that produce abroad may be at a disadvantage because of the longer lead time needed to obtain supplies. This may be another reason to establish local manufacturing facilities within Japan.

In addition to prompt delivery, the Japanese expect free after-sale service. In general, the supplier in Japan is responsible for installation, training of operators (where necessary), and maintenance and servicing of products long after the official expiration of the warranty. In the West, if the warranty is for one year, then on the 366th day the supplier has no further obligation. In Japan the warranty period is almost unlimited. This difference may stem from the nonlegalistic mentality of the Japanese. In Japan it is common for the supplier to inspect and maintain its clients' machinery periodically, even ten or twenty years after the date of original purchase. Such periodic visits help maintain long-term relationships between supplier and customer, and obligate the latter in a sense to make future purchases from the original supplier (*Keys to Success*, 1980). Besides maintenance, it is common in Japan to visit one's clients even if there is no particular business transaction in mind: "It is good to just come over and make a call. The Japanese love it" (*Keys to Success*, 1981, p. 23). This practice is often referred to as "selling one's face" (Van Zandt 1970).

Avoidance of Extremes

Because of the overriding concern with maintaining harmony, the Japanese tend to avoid extremes and prefer to adopt a middle-of-the-road attitude. This attitude is immortalized in the words of Miyamoto Musashi, a samurai of the late sixteenth and early seventeenth centuries: "Always be in the same way in any situation, and to keep your mind in the Middle Way attitude" (*Musashi* 1982, p. 30). Musashi's teachings and advice to the warrior class of his time are contained in his writings, entitled *The Book of the Five Rings* (trans. ed., 1982). His teachings still have a wide audience among members of the Japanese government and business communities. In 1982 his work was lauded by some U.S. journalists as "Tokyo's response to Harvard's M.B.A.," the "real art of Japanese management," and "a guide to winning strategy." While his advice was directed at samurais, it could be transferred to business negotiations. Avoidance of extremes is generally exhibited in one of several forms, such as concealment of emotions, a general reluctance to say "no," vagueness of responses, and prolonged periods of silence. Each of these characteristics will be discussed briefly.

Concealment of Emotions

The Japanese are not devoid of emotions; they cherish friendships and long-standing relationships, perhaps more than in the West. The difference is in terms of the expression—or, rather, concealment—of such emotions. The emotions of an Italian, for instance, may reflect a person's feelings at a particular time, are generally highly visible, and may have no relationship to others. The emotions of a Japanese, on the other hand, may be directed against or toward others and are generally well concealed from the public eye (Van Zandt 1970). Without understanding this distinction, a foreigner could easily assume that the Japanese are unfeeling and hence could insult them without being openly reproached for such abrasiveness. The Japanese prefer to be indirect, even with respect to compliments. For example, instead of directly praising a person's good taste and sophistication, a Japanese would usually single out and comment on one aspect of the office or home to reflect the person's taste (*Doing Business*, 1982).

Reluctance to Say "No"

The tendency to avoid extremes and the desire to save face often translate into an aversion to use the word *no* in conversations. Chie Nakane, a professor at Tokyo University and a respected authority on Japanese culture, indicates that the word *no* is almost never used except in completely reciprocal or superior-subordinate relationships. "You rarely receive a *no* from a Japanese, even when he means no he would use *yes* in the verbal form" (Van Zandt 1970, p. 49). Van Zandt offered certain cues that will help one recognize when a Japanese is genuinely negative about a given issue. Such cues could include the drawing of breath between one's teeth and saying *sah*, which does not carry any meaning; or the Japanese will indicate that something is "very difficult." In the words of Mr. Yoshio Terasawa, the chairman and chief executive officer of Nomura Securities International Incorporated, if a Japanese says "I will consider it," the probability is 99 percent that he means "no" (Tung 1984). Conversely, if a Japanese uses the term *yes*, it may not be truly an affirmative. To avoid possible misunderstandings, non-Japanese should try to recognize some of the cues described here and should emphasize to the Japanese party the need to express opinions frankly in order to avoid misunderstanding and discord later. In one of the firms interviewed, it took the U.S. partner a full two weeks to get one of the Japanese employees to say "no" when he disagreed with a particular issue. Even then such requests have to be repeated periodically so that the Japanese employee will not return to his former habits.

Vagueness of Responses

The tendency to avoid extremes is also characterized by a general vagueness in responses. In negotiations the Japanese will carefully study the opinions of the other side, while remaining deliberately vague about the stand that will eventually be adopted by his party (*Doing Business*, 1982). This vagueness may be due to the need to obtain consensus in decision making and the desire to save face, in case a reversal of position needs to be made at a later time. In one of the firms interviewed, the U.S. partner expressed a "feeling that you never get a straight answer. You never really know how the Japanese executives feel. . . . Instead of getting the differences out on the table, with each side learning from the other and coming up with a synthesis (which in many cases is better than either of the original ideas), the Japanese are just submissive and do what they are told, which may be unfortunate in some cases. . . . Japanese executives pay lip service to the foreign executive while he is there. They know that in two weeks you are going to be back in the States and they can continue to do things the way they want. You think you have a problem resolved, you think you have people aimed in the right direction, and you find that nothing has been done. If there are problems, they are never brought to you. I like people to bring their problems to me, not just all their successes and achievements. Yet the Japanese are very reticent to bring a problem to you. They don't like to talk about negative things. Sometimes the answers they give you are not really what they are thinking about. Sometimes three or four objections are brought to you, but those may not really be the issues because the person may be embarrassed to bring up the real objection. It is a challenge. . . . We have done business in Singapore, and the Singaporeans are pretty up-front people. If something is not going to work, they say 'this isn't going to work.'

The Japanese, on the other hand, does not want to say that. What he is trying to do is say to you *no*, but you don't understand it that way.''

This general vagueness and avoidance of extremes are also exhibited in the completion of questionnaires. Where 5- or 7-point ranking scales are used (ranging from strongly positive to strongly negative opinions on a certain issue), most Japanese respondents generally avoid the extremes and have a tendency to check a 3 or a 4 instead.

Prolonged Periods of Silence

Vagueness in responses in negotiations is sometimes accompanied by prolonged periods of silence. In Japan the maxim that "silence is golden" still holds. This may stem from the Japanese desire to avoid confrontation, which is deeply imbued in individuals from childhood. Kanji Hatano, another noted authority on Japanese culture, compares children's quarrels in various European countries with those in Japan. In general, "prompt retort" was expected in the European countries, whereas Japanese children generally remained quiet even if they felt they were right (Van Zandt 1970, p. 50). When an impasse is reached in a negotiation, the typical Japanese response is either silence, withdrawal, or a change of subject (Graham 1981). To the Japanese, a period of silence may allow matters to cool off and give both sides an opportunity to rethink the issue. Americans, on the other hand, may feel uncomfortable and have the urge to say something. At these crucial junctures Americans are most susceptible to committing tactical errors (Van Zandt 1970).

Long-Term Relationships

Japanese people may not befriend others as quickly and easily as their counterparts in the United States; but friendships, once established, generally last much longer. This difference has two implications for the foreign firm: (1) the need to develop long-term relationships in Japanese industrial society, and (2) the differences in corporate time horizons between Americans and Japanese.

The Need to Develop Long-Term Relationships

Earlier we discussed the strong sense of loyalty among Japanese employers, consumers, and industrial users, and emphasized the need to develop long-term relationships. In Japan business transactions, like marital relations, are not viewed as a passing fancy or temporary bond between two partners. They are lifelong relations involving obligations and responsibilities on both sides, even under adverse conditions. This is manifested in the system of lifetime employment; the phenomenon of the old boys' network, which is more pervasive than that in the United States; and the longer time it generally takes to reach a contractual agreement with a Japanese partner for the establishment of a business venture.

The Japanese tend to describe non-Japanese business relationships as "dry" because they hinge entirely on the profitability of the venture and the benefits that accrue to either partner. Once these conditions cease to exist, the relationship is terminated. Using this analogy, the Japanese have described their own business relationships as "wet" because they are built on personal ties that have developed over the years and may not be based entirely on profitability. Such "wet" relationships are more permanent and will persevere under adverse conditions (*Doing Business*, 1982, p. 19). Of course, there are exceptions, as is evident in chapter 8, which deals with the dissolution of a joint venture because of bleak prospects for financial profitability.

Given this presumed difference in business relationships between the United States and Japan, the question is how long does it take to develop the Japanese kind of relationship? In the words of the vice-president of Dentsu Corporation, the largest advertising agency in Japan, "twenty years in Japan isn't long enough to develop personal contacts" (*Foreign Companies*, 1982, p. 11). Such relationships, once formed, however, generally endure the test of time.

For example, when I was in Japan to collect data for a research study, I solicited the assistance of a professor at a renowned university to obtain access to certain large industrial firms. The senior officer of one such company told me that he had not been in touch with this professor, who was his classmate at university, for twenty years. When he received the call from his former classmate, however, he immediately recognized him and consented to the interview with no qualms whatsover. This kind of response is almost unheard of in the United States. The phenomenon of *naniwabusi* was in operation here. *Naniwabusi* refers to a condition whereby a person is on very good personal terms with another and hence is able to obligate the other to perform favors on his behalf (Van Zandt 1970). Such a phenomenon could prove very beneficial in business relations.

How should a foreign firm go about nurturing long-term relationships? There are several ways: patience in negotiations; less frequent rotation of U.S. expatriates in Japan so that the Japanese employees and customers can truly get to know the Americans; maintenance of frequent contacts with one's customers and suppliers; socializing with the Japanese outside of office hours; and the exchange of gifts. Some of these areas were addressed previously. The discussion here will center on socializing with the Japanese and on the tradition of gift-giving.

Because of the emphasis on developing good personal relationships in Japan, most male workers tend to fraternize with each other in restaurants and bars after office hours, primarily to solidify the ties that prevail among them. This accounts for the substantial entertainment expense accounts of Japanese businessmen. Advertising agencies, for example, spend approximately 1.8 percent of their gross revenues on entertainment (Van Zandt 1970). This socialization is often extended into business relations with foreign businessmen. In Japan it is common to discuss business after office hours or on weekends in a social setting such as a golf course, restaurant, cabaret, or geisha party. To the Japanese, such after-hour socializing is considered a "necessary carry-over" from the regular business meetings from 9:00 to 5:00, and helps "cement the ties that bind the parties together" (Hahn 1982, p. 22).

In these social contexts the Japanese feel less inhibited and may be more willing to express their emotions and perhaps even to reveal their human frailties. For example, flirting with cocktail waitresses and drunkenness are fairly common and are condoned by one's colleagues to a much greater extent than in the United States and Europe (Richardson and Ueda 1981). Sometimes a Japanese may use the guise of drunkenness to express his real feelings to his superiors (Ouchi 1981). In the course of after-hour socializing the Japanese may burst into sing-along sessions at a cabaret. If a foreign businessman can tolerate or perhaps even participate in this buffoonery, he has "accomplished the same feat as taking a hot bath naked together" (Tsurumi 1981c, p. 320). The Japanese will interpret this as a genuine willingness on the part of the foreigner to break down the barriers between them.

Unlike in the West, most entertainment and socializing take place outside of the home because of the housing situation in Japan and also because wives are generally excluded from such activities. Most socializing is done in restaurants; in Tokyo alone there are over 100,000 restaurants. In fact, most aspiring Japanese businessmen do not go home until 10:00 or 11:00 every evening. Late every evening the streets of the Ginza area in Tokyo are congested with taxis that swarm to the region to pick up businessmen who are only then setting out for home.

Besides after-hour socializing, the Japanese enjoy exchanging presents, particularly in the traditional gift-giving seasons of July and December. In a business relationship such gift-giving is usually reciprocal and helps to develop a warm, trusting relationship between partners (Richardson and Ueda 1981). Gifts could range from very expensive items such as mink coats to the more common fine-quality Scotch whisky and other imported alcoholic liquors. Van Zandt (1970), for example, notes that many government officials receive gifts of cases of soft drinks in July and smoked salmon in December. These should not be construed as bribes because most of these items are inexpensive and the gift-giving is usually reciprocal. Traditionally, the giver apologizes for the lack of grandeur of the item, and the recipient is not supposed to open the present in the presence of the giver (Hahn 1982).

Besides socializing and gift-giving, another way to facilitate relationships is through an influential intermediary who is a mutual friend. Given the strong old boys' network in Japan, a former classmate could be called on to serve as a go-between. Most Japanese businessmen tend to consider proposals from a new business associate more seriously and favorably if an influential go-between is used (*Doing Business*, 1982). This is generally attributable to the phenomenon of *naniwabushi* described earlier.

The Differences in Objectives

This longer time perspective on the part of the Japanese businessmen often translates into differences in corporate objectives between U.S. and Japanese partners to a business venture. In general, U.S. firms are more oriented to the short term and display a greater concern for immediate profitability and return on investment. This is primarily because quarterly and yearly earnings are translated into dividends and hence affect investors' perception of the attractiveness of a given company. The shares of Japanese firms, on the other hand, are generally held by large financial institutions. Consequently, the Japanese may be prepared to take a longer-term perspective and are more concerned with developing market share as a key objective. This latter goal generally takes time and may involve losses for a number of years initially. This difference in objectives could pose problems in forming and operating joint ventures between U.S. and Japanese entities. In the case of SmithKline·Fujisawa, for instance, this *perceived* difference in objectives (even though in that particular case it proved to be unfounded) posed a major stumbling block in the negotiations and delayed progress for a number of months.

Language

The Japanese language is unique; its written form bears little resemblance to any except written Chinese, and its spoken version has no relationship to any other. Furthermore, the language is complicated by the fact that there are several levels of formality, one for equals, one for superiors, and one for subordinates. Consequently, very few foreigners know enough to negotiate in Japanese. Because it is intricate and subtle, most experienced negotiators caution foreigners against using it in business unless they are thoroughly proficient in the language; otherwise they risk insulting the Japanese partner through inappropriate words and manner of address (Hahn 1982). Most negotiations are conducted in English or through interpreters. When interpreters are used, the foreign firm must know that its message is adequately translated. When the foreign firm has to rely on the translation services provided by the Japanese partner, it may be at the mercy of incompetent interpreters who either have inadequate command of English or who are unfamiliar with the technical terms. It is best for the foreign firm to include a bilingual member in its negotiating team. The bilingual team member can interpret or if an interpreter is used, check on his accuracy. The use of interpreters and bilingual team members is discussed in the questionnaire survey reported in chapter 3 and in some of the cases.

Status and Face

Given the strong group emphasis in Japanese society, a person's status in any business or social setting is defined in relation to his rank in a hierarchical order. Individuals seldom relate to each other as equals, but rather as superiors or subordinates (Haitani 1976).

This emphasis on status has three primary implications for the foreign firm. First, even though the details of a negotiation may be conducted by someone lower in the organizational hierarchy, the most senior officer of the foreign firm should meet with his Japanese counterpart, preferably early in the process. This will help establish relationships between the two parties and indicate that the business transaction has the endorsement of the respective companies. In the questionnaire survey reported in chapter 3, most U.S. companies reported that they included at least one senior ranking officer in their negotiating teams.

A second implication of the emphasis on status is the importance of business cards or *meishi* in Japan. A Japanese must be able to determine immediately how he ranks in relation to another individual to whom he has been introduced, so that he can decide the appropriate angle of bowing and the level of formality required in the conversation. The business card immediately informs the other person of one's rank in a given organization. *Meishi* are standard business cards that are printed in English on one side and in Japanese on the other. Business cards may be used more widely in Japan than in any other country. One middle-management executive informed me that he typically uses 250 business cards in any given month, which is high by U.S. standards. Furthermore, there are protocols associated with the exchange of business cards. First, the younger or lower-ranking person is supposed to offer his card first. Second, when the card is extended, it should be turned so that the recipient can immediately read the fine print on it as he accepts it. Third, damaged cards or ones that bear messages not intended for the recipient should not be used; they are considered impolite. Fourth, business cards for women should be smaller than those for men. This last protocol, however, does not apply to foreign business women (*Nippon*, 1982).

As for bowing as a form of greeting, foreigners are generally not expected to do so. In most instances a handshake will do. If a Westerner chooses to bow, however, a nod of the head or a slight inclination of the body is considered acceptable.

A third implication of status is the heavy emphasis on face and the use of face-saving devices in the Japanese context. Although face-saving is important in any country—nobody wants to be humiliated or insulted in public—the difference lies in the degree of sensitivity. Americans like to address issues directly and are more prone to confront others on given matters. The Japanese, on the other hand, shy away from direct confrontation. As noted previously, the Japanese are deliberately vague on specific issues in the early stages of a negotiation, so that any later reversal will not result in loss of face. Given the increased sensitivity in Japan, an American should be careful not to affront the Japanese. An outright rejection of a proposal made by the Japanese side would result in a loss of face to the latter (Hahn 1982). In negotiations the Americans should never back the Japanese partner into a corner but should always give the other side sufficient room to maneuver and change positions without a loss of face. This is very similar to the situation in negotiating with the Chinese (Tung, 1982a).

It may also be unwise for Americans to pressure a Japanese partner for an answer when a stalemate is reached in a negotiation. As pointed out previously, the Japanese prefer to have a period of silence to let matters cool off and give either side an opportunity to rethink the issue. Aggressiveness and pressure on the part of Americans are generally negatively received by the Japanese partners because such tactics could cause a loss of face (Van Zandt 1970). U.S. negotiators should be careful not to transgress on any issue that may result in a loss of face to the other party. They should remember that what is acceptable in the West may be considered insulting in Japan. Hence they should adjust their level of sensitivities in operating in Japan.

This chapter has examined the distinguishing characteristics of doing business in Japan, and has highlighted the salient cultural differences that affect business practices in Japan. A foreign firm has to understand these differences and operate within such constraints. As evident from the findings of the U.S.-Japan Study Group published in early 1983, the inroads by U.S. manufacturers into the Japanese market may be more prevalent than is generally assumed. Although having a product that appeals to the Japanese consumer is important to success in the Japanese market, it is a necessary but insufficient condition for successful operation. An innovative product must be accompanied by a genuine willingness on the part of the foreign firm to understand the peculiarities of the Japanese system and, more important, to adapt to them. Only then can a foreign manufacturer hope to succeed in the Japanese market. The case studies presented in the book will document this assertion.

3

Questionnaire Survey Findings

This chapter reports the results of a questionnaire survey conducted in the last quarter of 1981 on the subject of U.S.-Japan business negotiations.

A 13-page, 45-item questionnaire was developed to identify various aspects of practices, procedures, and outcomes pertaining to U.S.-Japan business negotiations. Specifically, information was gathered on the following:

1. The nature and extent of present trade/contractual agreements with Japan.
2. The criteria used in selecting a Japanese partner.
3. The importance of business relations with Japan to the company's overall profitability.
4. The composition of the U.S. and Japanese negotiating teams.
5. The company's satisfaction or dissatisfaction with the quality of past negotiations.
6. Areas in which U.S. companies hope to see major improvements in the future.
7. Perceived differences in the decision-making and negotiating styles of the Japanese negotiating team vis-à-vis the U.S. team.
8. Areas of conflict between U.S. and Japanese partners and means for resolving such differences between the parties.
9. The success rate of business negotiations with the Japanese.
10. Factors accounting for the success and failure of such negotiations.
11. Programs that help firms prepare for the negotiations.

The questionnaire was pilot-tested and subsequently revised. The revised questionnaire (see Appendix) was sent to approximately 582 firms listed in Angel's *Directory of American Firms Operating Abroad* (1980) that had subsidiary or affiliate operations in Japan. Of the 165 responses, 114 questionnaires were usable. The questionnaires were completed by the vice-president for foreign operations or someone similarly designated in each organization.

The firms were of diverse sizes, measured in terms of the company's 1980 assets. Thirty-five percent of the respondents came from companies whose 1980 assets were over $1 billion; 13 percent of them were from companies whose assets ranged between $500 million and $1 billion; 23 percent were from companies whose assets were between $100 million and $499 million; and 33 percent of the respondents came from companies whose assets were below $99 million. The respondent firms were engaged in a wide variety of industries and business activities, including electronics, seeds, consumer products, automotive vehicles and parts, food processing, broadcasting, engineering, aerospace, sporting goods and equipments, livestock, steel and metalworks, ship chartering, insurance, chemical manufacturing, forest products, advertising, news gathering, and accounting/tax-consulting services.

There are several limitations associated with the procedure used in obtaining data for the study. First, the length of the questionnaire may have affected the response rate, although the final sample of 114 firms is large enough to permit meaningful analysis of the data. Second, the respondents may be somewhat self-selecting. Only 9 percent of respondent firms had success rates of 40 percent or below; the overwhelming majority of respondent firms were relatively successful in their operations in Japan. This possible bias in the sample, however, may further a primary purpose of the study: to obtain a better understanding of the factors that contribute to successful U.S.-Japan business negotiations. Nevertheless, the findings should be interpreted in light of these possible biases in the final sample, which may not be representative of all U.S. firms that actually have business relations with Japan.

Findings

History of Negotiations with Japan

The first section of the questionnaire sought to examine the history of each company's negotiations with Japan. Information was gathered on the nature and extent of present trade/contractual agreements with Japan, the nature and frequency with which the company entered into business negotiations with the Japanese, which side took the initiative in contacting the other party to discuss the prospects of trade between the two parties, and the Japanese agencies that the U.S. investor have to deal with in establishing trade/contractual agreements in Japan.

Many of the respondent firms had entered into more than one form of trade/contractual agreement with the Japanese. Thirty-seven percent of the respondents had entered into joint-venture agreements of various types; 44 percent had equity ownership with manufacturing facilities within Japan; 23 percent had equity ownership with no manufacturing facilities. Thirty-seven percent of the respondents were engaged in exporting to Japan and 25 percent in importing from Japan. Sixty-one percent of the firms were engaged in licensing, and 34 percent provided technical assistance. None of the firms were engaged in franchising or turnkey-plus operations. Only very few firms were engaged in consortia, lease agreements, turnkey operations, and management contracts.

Besides showing the diversity of business agreements between U.S. and Japanese firms, the response also indicates whether there were significant differences in success rates among firms that pursued different types of trade relationships with the Japanese. No statistically significant difference was found. This suggests that neither party would restrict itself to one particular form of economic cooperation or relationship as long as an arrangement was mutually beneficial. It is interesting, however, that although the Japanese government has allowed 100-percent foreign-equity ownership in most industries since May 1, 1973, only 12 percent of the respondents had 100-percent equity ownership with manufacturing facilities established within Japan. This could be attributed to the problems of operating wholly owned subsidiaries in Japan, given the complexities of the distribution system and the difficulties of recruiting capable Japanese college graduates to work for foreign firms.

The next question asked how many Japanese enterprises or partners the company was involved with for trade and other forms of economic cooperation. The majority of respondents are at present involved with 4 or fewer Japanese partners or enterprises: 44 percent of the firms have 2 to 4 partners, whereas 30 percent have only 1. Eight percent of the respondents are currently involved with 5 to 7 Japanese partners; 3 percent have 8 to 10 Japanese partners; and 16 percent have more than 10 Japanese partners. These responses indicate the extent of involvement by U.S. firms in the Japanese market.

Nearly half the companies (44 percent) have entered into negotiations with the Japanese more than 10 times over the past 10 years. One-third of the firms have entered into 1 to 3 negotiations with the Japanese during the past 10 years. This question was designed to determine whether experience in negotiating with the Japanese would increase the success rate for such negotiations. Given the vast cultural differences between the United States and Japan, a U.S. firm may not know how to proceed. This may affect the outcome of negotiations. One would generally expect that companies that have engaged in previous negotiations with the Japanese would be more knowledgeable and skilled in discussing terms of trade with the Japanese, which may positively influence the outcome of the negotiations.

T-tests of significance showed that the firms that engaged in more than 10 negotiations with the Japanese experienced significantly higher incidences of success in obtaining trade agreements with the Japanese ($p \leq .005$). An alternative explanation could be that firms that were successful in their initial dealings with Japan would be encouraged to pursue further business relations with the Japanese.

Approximately 20 percent of the negotiations were for the conclusion of licensing agreements, and 18 percent were for the establishment of joint ventures. Other companies engaged in negotiations to establish manufacturing facilities in Japan (12 percent); to conclude commercial and service contractual arrangements (10 percent); to establish manufacturing facilities in the United States (4 percent); to export to Japan (27 percent); and to import from Japan (8 percent). The balance of the negotiations were to discuss miscellaneous agreements, including change in equity position and termination of joint-venture agreements.

Although a greater percentage of the negotiations were for the establishment of manufacturing facilities in Japan than for the establishment of similar facilities in the United States, it is interesting to observe changes in the pattern of Japanese foreign direct investment overseas. Initially, Japanese foreign direct investment was confined to the neighboring Southeast Asian countries and the developing nations. From the early 1970s on, as Japan made rapid economic and technological strides, it began to look to the developed countries for investment opportunities. This is, however, still a relatively new phenomenon. As of the end of 1980 Japan had controlling interests in only 210 manufacturing companies in the United States (Hahn 1982, p. 21). This accounts for the limited percentage of negotiations for the purpose of establishing manufacturing facilities in the United States.

In the 1980s, when an increasing number of Western nations are burdened with high unemployment and slow economic growth, there are strong demands to curb Japanese imports. To respond to these changing world conditions, Japanese firms increasingly must establish manufacturing facilities in the developed nations to maintain their market positions. Consequently, negotiations to establish manufacturing facilities in the United States are expected to increase in the future. Although the questionnaire did not specifically examine the differences between negotiations for the establishment of facilities in Japan as opposed to the United States, it would be interesting to investigate whether such differences exist and, if so, how these differences affect the outcome of such negotiations.

The next question examined the physical location or site for the conduct of business negotiations. Nierenberg (1973), for instance, discusses the advantages and disadvantages of conducting negotiations in home territory as opposed to foreign soil. Most of the negotiations were conducted in Japan. Approximately half the firms indicated that 80 percent or more of the negotiations took place in Japan; only 14 percent indicated that 80 percent or more of the negotiations were conducted in the United States. This is understandable, since the majority of the negotiations were for the provision of facilities in Japan.

Given the heavy volume of annual trade between the United States and Japan and their mutual importance as major trading partners, it appears that enterprises from both countries are equally anxious to initiate business and other cooperative arrangements between the two nations. This was the perception of half the respondent firms, which indicated that both sides took the initiative in establishing business relations. On the other hand, 36 percent of the respondents said that the U.S. side took the initiative in contacting the other party to discuss prospects of trade between the two countries. This could stem from the recognition by U.S. investors that investment opportunities abound in the Pacific Rim countries, particularly Japan, because of the existence of a vast and still largely untapped market. Because of tariff and nontariff restrictions, many foreign firms (with a few notable exceptions) have so far failed to make significant inroads into the Japanese economy. There is a consensus that in the 1980s, more than ever, the Japanese government is generally receptive to increased foreign investment (*Foreign Companies,* 1982).

One misconception about the Japanese economy pertains to the persuasive influence of government in industry and the complexities of dealing with Japanese ministries. The next set of questions examined the role of the government and the ministries in business negotiations to establish collaborative arrangements between U.S. and Japanese partners or entities. Most U.S. firms indicated that they had to deal with one or more of the following Japanese agencies in establishing trade or contractual agreements with the Japanese: the Ministry of International Trade and Industry (MITI), the Japanese government, the Japan External Trade Organization (JETRO), and miscellaneous ministries and public agencies. Only 37 percent of the firms indicated that they had no dealings with any of these agencies.

Although most firms had to deal with the aforementioned Japanese agencies, the majority felt that none of these were active participants in the negotiations. The responses to these items illustrate the role of Japanese government involvement in foreign investment through the principle of administrative guidance, discussed in the previous chapter. Although the extent of economic cooperation with foreign entities is dictated by the Japanese government and its ministries, these agencies do not play an active role in the actual negotiations. Except in strategic industries and in collaborative projects that involve the government itself, representatives of these ministries and agencies are seldom, if ever, present at the negotiations. It can be assumed, however, that the ministries are briefed about the progress of such negotiations.

The role of the Japanese government and its ministries in actual negotiations is highlighted in the cases of Nippon Univac Kaisha and Boeing Commercial Airplane Company. The former case deals with the formation of a joint venture between the Mitsui Trading Company and Sperry Univac Corporation in 1958 for the manufacture of mainframe computers at a time when computers were designated a key industry to be fostered in Japan. The latter case deals with a joint program between Boeing Commercial Airplane Company and the Civil Transport Development Corporation, a quasi-Japanese government entity for the manufacture of parts used in the production of 767s, the newest line of Boeing commercial airplanes, which began delivery in late 1982. The Boeing negotiations took place at a time when the Japanese government was committed to the development of an aerospace industry and to heavier spending for national defense.

The next set of questions dealt with the extent to which the U.S. firms were satisfied or dissatisfied with the quality of past negotiations, and the major sources of dissatisfaction. The overwhelming majority of firms (90 percent) were "satisfied" or "very satisfied" with the quality of past negotiations. Of the 10 percent that were "dissatisfied" or "very dissatisfied" with the quality of past negotiations, the major sources of dissatisfaction cited were: differences in negotiating styles (10 percent); language barrier (9 percent); delays in decision making (9 percent); cultural differences (7 percent); lack of control over pace of negotiations (7 percent); lack of authority on the part of the Japanese negotiating team to make major decisions (5 percent); inquiries not fully answered (5 percent); inquiries not promptly answered (5 percent); lack of control over content of the negotiations (4 percent); and insincerity on the part of the Japanese negotiation team (4 percent). Most of these factors were studied further in the survey. None of the respondents who were dissatisfied with the quality of past negotiations cited "poor negotiating skills of the Japanese" as a source of discontent or dissatisfaction. This supports the popular belief that Japanese negotiators are astute negotiators who should not be underestimated.

Although most of the U.S. firms were satisfied with the quality of past business negotiations with the Japanese, many did indicate that there could be room for improvement. The areas in which U.S. firms hoped to see major improvements were as follows: improved communication between the parties (40 percent); the ability to make more rapid decisions (35 percent); greater control over the pace of the negotiations (26 percent); inquiries answered more fully (18 percent); greater trust between the two parties (11 percent); inquiries answered more promptly (11 percent); and more control over the content of the negotiating sessions (5 percent). The responses suggest that in conducting negotiations with the Japanese, U.S. firms should be aware of potential communication problems between the parties and of the general slowness of the negotiations. Communication problems could arise from differences in culture, corporate objectives, and language, and from the sheer physical distance between the United States and Japan. U.S. businessmen should be prepared to cope with these factors.

The next set of questions examined the importance of business relations with Japan and the criteria used by U.S. firms to select a Japanese partner for trade or contractual agreements. When asked to characterize the importance of business agreements with Japan to the overall profitability of their company, only 3 percent of the respondents indicated such agreements were "very important." Thirty-seven percent of the firms described such agreements as "important" to the company's overall profitability; 41 percent perceived such agreements as "moderately important"; and 19 percent viewed the agreements as "unimportant" to the overall profitability of the company.

A key to understanding these responses is to distinguish between long- and short-term profitability. No business firm would undertake a venture if the prospects of making a reasonable return on its investments were low. Given the difficulties of establishing operations in Japan, many U.S. firms have been unable to capture a significant portion of the Japanese market. Furthermore, it takes time and patience to develop business relations with Japanese firms. Consequently, U.S. companies may perceive their operations in Japan as less profitable in the short run than their business at home or in other parts of the world.

With respect to the criteria used by U.S. firms to select a Japanese enterprise or agency as a partner in trade or economic cooperation, 72 percent of the respondent firms indicated "access to Japanese market" as an important yardstick. This highlights the difficulty of penetrating the Japanese market without assistance from a local partner. Other important criteria mentioned for selection of a partner included technological expertise (40 percent), capital contribution (17 percent), connections with Japanese government (11 percent), access to Southeast Asian market (8 percent), and manufacturing expertise or capability (5 percent).

Composition of Negotiating Teams

To give business firms with little or no experience in negotiating with the Japanese an overview of what to expect in actual negotiations, the questionnaire contained items pertaining to the size and composition of the negotiating teams and the use of third parties or agents in doing business with the Japanese.

Of the companies, 81 percent indicated that the U.S. negotiating team had between 2 and 4 members. Sixty-three percent indicated that the Japanese team had 2 to 4 members; 31 percent observed that the Japanese team had 5 to 7 members. An overwhelming majority of the firms were satisfied with the current sizes of their negotiating teams. Only 4 percent indicated that they wished the respective teams were smaller.

The compositions of the U.S. and Japanese negotiating teams were fairly homogeneous. The U.S. negotiating teams included: technical specialists (68 percent), attorney (46 percent), chief executive officer or owner of organization (45 percent), accountant (19 percent), industry representative (4 percent), government representative (0 percent). The Japanese negotiating team contained: technical specialists (77 percent), attorney (32 percent), accountant (31 percent), industry representative (6 percent), and government representative (4 percent).

The majority of negotiating teams included at least one technical specialist. This could reflect the nature of the contractual agreements entered into between U.S. and Japanese partners, coupled with the Japanese preference for specific, detailed technical information. In contrast to the typical negotiation between two U.S. firms, where both sides would invariably be represented by legal staff, the role of attorneys is downplayed in negotiations between U.S. and Japanese firms. This could reflect the traditional Japanese distaste for formal legal representation in negotiations.

None of the U.S. firms cited government representation on the U.S. team, and only 4 percent indicated the presence of industry representatives. This compares with 6 and 4 percent of the respondent firms who described their Japanese partners' teams as comprising industry and government representatives, respectively. This suggests that some U.S. firms feel that their Japanese counterparts can solicit the assistance of their industry and government in important negotiations. The fact that only a very small percentage of the U.S. firms cited the presence of government representatives in the Japanese negotiating team reinforces the earlier observation about the role of the government in actual negotiations.

Fifty-six percent of the U.S. firms included a bilingual member in their negotiating teams. Most of these firms (77 percent) indicated that the bilingual member's role was primarily that of an interpreter. Only 20 percent indicated that the bilingual member was actively involved in making important decisions during the negotiations. An overwhelming majority of the firms (87 percent) felt that the presence of the bilingual member improved the quality of the negotiations, and an almost equal number believed that the presence of the bilingual member increased the speed of the negotiations. Of those who did not have a bilingual member on their team, half indicated that they wished they had had one. The majority of firms that had no bilingual person on the team intended to do so in the future and perceived this is an important factor in affecting the outcome of the negotiations.

In most instances the Japanese negotiating team furnished interpreters. Half of the respondent firms were "satisifed" or "very satisfied" with the interpretation services rendered by their Japanese parnters. For those who were "dissatisfied" or "very dissatisfied" with the translation services, the principal sources of dissatisfaction were lack of command of the English language, unwillingness to present the U.S. firm's points of view, failure of the interpreters to make exact translations, and a feeling that there were "only indirect communications" between the parties. Given such potential problems and the fact that the oral English capabilities of the Japanese negotiators vary, it may be worthwhile for a U.S. firm to include a bilingual member on its negotiating team. Misunderstanding due to inadequate interpretation services impedes the progress of negotiations and may completely disrupt them because the perspectives of both sides cannot be presented accurately. Besides mere interpretation, a bilingual person familiar with Japanese culture can also interpret the "silent language" of various terms and gestures (Hall 1973) for the U.S. side. In addition, a bilingual member could make suggestions about the best way to present certain points of view where there are cultural differences in discussing various viewpoints (Brislin 1976). This is particularly important given the Japanese emphasis on face-saving and avoidance of direct confrontation.

The respondents were asked whether they used the services of a third party or agent. Only 41 percent engaged the services of a third party, primarily an attorney or a trading company. Of these, approximately half indicated that they will continue to use the services of such third parties or agents in the future. For those who chose to discontinue the services of a third party, the primary reasons given were dissatisfaction with the services rendered by the agent and lack of control over the third party or agent.

Differences in Decision-making and Negotiating Styles

The next set of questions asked respondents to characterize the decision-making style of the Japanese negotiating team and to report perceived differences in negotiating styles. The majority of U.S. companies perceived major differences in decision-making style but were divided in their perceptions of how decisions were made among the Japanese negotiating-team members. Of the companies, 37 percent indicated that there appeared to be no single key decision maker and that every member of the team seemed to have an equal say in the final decision. Nineteen percent of the respondent firms felt that none of the members of the Japanese negotiating team appeared to have the authority to make the decision. Another 37 pecent of the U.S. firms characterized the decision-making style of the Japanese team as very slow and unhurried. This slowness could be attibuted to the need to reach consensus. Other perceived differences in decision-making styles were described as follows: No one in Japan likes to say "no"; the Japanese have a strong desire to be "agreeable and cooperative"; although the Japanese strive for a consensus, if the matter is of sufficient importance, the senior person has the authority to make major commitments; and the Japanese are very thorough and proceed cautiously. A few U.S. firms believed that the decision making went beyond the "team within the company, and that entire industry and trade segments act in concert most of the time." These firms indicated that negotiations were subject to "final corporate and governmental approvals, and the frequent negotiation breaks allow for caucus and consultation."

Besides differences in decision-making style, the overwhelming majority of U.S. companies (93 percent) perceived major dissimilarities in negotiating styles between U.S. and Japanese teams. The principal reported differences were: the Japanese like to avoid direct confrontation on issues (67 percent); the Japanese take longer to make major decisions (49 percent); the Japanese negotiators seemed to be more concerned with establishing long-term associations (37 percent); the Americans are more flexible (33 percent); and the Japanese place heavy emphasis on face-saving (32 percent). Other perceived differences included the following: the Japanese have a greater tolerance for silence; the Japanese are more flexible and are "exceedingly accommodating"; the Japanese prefer "more general wording of agreements"; and, although the Japanese may take longer to reach a decision, they "move more quickly and efficiently" thereafter. These reported differences in decision-making and negotiating styles are largely culture-based. This points to the need for U.S. companies to be aware of such differences and cope with them.

*Factors Responsible for Success or
Failure of the Negotiations*

The questionnaire then examined the success rate of U.S. firms in obtaining business agreements with Japan, and the factors that were perceived as important for success or failure of the negotiations.

With respect to the success rate of business negotiations, 5 percent of the firms indicated a 100-percent success rate; 41 percent indicated an 80–99 percent success rate; 34 percent indicated a 60–79-percent success rate; 13 percent indicated a 40–59-percent success rate; 5 percent indicated a 20–39-percent rate; 2 percent indicated less than a 20-percent success rate; and 2 percent indicated zero success rate. Although the successes far outnumbered the failures, there is considerable room for improvement.

Tables 3-1 and 3-2 examine the extent to which the firms perceived certain items to be responsible for the success or failure of the negotiations. The ten items cited as responsible for the success of business negotiations were subjected to factor analysis. The results of orthogonal quartimax rotation were compared with those obtained from oblique oblimin and orthogonal varimax rotations. The various factor matrixes were found to be fairly consistent. Only the results of orthogonal quartimax rotation are reported here. Six separate factors were extracted. The eigenvalues, which are the

Table 3-1

Factors Responsible for the Success of Business Negotiations

	Factor Loadings	Very Important[a] (%)	Important[a] (%)	Moderately Important[a] (%)	Total (%)
Attitude of U.S. firm					
Preparedness on part of U.S. team	.8156	67	23	5	95
Patience on part of U.S. team	.8403	59	30	8	97
U.S. team's sincerity, good faith, honesty	.8141	59	28	10	97
	Eigenvalue: 3.7971				
	% of var.: 34.5				
	Cum. var.: 34.5				
Cultural awareness					
Familiarity with Japanese business practices	.6403	31	38	26	95
Familiarity with Japanese customs	.8131	22	31	33	86
Uniqueness of Japanese product/service	.5199	13	28	38	79
	Eigenvalue: 1.3038				
	% of var.: 11.9				
	Cum. var.: 46.4				
Attitude of Japanese firm					
Japanese team's sincerity, good faith, honesty	.7003	56	27	15	98
	Eigenvalue: 1.1880				
	% of var.: 10.8				
	Cum. var.: 57.2				
Product characteristics					
Uniqueness of U.S. product/service	.7076	40	37	16	93
	Eigenvalue: 1.006				
	% of var.: 9.1				
	Cum. var.: 66.3				
Personal relationships					
Personal ties built up over the years	.5846	33	38	18	89
	Eigenvalue: .9861				
	% of var.: 9.0				
	Cum. var.: 75.3				
Technical expertise					
Technical expertise provided by U.S. firm in the past	.4982	29	39	19	87
	Eigenvalue: .8120				
	% of var.: 7.4				
	Cum. var.: 82.7				

[a]Figures indicate the percentage of firms in the total sample that perceive the extent to which the respective items were important to success.

Table 3-2
Factors Responsible for the Failure of Business Negotiations

	Factor Loadings	"To Some Extent" to "To a Very Great Extent" (%)[a]	"Not relevant" to "To a Little Extent" (%)[a]
Cultural differences			
Differences in social customs	.7750	44	33
Communication breakdown	.4906	69	19
Insurmountable cultural differences	.7260	21	44
Differences in negotiation styles	.6933	58	20
Differences in business practices	.6594	59	17
Insincerity on part of Japanese	.4424	42	30
	Eigenvalue: 2.9341 % of var.: 55.6 Cum. var.: 55.6		
Product characteristics			
Japanese did not need products/services	.7979	83	9
Too many competitors all offering same products/services	.7004	73	13
	Eigenvalue: 1.0860 % of var.: 20.6 Cum. var.: 76.1		

[a]Figures indicate the percentage of firms in the total sample that perceive the extent to which the respective items were responsible for failure.

measures of the relative importance of the respective factors, are presented in table 3-1. The first factor, labeled "attitude of U.S. firm," included items pertaining to the preparation of the U.S. firm, patience on the part of the U.S. team, and the latter's sincerity. All these items are related in some way to the willingness of the U.S. firm to devote time and effort to cultivating a business relationship with the Japanese partner. This was perceived by the majority of firms as the most important factor in the success of the negotiations. This finding points to the need for U.S. firms to exercise patience and develop a longer-range perspective when investing and doing business in Japan.

The second factor could be labeled "cultural awareness" and included such items as familiarity with Japanese customs and business practices. The item "uniqueness of product/service that Japanese firm could offer" loaded highly on this factor. A possible explanation is that where a Japanese product or service is unique, the U.S. firm would tend to be more accommodating and hence exhibit a greater willingness to adapt to cultural differences in order to obtain access to the product and/or service. This factor was perceived by most U.S. firms as less important than factor 1 ("attitude of U.S. firm")—a finding consistent with previous research on the importance of being able to bridge cultural gaps (Tung 1982a). Familiarity with a foreign culture is a necessary but insufficient condition for success. There must be a genuine willingness on the part of both sides to work toward some common ground—that is, to accommodate the needs of the other party.

A third factor, which could be labeled "attitude of Japanese firm," included a single item pertaining to the sincerity, honesty, and good faith exhibited by the Japanese partner in the negotiations. Negotiations require the mutual cooperation and efforts of both parties.

A fourth factor, labeled "product characteristics," consisted of the uniqueness of the product or service offered by the U.S. firm. Given the difficulties encountered by foreign investors in establishing operations in Japan, and the general competitiveness of Japanese producers, it is important that the product or service offered by the U.S. firm be truly unique. Otherwise, the chances of a U.S. firm's gaining successful entry and penetration into the Japanese market may be severely hampered.

A fifth factor, which could be labeled "personal relationships," included the friendly ties built up between the parties over a number of years. This again points to the need for patience and the importance of cultivating and developing personal ties to ensure the successful operation of joint cooperative arrangements between the parties. In Japan, human relations, as characterized by the close bonds between superior-subordinate and among peers, play a significant role in the smooth operation of any human endeavor. U.S firms should pay due respect to this factor.

A sixth and final factor perceived as contributing to the success of business negotiations was the technical expertise provided by the U.S. firm to the Japanese partner in the past. This factor reflects a combination of the previous two factors, "product characteristics" and "personal relationships." In the early years after World War II, a significant technological gap existed between the United States and Japan. In those days Japan imported a lot of technology in the form of licensing agreements and was a major recipient of U.S. technical-assistance programs.

Although the Japanese have made remarkable strides in technological development since then, many remain grateful for the initial assistance provided them after the war; others concede that the United States still have a technological edge in certain areas. Consequently, technical expertise provided by U.S. firms to their Japanese partners in the past is viewed as a contributing factor to the success of business negotiations. In the case of Merck and Company, which introduced streptomycin (a cure for tuberculosis) into

Japan after the war, when the country was plagued with the disease, P. Reed Maurer notes that even today Japanese come up to him to express their appreciation to Merck for manufacturing the vaccine that saved members of their families.

Other write-in items perceived by U.S. firms as contributing to the success of business negotiations included the following: availability of a mutually respected go-between, meeting national objectives, congruence of interpreters on each side, U.S. capability for alternative business actions, and "being able to drink after work and go to work the next day." Most of these factors are discussed elsewhere in this book.

The eight items identified as being responsible for the failure of business negotiations were also factor-analyzed (orthogonal quarimax rotation). Two factors were extracted. The eigenvalues of the respective factors are presented in table 3-2. Factor 1, labeled "cultural differences," included items pertaining to communication breakdown and differences in business practices, negotiating styles, and social customs. The item "lack of sincerity on the part of the Japanese" also loaded highly on this factor. A possible explanation for this finding is that perceived insincerity on the part of the Japanese negotiators could be attributed in part to cultural differences. For example, in the United States, eye contact during hand-shaking and conversation is considered a sign of honesty and sincerity. In Japan, on the other hand, eye contact is not common in greeting or conversation. Many Japanese deem it inappropriate to establish eye contact during the exchange of greetings or in the course of conversations. As a result, many Japanese international firms have considered it necessary to include a course in "How to Shake Hands with Occidentals" in their training programs for preparing employees for overseas assignments. In the words of a Japanese executive, his employees are taught that in the West it is good manners to "watch the eyes of the person whose hand you are shaking" (Tung 1984). Hence behavior patterns that are specific to a given cultural environment may be misconstrued by the U.S. negotiators as indications of insincerity and dishonesty on the part of the Japanese negotiators.

Two points with regard to cultural differences deserve mention. First, although "cultural differences" may be viewed as less important than "attitude of U.S. firms" in the success of business negotiations, ignoring such differences may be detrimental to the outcome of negotiations. Unfamiliarity with cultural differences and inability to bridge the cultural gap can lead to the collapse of business negotiations.

Second, the specific item "insurmountable cultural differences," which loaded on the factor entitled "cultural differences," was perceived by approximately half the respondent firms as either irrelevant or responsible "to a very little extent" for the failure of business negotiations. This suggests that although differences in social customs, negotiating styles, and business practices may pose tremendous obstacles to the progress of negotiations, most respondents perceive these barriers as surmountable. U.S. firms should realize that with careful preparation and proper understanding, cultural differences need not impede progress or negatively affect the outcome of business negotiations.

A second factor responsible for the failure of business negotiations was labeled "product characteristics" and included two items: "Japanese did not need products/services offered by the U.S. firm" and "too many competitors all offering the same products/services that U.S. company supplies." The first item, "Japanese did not need products/services offered by the U.S. firm," was perceived by 83 percent of the respondent firms as being responsible for the failure of business negotiations. This was by far the most frequently mentioned item. This finding again points to the extreme competitiveness of the Japanese market and the need for U.S. firms to offer unique products or services in order to make significant inroads into the Japanese economy.

Other write-in items that were perceived by U.S. firms as contributing to the failure of business negotiations included: restrictions imposed by the Japanese government; physical distance between the two countries, which compounded problems of communication and control; and differences in profit standards. These factors are examined in greater detail elsewhere in the book.

Conflict and Conflict Resolution

The next set of questions examined areas of conflict between the parties and the means for resolving such differences. The principal areas of conflict were: differences over contribution (for example, technological know-how, machinery, and so on) by either party (27 percent); differences over extent of management control (21 percent); differences over equity ownership (19 percent); differences over remuneration policies for Japanese and U.S. personnel (11 percent); differences in opinion about the rights and responsibilities of management and labor (7 percent); and differences over pricing of products (5 percent). Other areas of conflict mentioned by the respondents included differences in areas of market interest between the two partners, and divergences in corporate objectives, such as return on investment, market share, and profit margins. As noted in chapter 2, there could be significant differences between Japanese and U.S. firms with respect to corporate objectives, the measure of profitability of an operation, and the time horizon used in planning. If not properly addressed, these differences could debilitate the existing collaborative arrangements between the parties and lead to the eventual dissolution of such cooperative agreements between U.S. and Japanese firms.

Although conflicts appear to be inevitable in any partnership, they need not be destructive as long as effective mechanisms are available for resolving them. Hence there is a need to examine the means for resolving such conflicts when they arise. The respondent firms were asked to identify the methods their companies have found useful in resolving conflicts. A full 74 percent cited friendly discussion as a useful mechanism for ironing out such differences; 65 percent resorted to compromise. Given the traditional Japanese distaste for litigation and emphasis on face-saving, the parties seldom resorted to arbitration (4 percent) or open confrontation (11 percent) as means of conflict resolution. Ten percent of the firms sought the assistance of a mutually respected third party to resolve differences.

Preparation for Negotiations

In preparing for negotiations with the Japanese, U.S. firms used the following techniques (the figures in parentheses indicate the percentage of firms that considered each of these techniques "important" or "very important" to improving the quality of the negotiations): read books on Japanese business practices and social customs (74 percent); hired experts to train negotiators (53 percent); and used simulated negotiations (32 percent). Other preparatory procedures included the use of their Japanese staff to assist in the negotiations (7.5 percent); study of the Japanese language; and extensive prior discussions with business consultants, banks, trading companies, academics, and other negotiators.

Since "cultural differences" were seen as a major factor in the failure of negotiations, it is natural that firms would perceive reading books about Japanese business practices and social customs as very important to improving the quality of the negotiations. Similarly, hiring experts to train negotiators (including the use of legal and business advice from professional firms in Tokyo) was seen as an important device by approximately 53 percent of the firms. Where the company does not have in-house facilities, it may be necessary to hire experts to provide assistance. Given the language barrier and the tremendous cultural differences, some U.S. firms simply relied on their Japanese staff to handle the negotiations.

Those firms that did not sponsor formal preparatory procedures for negotiating with the Japanese cited the following reasons: prior experience in trading with Japan (60 percent); lack of time (13 percent); doubt about effectiveness of such procedures (12 percent); and feeling that negotiations were not important to overall profitability of the company (6 percent).

Regression Analysis

The study then sought to examine the relationships between incidences of success (y) and number of previous negotiations with the Japanese ($x1$); type of industry ($x2$); type of trade relationship ($x3$); assets of U.S. firm ($x4$); and types of programs used in preparing for the negotiations ($x5$ = read books on Japanese business practices and social customs, $x6$ = hired experts to train negotiators; $x7$ = simulated negotiations). The results of regression analysis are presented in table 3-3.

As expected, having had previous negotiations with the Japanese and reading books on Japanese business practices and social customs were significantly ($p \leq .05$) associated with success rates. The other explanatory variables, such as the type of industry, type of trade relationship, assets of U.S. firm, hiring of experts to train negotiators, and the use of simulated negotiations, were not significantly related to success.

To corroborate these findings, T-tests were run to determine whether there were significant differences between those firms with a high incidence of success and the aforementioned independent variables. Significant differences (at the .005 level or better) were found for the two explanatory variables of number of negotiations and reading books on business practices. A marginally significant difference (at the .010 level) was found for those firms that were engaged in high-technology industries such as engineering, aerospace, and electronics.

Implications of Findings

Based on the results of this study, the following inferences for business practices could be drawn:

Table 3-3
Relationships between Incidence of Success and Practices and Procedures for U.S.-Japan Business Negotiations

	Number of Negotiations	Type of Industry	Assets of U.S. Firm	Read Books	Hired Experts	Simulated Negotiations	Type of Trade Relationship
Incidences of Success	.6314** (.005)	.2185 (.010)	−.1711 (N.S.)	.6407** (.005)	.2987 (.010)	.2793 (.010)	−.1288 (N.S.)

Notes:
  F Value = 5.13 (p<.005)
  R^2 = .6281
  R^2 = .5674
  p** < .05
  Figures in parentheses indicate *t*-tests of significance.
  N.S. = not significant

1. Most U.S. firms perceive major differences between the decision-making and negotiating styles of the U.S. and the Japanese negotiating teams. Many of these differences are culture-based. The results of regression analysis and T-tests of significance indicate that reading books on Japanese business practices and social customs could improve cultural understanding and thus increase the probability of success of future negotiations. As noted previously, the analyses of factors responsible for the success or failure of negotiations suggest that familiarity with Japanese business practices and social customs is a necessary but insufficient condition for success. Its absence is perceived as a primary factor in the failure of the negotiations. Knowledge, however, must be combined with a genuine willingness to work toward a common goal. The findings on perceived differences in negotiating styles between the U.S. and Japanese teams should prove useful in assisting U.S. firms to be cognizant of such dissimilarities and consequently to cope with them.

2. The analysis of factors responsible for the success of business negotiations indicates that the attitude adopted by the U.S. firm has a significant impact on the outcome of the negotiation. This is where preparatory procedures designed to familiarize understanding of the Japanese culture would be useful. As noted previously, reading books on Japanese business practices and social customs could significantly increase the incidences of success. Although the other preparatory procedures, such as hiring of experts to train negotiators and use of simulated negotiations, were not significant explanatory variables in the regression analysis in accounting for success, T-tests of significance showed that there were significant differences (at the .010 level) in the incidences of success between those firms that hired experts to train negotiators and those that did not. A similar finding was obtained between those firms that used simulated negotiations and those that did not.

3. Results of regression analysis and T-tests of significance indicate that experience in negotiating with the Japanese increases the probability of success of future negotiations. Those firms that plan to enter into trade would benefit from learning about other companies' experiences and thereby trying to avoid pitfalls.

4. Regression analysis and T-tests indicate that the type of industry, type of business relationship, and assets of the U.S. firm do not appear to matter. Firms in various industries and of different sizes could be successful in doing business in Japan. In light of the findings on factors responsible for the success and failure of business negotiations, however, and in view of the extreme competitiveness of the Japanese market, U.S. firms should try to offer only those products and/or services that are truly unique. Otherwise their chances of successful entry and penetration of the Japanese market would be minimized. Furthermore, the T-tests of significance showed that

there were significant differences (at the .010 level) in the incidences of success between those firms that were engaged in the high- as opposed to low-technology industries. This finding is in line with the present commitment by the Japanese government and various Japanese enterprises to further the country's research and development capabilities. In the fiscal year ending March 31, 1983, Japanese companies plan to increase their research and development budgets by a minimum of 13 percent (*Wall Street Journal*, 10 September 1982, p. 32). Several rural villages 37 miles outside of Tokyo have been transformed into a "science city" to concentrate on research and development in the areas of robotics, bionics, lasers, and sophisticated electronics (*U.S. News and World Report*, 10 January 1083, p. 40).

5. Last but not least, many U.S. firms agree that the Japanese generally take longer to make decisions; that the Japanese place a high value on developing business and personal relationships over a period of time; and that Japanese firms tend to emphasize market share over short-term profitability and immediate return on investments. These factors reinforce the popular belief that the Japanese take a longer-range perspective in business dealings than do their U.S. counterparts. Consequently, U.S. firms should cope with such differences and be prepared to invest time and money in building a long-term relationship with the Japanese.

4 Collaboration in the Computer Industry

After Japan's military defeat in 1945, the postwar Japanese government immediately embarked on a series of measures designed to reconstruct and develop the country's industrial infrastructure. The policy of administrative guidance designated certain industries as strategic sectors, which would receive full government support in terms of resource allocation and protection from foreign competition. At first, basic industries such as steel, coal, and electric-power generation were placed under government auspices. In the mid-1950s, when these basic industries had established a sufficiently solid base for subsequent development, the government turned its attention to fast-growing and knowledge-intensive industries such as computers. In the late 1950s computers were added to the list of strategic industries receiving full support from the Japanese government, including tariff protection; duty-free import of raw materials and components; accelerated depreciation; and long-term low-interest loans from government banks such as the Industrial Bank of Japan, the Long-term Credit Bank, and the Reconstruction Bank (Rapp 1975). Under these protective auspices the computer industry flourished; by 1980 indigenous computer manufacturers accounted for half the total market share in Japan. In 1980 Fujitsu overtook International Business Machines (IBM) as the major supplier of computers in the Japanese market (*Nippon*, 1982). In 1980 the dollar value of mainframe computers sold by IBM in Japan reached $4,515 million, compared with a non-U.S.-manufacturer share of $9,664 million (*The New York Times*, 19 September 1982).

As the computer industry developed, it came under increasing pressure from foreign countries for liberalization of inward capital investment. In response, the Japanese government agreed to liberalize the industry in two phases: Effective August 4, 1974, up to 50-percent foreign-equity participation would be allowed; effective December 1, 1975, 100-percent foreign-equity ownership would be permitted (Yoshino 1975). Given the sensitive nature of the computer industry, it is interesting to trace the development of one of the earliest joint ventures between a U.S. firm (Sperry Univac Corporation) and a Japanese entity (Mitsui Bussan or Mitsui Trading Company) in this area. The joint-venture company thus formed is known as Nippon Univac Kaisha, Ltd. (NUK). Besides providing insight into the development of the computer industry in Japan, this particular joint venture has been lauded by both MITI and the Japan External Trade Organization (JETRO) as an exemplary model of cooperation between Japanese and U.S entities.

Consequently, it provides valuable insight into a successful cooperative agreement between two giant multinationals from the two countries. In fiscal 1981 Sperry Corporation's revenues reached $5.43 billion. Sperry's activities, though diversified, are primarily in high-technology areas. In 1981, for example, the company spent $336 million on research and development (R&D) activities, a 20-percent increase over the previous year. Approximately 85 percent of the company's R&D expenditures were channeled into electronics and related activities (*Sperry Annual Report*, 1981). The Japanese partner in the joint venture is Mitsui Bussan, the second-largest trading company (*sogo shosha*) in Japan. In fiscal 1976 Mitsui's revenues reached $3.61 billion, with $1.8379 billion in domestic sales, $7.764 billion in exports, and $2.594 billion in offshore business. The top 9 trading companies in Japan typically handle 50-60 percent of the country's import and export business. The sogo shosha are unique Japanese business institutions whose primary mission is to facilitate trade, develop industrial activities, and provide financing for such endeavors (*Unique World*, 1978). Mitsui is the oldest sogo shosha in Japan, dating back to 1673 (Roberts 1973).

The information presented in this case was obtained through interviews with Shiro Omata and L.J. Casanova. Omata is a second-generation Japanese-American who served on the negotiating team for the formation of the joint venture in 1958. He was subsequently appointed executive vice-president and managing director of Nippon Univac Kaisha, and was later president (1974-1977). Omata, now retired, continues to advise the operations of the joint venture. Casanova served as managing director of the joint venture when Omata was president, and is now the vice-president of Joint Ventures-Japan at Sperry Univac Corporation. Throughout the discussion, the example of another joint venture in the computer industry—between TRW and Fujitsu, in 1980—will be introduced for comparative purposes. The information on the latter joint venture was obtained as part of a course project by a group of students whom I taught at the Graduate School of Management, University of California, Los Angeles. I would like to thank Tal Ross, Henry Takata, Peter Wenzell, and David Winston for the information on the TRW-Fujitsu joint venture.

History

The relationship between Sperry Corporation and the Mitsui group dates back to the early 1920s, when Mitsui served as a distributor for Sperry's gyroscopes, typewriters, and other products in Japan. Sperry had also entered into a licensing agreement with Mitsui for the manufacture of its gyroscopes. During World War II all agreements were terminated. After the war the giant zaibatsus were disbanded in accordance with Allied wishes, but they were reorganized in the early 1950s in their present form. In 1954 a new Mitsui and Company was formed with Japanese government backing, and Sperry resumed its working relationship with the new entity. The reorganized Mitsui group consisted of Mitsui bankers, Mitsui real estate, and so on. The major difference was that the companies in the group were no longer majority-owned by the Mitsui family, but by the general public. The reorganized company groupings were essentially the same: Mitsui, Mitsubishi, and Sumitomo. The companies that make up a given group do not compete with each other; there is no intragroup competition. For example, within Mitsui, the top people in the satellite companies will not undertake a venture if another member firm has already embarked on a similar endeavor. The competition between groups, however—for example, between Mitsubishi and Sumitomo—is intense at times.

Sperry maintained its relationship with the trading company of the Mitsui group. In the early years, Sperry's computers (then called tabulating machines) were distributed through a very small company in Japan, not through Mitsui Trading Company. As the Japanese economy recovered rapidly from the devastating effects of the war, Sperry became aware of the limitations of a distributorship arrangement. In 1956 Sperry decided that for future growth, it was not in the company's best interest to be represented by a small firm. About this time the Japanese government began to take a strong interest in computers. Therefore, Sperry felt that a joint venture with a Japanese entity might be the most viable route for the company, and began its quest for a strong Japanese partner with which to collaborate.

Sperry already had good working relationships with Mitsui. Sperry took the initiative and approached Mitsui Trading Company for the possible formation of a joint venture between the two companies. Mitsui agreed to study the proposal. On March 31, 1958, both sides finally reached agreement. A joint-venture company called Nippon Remington Univac was established. At that time Sperry still had the Remington part of the business, but the Remington name was subsequently dropped from the joint-venture company as Sperry divested its interest in that division.

Mitsui took 70 percent of the original equity ownership of the joint-venture company, and Sperry held the remaining 30 percent. To promote the growth of the computer industry in the country, the Japanese government insisted that the joint venture should begin local manufacture of its products. Sperry was then prepared to share its know-how with the joint-venture company, provided it had controlling interest in the venture. Thus the issue of equity ownership was negotiated between the two partners. As a result of the lengthy negotiations, Sperry increased its share to 40 percent.

As time passed, the company got bigger. Given the strong nationalism of the Japanese and the government's designation of computers as a strategic industry, both partners decided it would be beneficial to give the joint venture a new image in the marketplace as a truly Japanese company, not U.S.-owned. The joint-venture company went public in 1972, and the shares of the company were traded on the Tokyo Stock Exchange. This change in corporate form necessitated a redistribution of equity ownership between the two partners. Both Sperry and Mitsui reduced their holdings to 34.7 percent apiece. In Japan's commercial code, an institution that holds one-third or more of the equity shares of a company may have the right of refusal to change an article of incorporation. This arrangement provided protection for either partner. This pattern of equity ownership has been maintained up to the present. Other minority shareholders in the company include Oki Electric, Mitsubishi Electric, and several other institutions. In retrospect, Casanova felt that the decision to go public was wise.

The initial contacts were made by the international division at Sperry Corporation. When serious negotiations began, the top people in both companies were involved. The senior Sperry officials included Harry Vickers and Frank Foster. General Douglas MacArthur was then chairman of Sperry. Later in the negotiations, Paul Lyet (who later became chairman of Sperry) and MacDonald were involved. There were always 3 to 6 people on the U.S. negotiating team. Mitsui always had about 6 people, including the president and the board executives. Since a basic function of a trading company is to provide financing, Mitsui wanted to assume that role in the joint venture, which was capitalized in the millions of dollars. The Japanese government was then very sensitive to the computer industry and wanted to minimize U.S. influence in a joint-venture company. It took 2 years to satisfy the government and Mitsui about the benefits that would accrue from the joint venture.

From its not-so-humble beginnings the joint venture flourished. Nippon Univac Kaisha (NUK) has been a very successful company. Initially the joint venture employed 242 employees and did several million dollars of business annually. In 1982 the company employed over 4,800 employees, and its revenues reached $369 million (Nippon Univac Kaisha, Ltd., *Report to Shareholders*, 1982). In July 1982 NUK announced its new line of computers, the Univac 1100-90 series, described as the "world's foremost types of giant computers." This series is designed to compete directly with IBM's latest model, the 8081k. The Univac 1100-90 series is claimed to have twice the capacity of IBM's 3081k and to occupy 20-30 percent less floor area than conventional models. The company hopes to sell 200 of these models in the Japanese market over the next 3 years, with shipments to begin in April to June 1983 (*Asahi Evening News*, 15 July 1982, p. 4).

The primary function of NUK is to market and service computers, including developing software for the Japanese market. Even today the Japanese computer industry lags behind that of the United States, primarily in software development. This allegedly prompted some Hitachi, Ltd., and

Mitsubishi Electric Corporation employees to try to steal technical secrets from IBM in 1982 (*U.S. News and World Report*, 23 August 1982).

Over the years and on the suggestion of the Japanese government, NUK began to manufacture certain selected products in Japan. For this purpose Sperry formed another joint venture, known as Oki-Univac, with Oki Denki, a manufacturer of communication equipment. Oki-Univac manufactures the smaller computers for sale in Japan through NUK. In this venture Sperry has 45-percent equity ownership, Oki Electric has 46 percent, and the balance is held by Mitsubishi Electric Corporation. Oki Electric is a closely held company whose shares are not publicly traded. This joint venture has also been successful and currently employs about 600 people, with sales revenue around $67 million.

Besides the joint ventures with Mitsui Trading Company and Oki Electric, Sperry entered into two other ventures, one with Tokyo Keiki Precision Company (TKC), and the other with Mitsui Trading Company and a large Japanese tractor dealership. In the venture with TKC, Sperry has 31-percent equity ownership; Mitsubishi Heavy Industries and Taiyo-Kobe Bank have minority interests in the company. This venture with TKC is also a public company, whose shares are traded on the Tokyo Stock Exchange. This venture handles products from the Hydraulics-Vickers division of Sperry Corporation, with annual sales around $200 million. A fourth venture is a company called New Holland-Japan, which markets farm equipment. In the New Holland-Japan joint venture Sperry owns 60 percent, Mitsui Trading Company owns 20 percent, and the remaining 20 percent is held by a large Japanese tractor dealership. The annual sales of this fourth venture are around $10 million.

The Sperry case illustrates that a U.S. manufacturer can successfully engage in simultaneous relationships with numerous Japanese partners. Despite the strong competition between trading groups, as noted earlier, Sperry's relationships with both Mitsui and Mitsubishi were not considered to conflict because different product lines were involved in the various ventures. Both TKC and Mitsubishi Electric are primarily manufacturing companies, whereas Mitsui Bussan is more of a trading company. Omata believes that Sperry is fortunate to have good partners in all four ventures, which helped the company achieve its objectives in the Japanese market.

The Role of the Government and Nationalism

Since computers were designated a strategic industry, the Japanese government exercised considerable influence on their development. Furthermore, the large trading companies generally have very strong ties with the government for reasons mentioned in chapter 2. To prepare for their eventual "descent from heaven" (*amakudari*), government bureaucrats tend to cultivate good relationships with large corporations to provide a haven for them when they retire from the government between the ages of 50 and 60. In their second career in the private sector, these former government bureaucrats serve as board members or in some advisory capacity until age 65. Another reason for the strong tie between government and industry is the old boys' network.

Under the principle of administrative guidance, the government has authorized the establishment of *kondankai* or three-way consultative mechanisms comprising the government, industry, and the financial sector. Such kondankai are available for the computer industry. According to Omata, consultation with the government is not done openly, but in the background. The Japanese partner, Mitsui Bussan, did all the actual negotiations with the government, although Sperry's representatives did attend some informal sessions and responded to certain queries of the Japanese government. Since the U.S. partner was generally not physically present in the official negotiations between the government and the Japanese partner, information had to be relayed back and forth, which was time-consuming. This accounted in part for the long time it took the two partners to reach agreement. Another reason the negotiations took two years was that the joint venture was formed before the liberalization of the computer industry. Consequently, the Japanese government wanted to minimize foreign participation in the venture.

Even after complete liberalization of the industry in 1975, the Japanese government continued to retain a keen interest in the formation of any joint venture involving foreign-equity participation in this sector. For example, in the formation of the joint venture between TRW and Fujitsu in 1980, MITI and the Ministry of Finance took an active interest, although they were not actually present in the negotiations. In fact, Japanese companies sometimes continue to use the government as an excuse for delays or as a negotiating ploy. In the case of TRW and Fujitsu, for instance, Fujitsu indicated early in the negotiation that for tax purposes a signed letter of intent must be submitted to the respective Japanese government agency by a certain date. TRW signed the letter of intent, believing that the document was a mere formality to facilitate progress. In subsequent negotiations TRW was surprised to discover that Fujitsu had actually treated the letter of intent as a legal document; the latter argued that since final agreement had been reached on the points covered therein, there was no need to negotiate them further.

Besides the role of the government, both Omata and Casanova emphasize the need to understand Japanese nationalism in order to operate successfully in Japan. In the words of Casanova: "Japan is really a socialist country. They say they are a democracy, but they are really a socialist state.

Everyone in Japan always asks himself: 'Is what I am doing good for Japan?' not 'Is it good for me or my company?' It is always in the back of everyone's mind that whatever one does, it has to be beneficial to the country. This permeates society—both government and industry. Some Americans view this as some sort of conspiracy between the government and industry. I think that it is just the Japanese way. They just feel that they have to work together as a unit in order to be successful. The idea of national survival leads to national unity.''

Although a close cooperative relationship exists between government and industry, this does not mean that the government will actually participate in the negotiations. Government influence is exercised through the principle of administrative guidance, which is unique to Japan. The cooperative relationship is not so explicit or blatant as "somebody had this meeting and tomorrow they are going to run over to MITI." Casanova noted that both MITI and industry are Japanese entities, and the Japanese always try to do everything as a country: "So you end up with this almost intuitive sense of cooperation that we are all going to do what is good for Japan." This explains, to a large extent, why the Japanese generally prefer to buy Japanese products, except for consumer items. In the United States, by comparison, people tend to buy the best product for their money. Casanova stated that the reason the Japanese purchase U.S. computers is that they need them to automate their industries. He believes that when the Japanese become completely self-sufficient in computers, "our joint venture could cease to work."

The Japanese Media

The Japanese news media can play an important role in the progress and outcome of negotiations. Even in the 1960s some U.S. officials complained of alleged bias in the Japanese press. According to the *Wall Street Journal*, most informed Americans and some Japanese admit that there is a definite nationalistic slant in the press coverage of major world events. "Like a cheerleader for Japan," the Japanese press has this tendency to report international events in a manner "that fits its view of Japan's interests" (*Wall Street Journal*, 9 December 1982, p. 16). In Omata's observations: "If it is something the Japanese industry needs, the media is all for it. But if they feel that it is not in the interest of Japan, then they will either turn against or ignore you. So you must be very careful in handling the media."

The Japanese press, compared with that in the United States, can have considerable influence on public opinion on certain issues. In the United States, many newspapers with different orientations and varying messages cater primarily to the interests of local audiences. In Japan, on the other hand, there are only five major national daily newspapers. Their circulation figures are staggering. The number-one newspaper, *Yomiuri*, has a readership of 8.58 million. The morning edition of the number-two newspaper, *Asahi*, has a readership of 7.43 million—greater than the combined circulation of six major U.S. newspapers: *The New York Times*, the *Washington Post*, the *Los Angeles Times*, the *Chicago Tribune*, the *New York Daily News*, and the *Wall Street Journal*.

There is a marked homogeneity in the messages conveyed by the five major Japanese newspapers. In general, Japanese television follows closely the opinions of the five major newspapers, with the possible exception of the public network, NHK, which hosts documentaries that tend to provide a more balanced treatment of world issues. The Japanese press generally portrays tiny Japan as a victim of the big bully, the United States. For example, in the coverage of the arrests of employees of Hitachi Ltd. and Mitsubishi Electric Corporation, involving alleged theft of IBM trade secrets, the Japanese press instinctively assumed that the employees of the two major Japanese corporations were innocent victims of entrapment by a conniving U.S. operation (*Wall Street Journal*, 9 December 1982, p. 16).

Another distinguishing feature of the Japanese press is that, although it devotes more attention to U.S. events than the latter does to Japanese news, the picture may be distorted to fit Japanese interests. A foreign firm in Japan must be very careful how it handles the press.

Management of the Joint Venture

The issue of management was addressed at the beginning of the formation of the joint venture. Mitsui was to be responsible for management and financing, and Sperry's contribution would be primarily in technology and product. The management of the company has always been totally Japanese, and its presidents have always been Japanese. At present NUK has approximately 4,800 employees, only 1 of them is an American, who sits on the board and represents Sperry from a technological viewpoint. This resident American assists the joint venture in product strategy and advises on the latest technological developments. While the American resident director is considered an outsider in the consensus decision-making process because he does not speak Japanese, he participates and is involved in decision making at NUK.

Besides this American who is resident in Japan, Sperry has two other board members, Paul Spillane, president of Sperry Univac, and L.J. Casanova. They are outside directors, not working members. In a Japanese company there is a real distinction between working and outside directors. The working, or inside, directors are involved in the day-to-day affairs of managing the company, whereas the outside directors are involved only in the firm's major decisions. In the joint-venture company there are two outside directors from Sperry and a similar number from Mitsui.

The board meetings of a Japanese company are very different from those of a U.S. company. When a decision reaches the board level in Japan, it has already been agreed to by consensus. The board meeting is a mere formality; there is never a "no" vote. The company is managed Japanese-style, by the *jomukai*, the Japanese version of an executive committee. This committee, which meets once a week, includes the working directors. The company's policy and management decisions are made at those meetings by the executive committee through recommendations from within the company and also from external sources, such as the American outside directors and customers. The executive committee is the decision-making body, and there is constant communication between both partners and the people on that committee. Thus management of the joint-venture company is Japanese-style, with input from the U.S. partner. Sperry Corporation has quarterly review meetings with the executive committee, where performance is discussed and projections made for the rest of the year. These sessions are sometimes attended only by the two American outside directors. On other occasions, depending on the issues at hand, the U.S. parent company may bring along a group of three, four, or ten people to Tokyo. For example, if a decision has to be made about a given product, Sperry would bring along experts, including personnel from the controller's office and legal department. In these sessions the U.S. partner provides input to the Japanese management and in turn receives feedback from the joint-venture company. Through this two-way communication process, Sperry is fully briefed on the latest events at NUK and in turn provides input into the management of the company.

To further promote dialogue between the joint-venture company and the U.S. parent corporation, there are regular exchanges of personnel. NUK sends its employees to the United States. At any given time there are approximately twenty to thirty NUK employees at Sperry's headquarters, most of them technical or product-oriented people. Given this regular exchange of personnel, there is a constant, almost daily, dialogue between the joint-venture company and the U.S. corporation. These informal dialogues are supplemented by the formal quarterly review sessions and board meetings. Casanova indicated that "because of the uniqueness of the Japanese mentality, we need to have this constant dialogue to avoid misunderstandings." He attributed the smooth operation of the joint venture in part to this constant communication between the parties.

Given this regular exchange of personnel between the U.S. parent company and the joint venture, it is interesting to see if there were problems in having the Japanese work alongside with the Americans. In Omata's opinion, difficulties would not arise if the functions of both Japanese and Americans were clarified in advance. In his words, "When you give too much leeway to inexperienced individuals, including Americans, then that leads to problems."

In chapter 2, the difficulty of attracting Japanese graduates of elite universities to work in a joint venture was discussed. This was one factor that prompted Sperry to organize a joint-venture company, publicizing the fact that the firm is majority-owned by the Japanese. The Japanese who are recruited by the joint-venture company (not just people from Mitsui or Sperry) are given a real opportunity to rise in the ranks of the organization. This is an incentive for Japanese to work for the joint-venture company. As noted previously, the presidents of the company have always been Japanese. NUK, like IBM, has been successful in attracting top people.

A key to success in recruiting talented young Japanese to work for a foreign firm or one that has foreign-equity participation is to adopt a Japanese style of management, particularly with respect to personnel matters. This includes providing financial assistance for employee housing, recreational facilities, and other fringe benefits typically offered by large Japanese companies. In a Japanese company there are definite obligations on the part of the employer and commensurate responsibilities by the employees. Loyalty, dedication, and honor are important attributes. These notions are alien to the Western mentality and may cause problems in staffing a joint venture with Americans. Besides language problems, Americans often have difficulty in accepting the concepts of seniority and cradle-to-grave employment as commonly practiced in Japan. In Japan, seniority is very important. In the United States it is possible to have a 35-year-old vice-president and a 40-year-old president; in Japan this is almost unheard of.

Resolution of Conflicts

The Japanese prefer to resolve differences through discussion, and the U.S. partner should respect the Japanese wishes. Should conflicts arise, these are usually discussed between the parties in lengthy sessions. Both sides will *try* to reach amicable solutions that will be mutually beneficial. In the process various trade-offs will be made. In short, both partners have to learn to give and take. In Japan issues are always resolved through negotiations. Casanova stated emphatically that it is important for U.S. businessmen to realize that "in dealing with Asia, matters are not resolved through votes. In Japan and Asia in general, if I have three votes on the board and someone else has four, it does not mean that the other partner will win on the issues. All our business in Japan has really been handled through lengthy discussions, from middle management all the way up to top management." The chairman of Sperry and the vice-presidents of the various divisions are usually actively involved in the negotiations: "These issues are resolved through many, many meetings, which could be very lengthy. Through the numerous lengthy sessions we finally arrived at a form of company that is mutually beneficial to the parties." According to Omata, the company, fortunately, has never been confronted with an issue that could not be negotiated; both sides have always been able to resolve their differences. Large companies like Mitsui or Mitsubishi are cosmopolitan in their outlook and hence are very accommodating to differing perspectives.

According to Casanova, one should distinguish between resolvable and unresolvable issues. From the Japanese standpoint, if an issue can be resolved, both parties will continue to negotiate until common ground is reached and the differences ironed out. An example of a problem that would require negotiations between the two parties is how to respond to the product needs of the Japanese market. Recently there arose a need in Japan to produce computers capable of processing Japanese characters (*kanji*). To operate as a native industry, the joint-venture company had to develop a kanji processor. The U.S. partner had to understand that and work with them. As a result, NUK developed a processor with kanji capability. This development was possible only after innumerable sessions between Sperry's development people and those of NUK.

Another type of problem that requires negotiations is the issue of quality. As noted in chapter 2, the Japanese are obsessed with quality; the zero-defect movement is strong in Japan. Sperry has to work with NUK's technical people constantly to respond to consumers' specifications. To resolve such issues, both sides must engage in long discussion sessions. Such negotiations may take a year or longer.

Casanova noted that in a joint-venture company some issues might be unresolvable: "If the issue cannot be resolved and we arrive at a confrontation point, we will sell out or we will buy them out." Even here, both parties would generally go through a long discussion period until it became obvious to one side that there was no solution. At that point the venture disintegrates. Some U.S.-Japanese ventures have, unfortunately, arrived at this stage. The Japanese process of conflict resolution is time-consuming and more drawn out than in the United States, where both parties typically bring in their attorneys and begin suing each other. That is unlikely to happen in Japan. Casanova believes that "the Japanese system works better when there is a possibility for solution because once you arrive at a decision, then you obtain total support from the two sides. But in a confrontation process where there is really no solution, the Western way is much better. Where there is a way to work out the differences, the Japanese system is better. We could here use the analogy of a divorce. In America, you might get a divorce that you really did not have to."

Casanova added that fortunately NUK never has to contend with such unresolvable issues. In his opinion the most dangerous problem for a joint-venture operation may occur when it becomes so successful that it threatens the parent company. At that stage the joint-venture company may feel that it should be granted autonomy to branch out on its own. The parent company will then find itself in competition with its joint-venture subsidiary in some geographic areas. This kind of situation has occurred among some Japanese joint ventures and poses tremendous difficulties for the parent company because, according to U.S. antitrust law, the parent cannot exclude its joint-venture subsidiary from embarking on such expansionary activities. For instance, if a joint venture decides to sell its product in Australia in competition with the products manufactured by the parent company, there is little the latter could do except persuade the former that the management of the parent company strongly opposes such action and desires the joint venture to refrain from such activities. According to Casanova, the way to keep this situation from developing is for the parent company to keep technologically abreast of the joint venture by at least one or two levels. In this way the activities of the joint-venture company can be kept in line, and the latter will be obligated to follow the directives of the parent company.

Differences between the American and Japanese Ways

Omata and Casanova were asked to comment on the most salient differences between U.S. and Japanese business practices with respect to the operations of a joint venture. Some of the differences reported here may not pertain to the specific joint venture between Sperry Corporation and Mitsui Bussan, but are issues between U.S. and Japanese partners in general.

Differences in Objectives

The Americans and the Japanese are very far apart in some of their philosophies. In general Americans tend to focus on bottom-line figures; the Japanese are more future-oriented, often concerned with events 5 years hence. Even in the late 1950s, when the joint venture was just established, the Japanese partner used to focus on events 3 or 5 years in the future. To accommodate this difference in time perspective, Sperry had to develop a long-range plan in discussing matters with the Japanese.

To make a joint venture work, the 2 parties must try to find some happy compromise; Sperry has learned to accept that. Omata believes that a major reason that many U.S. companies, including large ones, are divesting their interests from Japan is the complete difference in management philosophies between the U.S. and Japanese partners.

Although the Japanese tend to be more future-oriented, they are also concerned about profits. Future growth and market share are paramount, however, and profitability only secondary. The Japanese believe that profits will result once the company develops sufficient market share. The Japanese tend to emphasize the history of the company because it is extremely crucial in projecting future performance. U.S. companies focus more on immediate results: If they commit $100 million this year, what will that mean this year or, at the very latest, next year.

Differences in Decision Making

Although final decisions are made by the board in Japan, before reaching that level an issue will have obtained the concurrence of everybody involved, not just a majority. In Japan it is important that the proposal be endorsed by everyone before the decision is brought to the board level. Mr. Omata, though born in the United States, was raised by his grandparents in Japan from age 7 to 17. This enabled him to understand the Japanese philosophy. He emphasized that it is important to be aware of this difference in decision-making style. In his words, "You have to be able to understand them. You just don't come right down from the top, and say 'no' or 'yes.' One needs to have a very good *Japanese* reason to say 'yes' or 'no' in Japan."

By contrast, most decisions in U.S. companies are made from the top down, by strong presidents who truly decide. Sometimes the president may decide even without prior consultation or agreement from his staff. That seldom happens in a Japanese company. Of course, some top executives in Japanese companies do issue edicts through the mechanism described as "one screech of the crane" in chapter 2. Even in these instances, however, the executive feels the obligation to justify his actions to his subordinates. In general, decisions are made through the consensus process or some combination. The consensus process involves constant interrogation that progresses from top to bottom and vice versa until an agreement is reached. In general, Japanese executives consider it extremely important to obtain the full support of their subordinates in their decisions.

Given the fact that Omata was an employee of Sperry Corporation, it would be interesting to examine whether the Japanese parent company would question his objectivity in making decisions as president of the joint venture. In response to this question, Omata had the following observations: "I have always gone to both Mitsui and Sperry beforehand. Then, within the company, I always asked myself what is best for Nippon Univac.

You have to base your decisions on that. I may contradict both Mitsui or Sperry at times. Sure, you have to do that or you are going to get them into trouble. I have always operated on the principle that 'what is good for the goose is good for the gander.' I have always felt that what should be good for Nippon Univac should be good for the parent company.'' In order to make a joint venture work, it is imperative that neither partner think in terms of personal self-interest, but instead be genuinely concerned with the welfare of the joint venture.

Language

The negotiations were conducted in both languages. The Japanese negotiating team understood English quite well. It was almost a second language for most middle-management and technical personnel because many foreign words enter Japanese technical jargon. Most of the technical sessions are conducted in English with little problem. A language problem may occur at a higher level if a senior-management Japanese partner does not have a good command of English. Knowledge of Japanese by Americans is virtually nonexistent; only a very few Americans who are not ethnic Japanese can speak the language fluently and fully understand all its subtleties. Generally top management in Japanese companies are always accompanied by a few people in negotiating sessions with their U.S. counterparts. These individuals are employees of the company, generally perform administrative functions, and speak fluent English. In Casanova's opinion, these people function as explainers rather than interpreters. The explainer will sit at the session, listen, and then intercede to say, "I think what he really meant, or what you really meant, is such and such." Through such intercessions both parties arrive at an accurate understanding of the points made by the other side. When Omata was on the negotiating team to establish the joint venture, he always interpreted for the Sperry people. The Japanese would like to discuss certain things in Japanese, because they felt that some so-called Japanese nuances would be better understood. This highlights the importance alluded to in chapters 2 and 3 of including a bilingual member in one's negotiating team.

Casanova thinks that problems often develop because the Japanese like to use the term "I understand," which does not really mean that they understand the issue. Americans may come away from such sessions believing they have reached an agreement, when in fact they have not. This is where patience and socializing with the Japanese partners come in. Casanova believes it is important for a U.S. company to have the same individuals involved in the negotiations over time. Frequent changes in the composition of the negotiating team may lead to misunderstanding and disrupt the continuity needed to develop the personal relationships so important in Japan. To operate successfully in the Japanese market, people must get to know each other.

Differences in Negotiating Tactics

In general, the Japanese negotiating teams are larger than the U.S. teams. In a negotiation session there are usually 10 or more people on the Japanese side, compared with two or three on the U.S. side. Casanova did not feel that the smaller size of the U.S. team was a handicap "unless you allow it to be." Often members of the Japanese group will excuse themselves during a session by saying that they must caucus. This is true because they have to obtain consensus both within the team and within the company. In important matters they have to obtain government approval; the government does not like surprises, particularly in the computer industry. The Japanese partner briefs the government beforehand and gets its full understanding and support. Therefore, negotiations proceed at a slower pace; in general, the Japanese do not appear to operate with the urgency typical of Americans. The Japanese take as much time as they need, until they are absolutely sure of a decision and have reached consensus.

Members of the Japanese negotiating team tend to be inquisitive. They want to find out about the members of the U.S. negotiating team and assess their sincerity. They may ask embarrassing questions. Omata believes that "if one is honest, always above-board, and not trying to pull any wool over their eyes, they will be quite frank and above-board, will put their cards on the table, and there will be no problem. I never had any problem, not only because of my Japanese background. I always felt completely comfortable in Japan, just as I would in New York when I am with my own people."

Otherwise neither Omata nor Casanova perceived any major differences in negotiating styles. In the case of TRW and Fujitsu, the U.S. partner felt that its Japanese counterpart used the excuse of consulting with the government to get TRW to sign a letter of intent early in the negotiations that was later upheld as a legal agreement. For their part, TRW walked out on their counterparts in a negotiating session in Japan when they could not agree about the length of the maintenance contract. When the TRW team walked out, the Japanese relented; the issue was subsequently resolved to TRW's satisfaction.

Attitude toward Litigation

Japan is not a litigious society, and the concept of a very strict legal code does not exist there. As noted in chapter 2, arbitration and litigation are seldom used. The distaste for litigation pervades all aspects of Japanese society, including business contracts. The Japanese concept of an agreement is that it is valid as long as it makes sense and there is mutual benefit to be derived from the contract. When that ceases to be true, the agreement automatically disintegrates. This concept is foreign to the Western mentality.

An illustration of this problem is the air treaty between Japan and Taiwan. When Japan recognized the importance of establishing an air treaty with the People's Republic of China, it said that the contract with Taiwan was no longer valid. Americans might consider this dishonorable, but the Japanese believed that the differences could be resolved through other channels. They reneged on their contract with Taiwan and signed an agreement with China, and Japan Air Lines continues to fly to Taiwan under the name Japan Asia Airways. In the United States, similar incidents would have ended up in court.

This Japanase distaste for law is shared by the Chinese and other Asian societies. When U.S. firms want to establish operations in China, they are concerned about arbitration; since no such legislation has been promulgated by the Chinese, U.S. firms are skeptical about what would happen should they enter into a joint venture with Chinese firms (Tung 1982a). In general, the Western point of view is: "What will we do if we have a disaster?" The Asian view is: "Let's do what we have to do to make this successful, and if a disaster occurs (and we hope it won't), we will work it out in some way, because we always have." In Casanova's analogy, people in the United States prepare for a divorce at the time they decide to get married. The Asian viewpoint is that "if something unforeseen happens, we will find a way. We don't have to be specific at this time."

In the actual negotiations, although there were always six or more people on Mitsui's side, none of them was an attorney. Sperry, on the other hand, always brought its attorney along. The Japanese partner said that since Sperry always had its attorney, it would also introduce its own legal personnel. On the third day after the introduction of the legal personnel, Sperry's attorney asked about the legal training and background of his so-called counterpart. The Japanese legal man responded that he had no formal legal training, that he was really not an attorney but the chief legal person in the company.

In the negotiations, agreements are usually first reached verbally and then discussed. At this point the Japanese generally introduce their so-called general-affairs representatives with legal background. U.S. corporations do not have such departments. The general-affairs department in Japan takes care of corporate welfare and performs functions similar to those of the secretary's office in the United States. After the negotiations have been reviewed by the general-affairs department, the Japanese partner would then turn the matter over to its so-called legal department and their attorneys.

Although the Japanese are generally nonlegalistic, there are exceptions. For example, in the case of TRW and Fujitsu, it was noted that the Japanese partner held TRW to the letter of intent signed early in the negotiations. The important point is that although attorneys may be used, they should be seen as facilitators of the process rather than as representing the interest of a specific party.

Socializing

Given the need to develop personal relationships and generate dialogue, it is important to socialize with the Japanese to promote greater understanding and trust between the partners. Casanova indicated that Sperry's representatives were involved in after-hours socializing with the Japanese, and he considered this a good way for both parties to know each other better: "This is a common practice in Japan, and I think it is important that Americans learn to work within this system. If you go over there, have your session, break up around 5 p.m., and then get together with them at around 6 in a restaurant, you get to know the people much better. This is conducive to mutual understanding and cooperation. Similarly, what goes on in the golf course could be equally important. There has to be a willingness on the part of the Americans to do it the Japanese way, and I think that the Japanese will then be more willing to follow the American way when they are in the U.S."

In recent years more U.S. executives have become aware of the differences in business practices in Japan, and have come to accept them. Casanova believed that this "awareness comes from humility. It is very hard to understand the other side if one is arrogant, which has generally been the American posture for many years. We have finally arrived at a time when we realize that we must compete on an equal basis. Arrogance is a very poor ingredient in facilitating understanding and cooperation. Many Americans have matured." He further contended that if there is one ingredient that may make Japan fail, it would be when the Japanese become arrogant. Casanova observed that "For the first time now, we start to see this arrogance beginning to surface on the part of the Japanese. I think that Japanese arrogance has always been sublimated, but we saw that in World War II. As they become more powerful and more dominant, and the arrogance starts to surface, that could be the downfall of the Japanese. I think if we want to make this world work, we have got to understand the strong and weak points of both sides."

This is where patience and respect come in. Both sides have to accommodate the different perspectives of the other party. In order to understand Japanese characteristics and culture, Omata suggested that Americans spend more time with the Japanese people and learn about the environment. U.S. executives are typically busy and are able to spend only a few days in Tokyo, but they should also try to visit cities outside Tokyo: "I wish we could all learn to spend a weekend golfing or hiking together. That helps a lot. We often get more accomplished on the golf course. Part of the business is done in that type of environment. The Japanese do not like surprises, so before they meet formally for negotiations, they should have an understanding of the issues that will be discussed."

Omata offered the same prescriptions for the Japanese. He tells his Japanese friends that when they visit the United States, they should not only visit New York and Washington, D.C., because that is only part of the country. He urges them to visit places like Philadelphia, Chicago, Detroit, even the town of Fresno, and see what makes the United States tick. Omata agreed with Casanova that for the first time he had begun to detect a note of arrogance among some Japanese. He contended that "Japan thinks that they are the greatest now. I don't think so. In some areas we are way ahead of them. In other areas they could complement our shortcomings. We have to realize that in this world, we have to be able to coexist or coprosper." This can be attained only through patience and respect for each other.

In the case of TRW and Fujitsu, the representatives of both sides spent a lot of time socializing before the actual negotiations. Their informal discussions led to personal relationships between members of the two teams that helped reduce misunderstandings and facilitated progress in the negotiations. This theme is echoed throughout the cases reported in the book.

Factors for Success

By all definitions, NUK is the successful product of a joint-venture effort between two giant multinationals, Mitsui Bussan and Sperry Corporation. The factors responsible for this success will be summarized in this section.

Selection of a Partner

Mr. Casanova considered this the single most important factor in the success of the venture. This sentiment is shared by a number of firms in other cases to be presented. Casanova had the following advice for selecting a partner: "If you are a small company and are starting out cold, I think you have to talk to people and other companies that have experience in dealing with the Japanese. There are some expert people in the field, like the Boston Consulting Group. There are many companies, like Sperry, Xerox, and Caterpillar, that have been successful." The trading companies in Japan could also help because of their extensive network in Japan and throughout the world. Given the strong ties among alumni of universities and schools, Japanese acquaintances who have access to prospective partners would be of tremendous assistance. Of course, after selecting a partner, the U.S. company has to maintain dialogue with its partner and develop long-term relationships.

Long-Term Relationships

In the case of Sperry, its relationship with Mitsui dated back to the early 1920s. As noted in chapter 2, relationships with the Japanese tend to endure. Of course, both sides have to maintain such relationships through mutual understanding and respect.

Maintaining Dialogue

There was constant dialogue between Sperry and its Japanese partner and the joint-venture company. This minimized misunderstanding and helped promote a good relationship among the parties. Conversely, a hands-off approach to management by the U.S. parent may lead to problems, as will be evident in chapter 8, which discusses the dissolution of a joint venture. In response to the question of how to facilitate dialogue between the partners, Casanova had the following observations: "Typically, an American company has an international division that manages the whole world, part of which deals with Japan, part of which deals with China, and so on. The international division staff addresses the whole world in the same way. Also, many American firms believe that a trip a year to the various subsidiaries will keep headquarters briefed about activities around the world. Such practices are inadequate. There has to be an awareness on the part of the American company that to be successful in foreign markets, they have to see the various foreign markets from the eyes of the respective nationals. This is true not only with regard to Japan or joint ventures. It is very important that an American firm develop local management talent so that nationals can provide input to the parent firm and advise them accordingly about the courses of action to be taken. The local nationals should be in a position to say that 'this is the Philippines,' or 'in Singapore or Hong Kong, this is the way that things are done.' So corporate headquarters has to be receptive to ideas other than their own. The attitude that 'if it sells in Des Moines, Iowa, it will sell anywhere' doesn't work, and I think we have proved that to ourselves. Americans, on the whole, have not done a very good job in exporting from the United States. I think there is a need for the U.S. corporation to be truly global in its orientation, with a willingness to accept different ideas and to involve nationals of other countries in management and the decision-making process. Fortunately, Sperry has always adopted an international outlook and orientation. I think we have been lucky; Paul Lyet and Frank Forster before him have always promoted this world orientation. But there are certainly a lot of U.S. companies that will adopt an ethnocentric attitude. That is inappropriate. We just cannot, for example, sell huge refrigerators in a country where the houses are small and there are differences in voltage.''

As noted earlier, Sperry's primary contribution to the joint venture was in product and technology; hence the Japanese were very concerned about Sperry's technological developments. Mr. Omata believed that exchange of information ''that is mutually important and interesting should be done constantly at the top- as well as the middle-management level, so they will know where we are going, and we will know what they are doing. We can learn from them in some things.'' This principle has been followed in Sperry's Vickers division and in the software end of Univac.

In the case of TRW and Fujitsu, to prevent misunderstanding, each party would prepare and submit a proposal to the other side before each negotiating session. This exchange of proposals and counterproposals minimized the possibility of loss of face resulting from overt criticism of the other party's position. This practice also reinforced the positive aspects of the negotiations.

To ensure progress and promote communications between the parties, both sides agreed on a procedure for documenting successive agreements. At the close of each negotiating session, all the formal agreements arrived at during the meeting would be detailed in the minutes and initialed by both parties to indicate approval or consensus. Furthermore, TRW understood that since the joint venture with Fujitsu would have an indefinite life, the contract should be flexible enough to accommodate the changing conditions of the times. Consequently, rather than negotiating all the details of their present and future relationships, both sides agreed to ''create a living document which would serve as a framework for ongoing negotiations.'' This served two purposes: (1) by emphasizing flexibility in the terms of the agreement, TRW demonstrated its willingness to accommodate the Japanese concept of adaptability in an ongoing relationship; (2) by omitting the details of the future relationship, the parties were able to reduce the amount of time required to reach a formal agreement.

There is always a possibility that vagueness in the terms of the contract may lead to disputes should the relationships deteriorate, as will be discussed further in chapter 8. Given the Japanese distaste for litigation, however, and the fact that computers are a growth industry, no contractual agreement could possibly encompass all the contingencies that might arise in a dynamic sector.

Cultural Understanding

To maintain dialogue, Casanova argued that there must be respect for cultural differences and the varying needs of consumers. Therefore, the joint venture has always been managed by Japanese presidents. Sperry was fortunate to have Omata, who, though a *nisei*, was raised in Japan during his formative years and hence had a thorough understanding of the Japanese way. Omata suggested that to promote cultural understanding it is important to learn the history of the country. U.S. companies tend to sponsor a crash program in the Japanese language for their expatriates. Omata contended, however, that it is more important for expatriates to study Japanese culture and history than the language: "By doing so, I believe they can learn much more about the Japanese characteristics—why do they think in that manner? I think that works the other way round, too. I have been advocating to my Japanese friends that it is important for them to study American history and understand what made America such a great nation. I think this is a very important part of the business, especially when we have so many cultural differences."

Cultural understanding would lead to an increased ability to adapt to a foreign way of doing business. For example, in Japan, when top management conceive of a plan, they do not simply ask their subordinates to follow it. Instead, they probably start to discuss the idea with people at the middle-management or departmental level. In this fashion, the initiative appears to come from below rather than from the top down: "So, everybody gets on the bandwagon. There may be some objections and opposition to it, but never just override them. I always had them talk to each other at their level and convince the opposition that this is best for the company."

U.S. companies also have to understand the importance of human relations in Japanese companies. In the United States the shareholders are foremost in top management's mind; in Japan, on the other hand, the employees are at least as important, if not more so. Omata believes it is imperative for Americans to understand these differences in the Japanese system: "Unless we are willing to learn from them and make necessary changes, the venture is bound to fail. Frank Forster and I used to talk about this matter. He would ask: 'This is your thought, isn't it?' I say, 'Yes, this is the way we do things in Japan.' But this is what I call dynamic management, where a person can make a 180-degree turnaround. I think Japanese management also has to learn and understand American management philosophy, then arrive at a compromise that is mutually acceptable to both sides."

A second important difference is that the Japanese tend to be ambiguous at times, as discussed in chapter 2. Omata contended that Americans have to learn to trust their Japanese partners even when matters are not clearly spelled out.

Omata was asked whether the Americans ever wondered which side he was really on (the Japanese or the U.S. side), since the negotiations to establish the joint venture took place shortly after World War II, and he was an ethnic Japanese who had spent his formative years in Japan. In response, Omata remarked: "I think that's where some people have difficulty. If you can carry on an intelligent and sincere conversation with your own people in the States, I believe one will win the confidence of top mangement people. In Japan, the same holds true. Being a *nisei* never bothered me. Looking back, Sperry was good to me, and so was Mitsui. Their confidential trust in me made this joint venture a success. One of our Sperry people asked, 'When you are speaking to the Japanese, are you thinking in English or Japanese?' I said, 'When I am talking in Japanese, I am a Japanese. That is the only way that you can get your points across.' The same applies when I speak in English; I am an American." Omata stated emphatically that it is necessary to accept the differences between the two cultures. "If you accept the fact that this is Japan and this is the way business should be done, then there will be no difficulties. This has to work both ways, however."

Similarly, in the case of TRW and Fujitsu, cultural awareness was crucial to the success of the venture. Although the members of the TRW negotiating team did try to familiarize themselves with Japanese business practices, the Japanese partner should really be credited for this mammoth undertaking. Most of Fujitsu's technical and legal personnel were educated in the United States and hence were thoroughly familiar with U.S. business and legal practices. Besides this understanding, TRW's liaison office in Japan was staffed by Japanese nationals who provided valuable insight into the situation and advised the TRW negotiating team on how best to proceed.

Product Characteristics

Given the nationalism of the Japanese, they prefer to buy domestic products unless a foreign item is unique in some way. A company can obtain a dominant share of the Japanese market only if indigenous firms cannot manufacture the same item. This point was elaborated on in chapters 1 and 2. Casanova noted that it is important for the foreign firm to ask itself: "Is what I make and sell unique? Whom would I be competing with? Will I ever be able to penetrate and obtain a satisfactory market share?" A foreign firm has to evaluate whether Japanese consumers need and want the company's products or services. For consumer items, this is not as true. Paris fashions sell well because of their snob appeal. In general, imported luxury items are well received by Japanese consumers.

For a joint venture to work, the needs of the partners must converge. In the case of Nippon Univac Kaisha, Ltd., Mitsui provided financing, management, and access to the Japanese market. Furthermore, since this is designated a strategic industry by the government, it was not completely liberalized for inward capital investment until 1975. Consequently, 100-percent foreign-equity ownership was not possible in the late 1950s. Sperry, on the other hand, provided the much needed technology and product. Thus the contributions of the partners were complementary; each side needed the other.

In the case of TRW and Fujitsu, each side could provide something the other lacked. By the late 1970s the Japanese computer industry had developed to the point where it seriously challenged U.S. dominance in the field. In 1980 Fujitsu overtook IBM as the major supplier of computers in the Japanese market, but the company had difficulty penetrating the U.S. market. By establishing the joint venture, Fujitsu could obtain access to the U.S. market through the 3,000-person data-processing maintenance network provided by TRW, without the expense of having to develop its own distribution system. This would allow the company to compete not only with indigenous U.S. firms, but also with other Japanese firms that had entered into similar agreements with other U.S. manufacturers. For example, Hitachi, Ltd., the second-largest Japanese manufacturer, entered into a joint-venture agreement with National Semiconductor Corporation at around the same time.

TRW, for its part, has tried to enter the field of data processing, which could be viewed as a natural extension of its high-technology systems business. Its sales of banking and other point-of-sale systems were scarcely profitable; the company's principal weakness lay in its inability to develop cost-effective reliable hardware. Consequently, TRW sought a partner that could fulfill this role. Fujitsu, with its impressive line of computer equipment, seemed to fill the bill. Fujitsu's products range from small business computers selling at around $100,000 (these were among the products initially marketed by the joint venture) to the MF mainframe series, which competes with the IBM 4300 models. As one TRW executive described it: "I'm like a kid in a candy store, looking at all that Fujitsu hardware." To capitalize on the economies of scale in production needed to compete successfully with IBM in Japan, Fujitsu was eager to enter the U.S. market. Furthermore, the joint venture would provide Fujitsu with software technology, an area in which Japanese computer manufacturers are still relatively weak. Thus both Fujitsu and TRW stood to benefit from the joint venture.

Patience

Things tend to proceed at a slower pace in Japan. Consequently, patience is of paramount importance. In fact, Omata considered this "one of the most important ingredients'' in success. As Casanova noted earlier, some of the negotiations took a year to a year and a half before agreement was finally reached. Although Sperry often felt pressure to resolve matters, it also realized the importance of resolving them to the satisfaction of both parties. Consequently, the U.S. negotiators had to convince their management at home that they needed time. The team had to impress on management that if undue pressure was applied, bad decisions might result. Compounding this difficulty was the physical distance between the two countries. It takes approximately 14 hours by plane to travel from the east coast of the United States to Tokyo. Consequently, the next morning may not be the best time to make important decisions. To alleviate this problem, Casanova tries to get the Japanese to come over to the United States at times: "We will say: 'Okay, we came last time. Next time, you come.' I guess we understand that it will take time, and that it is frustrating. Patience is of utmost importance in negotiating with the Japanese."

The TRW team also indicated the importance of coping with changes in time zones and delays in decision making. During their trips to Japan, the TRW negotiating team tended to underestimate the fatigue resulting from jet lag and the amount of time it generally takes to make decisions in Japan. The TRW team contended that unless these factors are taken into consideration, it could jeopardize the effectiveness of the negotiating team.

Modes of Entry

Given the sensitivity of the Japanese government in the computer industry and the tremendous differences in business practices between the two countries, Casanova believed that a preferred method of entry into the Japanese market would be through joint venture: "For an American firm to try to understand the Japanese market on its own, it would take ten to fifteen years. You do have to counsel and consult with people who have the experience." Of course, there are exceptions. IBM's operations in Japan are on a wholly owned basis, and they have been extremely successful in the Japanese market. IBM, however, is also beginning to see the potential benefits of a joint-venture arrangement. In February 1983, for instance, it agreed to discuss with Matsushita Electric Company the possible formation of a joint venture to develop and manufacture low-cost computer products. In March 1983 it was announced that Matsushita will manufacture the IBM 5550 multistation, designed for use as a kanji word processor and personal computer. Shipments are scheduled to begin in June 1983. Although IBM has previously marketed products made by other manufacturers under its own label (for example, the photocopiers manufactured by Minolta Corporation), this venture with Matsushita represents the first time that IBM will not supply any parts in the manufacture of a product it designed and plans to market. IBM's stated reason for entering this specific joint venture was that "its plants lack the capacity" (*Wall Street Journal*, 17 February 1983, p. 2; 16 March 1983, p. 8).

Concluding Remarks

Although U.S.-Japanese competition in computer technology has intensified over the past few years, this field could also provide a fertile area for collaborative efforts. As the Japanese have made major breakthroughs in computer technology, their manufacturers are well suited to complement some of the existing limitations of U.S. producers. If joint efforts could be arranged, manufacturers from both countries would benefit, as illustrated by the cases of Nippon Univac Kaisha, Ltd., and of the joint venture between TRW and Fujitsu. Perhaps in this world of rapidly changing computer technology, researchers from either country alone will be unable to cope effectively with all the challenges the future holds. Collaborative efforts between researchers and manufacturers may provide a key to advancement in this high-technology industry, as large producers in both countries are discovering.

The agreement concluded between the U.S. and Japanese governments in late 1982 to allow high-technology companies of either country to participate in tax incentives and government-sponsored research programs traditionally available to indigenous firms represents a major step in this direction. Such an agreement means that U.S. subsidiaries in Japan will be eligible to take part in the Japanese government-sponsored programs, such as the development of a "fifth-generation computer" with artificial intelligence (*Wall Street Journal,* 1 November 1982, p. 35). Before these joint efforts can come to fruition, however, many of the conditions outlined in this chapter must be met by partners from either nation.

5

Joint Program in Aircraft Production

In the 1980s a stated objective of the Japanese government is to focus on high-technology, rapid-growth industries (*White Paper,* 1981). Some of the industries targeted for growth or continued growth in the remainder of the twentieth century include computers, telecommunication equipment, and aerospace. In the case of the aerospace industry, Japan may have been prodded by the insistence of the United States that the former should increase its defense budget. Chapter 1 described the tensions that have developed between the two countries over the issue of defense. Although Japan's defense budget for fiscal 1983 fell short of Washington's expectations, its increased spending in this area (however moderate) has already resulted in rapid development of the military-armaments and aerospace industries. In 1982, for instance, Japan ranked as the eighth-largest military power in the world (*Wall Street Journal,* 22 November 1982, p. 1).

In general, developments in the military-aerospace sector precede those in commercial or civil aircraft, because there is synergy in terms of a "mutually beneficial technology interchange" between the two sectors. Many countries view development in commercial aircraft as a way to recoup investments in military technologies (Bacher 1981, p. 4). Furthermore, the Japanese Constitution prohibits the export of military armaments, whereas similar restrictions do not apply to civil aircrafts. Hence, although the latter may not be officially designated a strategic industry in Japan, it certainly has the potential to be one of the sectors that will receive increasing government attention in the future. The Ministry of International Trade and Industry (MITI) already supports the aerospace industry with low-interest, multimillion-dollar loans to domestic manufacturers, with repayment schedules to begin only after the ventures become profitable (*Wall Street Journal,* 18 May 1982, p. 35).

In fiscal 1982 Japan's exports of commercial aircraft were estimated to have increased by 25 percent, bringing its total aerospace sales to $1.7 billion. This trend is projected to increase in the future, according to an analyst at Daiwa Securities Research Institute, a reliable source of information in Japan (*Wall Street Journal,* 26 November 1982, p. 5).

A major difference in the aerospace industry, compared with, say, automobiles, is that in the former the Japanese government has encouraged joint cooperation with foreign manufacturers. This may reflect the fact that at this point in its technological development, Japan still lacks the capabilities to design a large aircraft. As will be noted later, the economics of production in the aircraft industry are unique. Consequently, the only viable route for Japan to follow may be joint production. As Mr. Minowa of the Japanese aerospace trade group indicated, "there is no way but international cooperation" (*Wall Street Journal,* 18 May 1982, p. 35).

This chapter will examine one such joint-production program. The program under investigation is the 767, Boeing's latest twin-engine, 210-passenger commercial jet aircraft, which was certified by the Federal Aviation Administration (FAA) in August 1982, with deliveries made in the same month. The discussion focuses on a series of negotiations that occurred over a five-year period pertaining to the production of the Boeing 767, with Japanese presence and involvement. It does not describe the actual sale of an aircraft. Such sales are common and are less interesting for examining collaborative efforts between entities from the two countries.

Since the Japanese lag considerably behind the United States in aircraft technology, the dynamics of the negotiating situation were quite different from those discussed elswhere in this book. Further, the cooperation here takes the form of a *joint program,* not a joint venture. This distinction will be defined later in the chapter. The case provides interesting insights into the role of the Japanese government, and how accommodating the Japanese partner could be in industries in which Japan is deficient. The information presented here was obtained through an interview with Thomas Bacher, director of international business at the Boeing Commercial Airplane Company. Bacher also provided a copy of his speech on the economics of the civil aircraft industry, delivered at a conference on the role of Southeast Asia in world airline and aerospace development held in Singapore on September 24–25, 1981. The speech provides valuable information and statistics on the civil-aircraft industry. To understand fully the intricacies of the joint program between Boeing and its Japanese partner, it is necessary to provide a brief overview of the aircraft industry.

Overview of the Aircraft Industry

Contrary to popular expectations, the aircraft industry is small in terms of dollar sales compared with a number of other industries. According to 1979 statistics, the world revenue for the commercial-aircraft industry (excluding those for the socialist-bloc countries) reached only $9 billion, below the figure for raw steel, automobiles, computer hardware, cigarettes, and television receivers. In 1979 the total revenue for the commercial-aircraft industry was roughly one-fortieth that for the steel industry and one-twentieth that for the automobile industry (Bacher 1981).

A second distinguishing feature of the industry is that it is highly concentrated in terms of prime manufacturers of commercial aircrafts. According to the *World Aviation Directory,* there are only six major prime manufacturers of commercial aircrafts in the world. The United States has the largest capability; at present its manufacturers have the capacity to produce more commercial aircraft than total world market demands. In 1980, for example, sales of U.S. civilian-aircraft manufacturers accounted for two-thirds of total world sales, or over $50 billion.

In a typical program for the development and production of a commercial aircraft, more than half the costs are borne by subcontractors and suppliers. In the production of Boeing 767s, the Japanese partner's role exceeded that of a normal subcontractor in that they also assumed market risk for the end product. Although the number of prime manufacturers is limited, there are many subcontractors and suppliers: There are 50 major structure suppliers, approximately 70 engine manufacturers, 155 prime manufacturers for other aerospace products, 2,000 equipment suppliers, 2,000 component and parts suppliers, and innumerable suppliers of raw materials. Because of this pyradimal supporting structure and because of the inordinate risks associated with the manufacture of commercial airplanes, the neophyte country that seeks to enter the industry may participate originally as a subcontractor and supplier. Although Japan is not really a neophyte in the industry, it is still a latecomer. Consequently, although the Japanese partner originally wanted greater participation in the 767 program, it settled for the role of participant, rather than full-fledged partner. This was one of the major issues under negotiation in the joint program for the construction of the 767, and it will be explored in greater detail later. After the success of this initial cooperative effort, Boeing was willing to give the Japanese partner a greater role in a subsequent joint program, concluded in early 1983.

Besides concentration in terms of prime manufacturers of commercial aircrafts, the industry is also characterized by high concentration in terms of sales to airlines. Of the more than 300 air carriers in the noncommunist world, the 25 major ones account for over 60 percent of the world's traffic; Japan Air Lines is one of these (Bacher 1981). Consequently, by allowing the Japanese partner (a quasi-government agency) to participate in the program, Boeing hoped that the effort would increase the probability that Japan Air Lines would purchase Boeing's products.

A third distinguishing feature of the airline industry is that although many commercial air carriers are suffering from the effects of the worldwide recession of the early 1980s, the prospects for sale of commercial aircraft in the coming decade appears bright. Air traffic is projected to double in the next decade, with most of the growth to come from Asia, South America, the Middle East, and Africa. Furthermore, most of the 6,000 commercial jets now in service will be replaced within the next two decades, at an estimated cost of $90 billion. It is estimated that the number of commercial aircraft production programs will increase to above twelve during the

1980s, up from an average of eight in the 1960s and an average of twelve in the 1970s (Bacher 1981).

A fourth distinguishing feature of the commecial-aircraft industry is its volatility. There are reasons for this. One is fluctuations in demand. For example, from 1967 to 1972 the annual production of Boeing 707s declined from 118 to 4 per annum; that for Boeing 727s decreased from 160 to 33 per year. The production programs of other major U.S. manufacturers were also subject to such violent fluctuations. Air carriers tend to react drastically to increases or decreases in air traffic; orders are canceled or deferred indefinitely when air traffic declines.

Second, the industry requires high dollar investment but has low production volume, exacerbated by long lead-times. It is typically four years from the time a program has been given the go-ahead to the time of first delivery; it takes even longer to recoup the initial investment in research and development, engineering, and manufacturing. Of the production programs that have been embarked on by U.S. prime manufacturers and that have captured almost 85 percent of the market, less than half have reached the break-even point; even fewer are profitable.

Because of the high risks involved and the extreme competitiveness of the industry, of the four major U.S. prime manufacturers, one has withdrawn after incurring substantial losses, another has merged, and a third has sought financial support from the government. Consequently, the industry is generally unattractive from the economic standpoint for neophytes (Bacher 1981). Although the risks associated with the industry may be enormous, there is also the potential for substantial profits for experienced and well-positioned companies. In 1981, for instance, Boeing's net earnings exceeded $473 million (*Boeing Annual Report,* 1981). Although its profits in the second quarter of 1982 decreased by 49 percent to $71 million, much of the loss could be attributed to the worldwide recession, which affected demand, and the huge outlays on research and development incurred for the production of its 767 (*Wall Street Journal,* 3 August 1982, p. 7). The development of the joint program between Boeing and its Japanese partner should be examined against this backdrop.

Terms of Cooperation

Boeing's partner in the joint program is a quasi-government entity called the Civil Transport Development Corporation (CTDC). This entity was created under the sponsorship of the Japanese government, and its working entities are three giant multinationals—Mitsubishi Heavy Industries, Ltd.; Kawasakai Heavy Industries, Ltd.; and Fuji Heavy Industries, Ltd. The latter companies have the manufacturing capability for the airframe portion.

These three companies participated under the auspices of the CTDC, whose board of directors included financial interests, airlines, other manufacturers, and so on. The working relationship between Boeing and CTDC was designated as a joint program, with the latter as a program participant in the production of Boeing's 767. There were other program participants; the Italians, for example, produced the movable surfaces of the aircraft. The Italian participant was Aeritalia, which comprises a single company and is government-owned. Since this is the first joint program ever entered into by Boeing for the production of either commercial or military aircraft, it had to proceed cautiously so as to establish any precedent to which it would be held in the future.

The CTDC was specifically created to negotiate and implement this joint program with Boeing. Consequently, Boeing had had no previous dealings with this corporation, although it had had transactions with the three companies that constituted the working entity of CTDC. In Bacher's definition, these three companies "are not a part to it legally, but they get their directions and allocation of work from CTDC." These three manufacturers were to produce the body section panels (wing to body fairing and landing gear doors), and the Italian participant was responsible for the movable surfaces. Each of these two participants played an equal role in the production of Boeing's 767.

A joint program differs from a joint venture because the latter has a legal implication. The term *joint effort* is also inappropriate because it may more accurately describe the functions of a subcontractor. CTDC was more than a subcontractor because it also assumed a market risk, which will be explained later. The terms *program participants* and *joint program* were used because in Boeing's parlance these terms conveyed less than a joint venture but more than a major subcontractor.

The Boeing 767, an advanced-technology jet that could presumably use 35–47 percent less fuel than the aircraft it will replace, is a Boeing aircraft. It is not a product of joint design by a number of manufacturers. The joint program involves the development and production of 767s with an expected product life cycle of 15 to 20 years. The total duration of the joint program between Boeing and CTDC would be 20 to 25 years because it took approximately 5 years from the initial go-ahead to the first delivery of the aircraft. The Japanese partner's involvement represents approximately 7–8 percent of the program, largely in design. The Japanese partner was involved in the detail design but not in the configuration and selection. It had to pick up the production technology as well. Japanese aircraft companies manufacture some of the components of the body sections, which are delivered in body panels. They do not assemble the body sections, such as the fuselage of the aircraft. The Italian program participant played an equal role but built the movable surfaces such as the trailing edge flaps, spoilers, rudder, elevators, and so on.

The Japanese participation in the program occurred at two levels. The first is the airframe structure, which is significant because prime manufacturers of aircraft (such as Boeing) usually produce or subcontract this but purchase the engine, avionics, and other system items. Approximately half the cost of an aircraft is the airframe. Thus Japanese participation in building the airframe, which historically is built by the prime manufacturers themselves, was 15 percent. Since the airframe structure typically represents half of the total program, Japanese participation in the entire venture was approximately 7.5 percent.

The Japanese partner's contribution is primarily in the area of nonrecurring or one-time costs—what economists refer to as fixed cost. These nonrecurring expenses are incurred in the development or manufacture of the components the Japanese partner furnishes, which essentially involve the design engineering and the tooling that are required to build them. Viewed from another angle, the Japanese investment would be costs incurred in their own detail engineering and the tooling associated with the parts they manufacture. The nonrecurring cost of designing, developing, and manufacturing a new medium-size aircraft is typically $1.5 billion (Bacher 1981, p. 7). Recurring costs, on the other hand, tend to decrease with successive units produced; that is, there is a learning curve phenomenon.

Since the form of cooperation is a joint-program arrangement and not a joint venture, profits are not calculated according to the 15- and the 7.5-percent participation in the airframe structure and the total program, respectively. The Japanese absorbed the costs related to the items they manufacture, and these investments are made at the beginning. Boeing then pays them an average unit price as the components are delivered. If the arrangement were to stop here, it would be a simple risk-sharing subcontracting arrangement. The difference in a joint program, however, is that the participant will also assume a market risk.

Boeing estimated the number of airplanes that will be delivered over a given time period. An average unit price was then negotiated between Boeing and CTDC based on these projected sales. If the aircraft did not sell at the rate Boeing estimated, then CTDC would assume a market risk because they would still receive the average unit price originally agreed on, even though they produced fewer units over the years.

Besides the market schedule and financial risks, CTDC also took on two other forms of risks—foreign-exchange and performance risk. Foreign-exchange risk was involved because payments for the components were designated in U.S. dollars and based on U.S. inflation rates. CTDC also undertook a performance risk because it operated on a fixed-price contract, which is common practice for all of Boeing's subcontractors. In a production program of this size and magnitude, the investment generally peaks around five to six years after the initial go-ahead for the program, and the cash-flow break-even point does not generally occur until the twelfth year of operation (Bacher 1981). Given all these factors, it is evident that CTDC assumed tremendous risks through its participation in the joint program, which perhaps shows the extent of concessions the Japanese were willing to make when it involved an industry in which they had a keen interest in acquiring expertise. For this reason, it is important to understand the motives behind CTDC's willingness to act as a joint participant in the Boeing 767 program, which is the focus of the following section.

Motives to Cooperate

In the theoretical framework of international business negotiations presented in Kapoor (1975), it was noted that to capture the dynamics of an international business negotiating situation, it is necessary to understand either partner's motives to enter into a cooperative agreement. An accurate gauging of the motives will assist in the projection of how accommodating or nonconceding a particular partner to the negotiation will be. If one party needed the agreement badly enough, it would bend over backward to meet the terms and demands of the other partner. As noted earlier, through participation in this joint program, the Japanese partner was very accommodating—not only in the area of terms agreed to, as discussed earlier, but also in its willingness to accept the U.S. style of confrontation in the negotiating process, which will be discussed later.

The Japanese government identified aircraft, both military and commercial, as a potential growth industry. In the 1980s there is a marked change in Japan's export orientation; the move is away from items that could be produced by its newly industrialized neighbors and toward the export of high-technology goods and equipment. The aerospace industry is high-technology, export-oriented, and hence worthwhile from the standpoint of Japanese objectives. Furthermore, for some time the U.S. government has prodded the Japanese to assume greater responsibility for its own defense. For the fiscal year beginning April 1, 1983, Japan has increased its defense budget by 6.5 percent. This outlay, though below Washington's expectations, nevertheless represents a commitment on the part of the Japanese government to develop its own capabilities in defense armaments, including military aircraft. There is a building-block sequence in the development of national-defense capabilities, with the production of military aircraft followed by the manufacture of commercial aircraft (Bacher 1981, p. 4). There is much complementarity between the production of military and civilian aircraft in terms of technological know-how and equipment. Furthermore, the production of commercial aircraft represents a viable route for recouping or recovering the costs of research and development on military defense.

The initiative to embark on the production of commercial aircraft came from MITI and was probably developed in conjunction with the industry in conformance with the latter's interest in expanding its aircraft sector. In the case of the three companies that made up the working entity of CTDC—Mitsubishi Heavy Industries, Kawasaki Heavy Industries, and Fuji Heavy Industries—the aircraft sector accounted for approximately 10 percent of each firm's total business activities. For example, Mitsubishi Heavy Industries is a major contractor for U.S. military aircraft, the F15s (*Wall Street Journal,* 18 May 1982, p. 35). Both Mitsubishi and Kawasaki are multibillion-dollar corporations and wield considerable clout in Japan.

There are several factors in Boeing's motivation to embark on a joint program with CTDC. One was risk-sharing. As noted earlier, because of the unique characteristics of the aircraft industry, there are tremendous risks involved in developing a new airplane. In Bacher's words: "the risk of starting a new program is a multibillion-dollar risk. A thousand airplanes is something like a 25 to 30 billion-dollar program." By allowing participation by others, Boeing would share that risk. In a typical program about half the costs of production are borne by subcontractors and suppliers.

A second aspect of Boeing's motivation is market access. The aircraft industry is highly competitive; although participation by a country does not necessarily guarantee the purchase of aircraft by a government-owned airline, it does create a more favorable market environment. Japan Air Lines is one of the top twenty-five air carriers in the world, which together account for over 60 percent of the world's air traffic. Hence Japan Air Lines is one of the major customers of commercial aircrafts.

A third aspect of Boeing's motivation is that by involving Japanese firms, it "keeps these companies (and countries) out of a competitive alignment." A distinguishing feature of the Japanese government's emphasis on the aerospace industry in the 1980s, compared with automobiles in the 1950s and 1960s, is that in the latter no foreign participation was allowed in the early stages. In the aerospace industry, on the other hand, the government has endorsed a policy of joint cooperation with firms from other countries. Besides this joint program with Boeing on the 767s and the more recently agreed on YXX series, Japan has also entered into an agreement with other U.S. and European firms to form a seven-firm consortium for the construction of a jet engine for use in a new 150-passenger airplane, with costs estimated around $2 billion (*Wall Street Journal,* 9 March 1983, p. 6).

In response to the question of which side took the initiative in approaching the other partner for the establishment of the joint program, Bacher indicated that it was "not black and white. There was some interest on the part of Boeing, bordering on a formal level. I would say that the initiative came from Japan, in a very subtle way." When Boeing started to develop the 767, it considered participants from other countries; its efforts with the Italians actually preceded those with the Japanese. The Italian government had a similar interest in developing its own aerospace industry. In Bacher's opinion, both the Italians and the Japanese chose Boeing, even though they also worked with McDonnell Douglas to a lesser degree, "because they saw Boeing as the instrument for achieving their objectives." For example, Japan currently manufactures McDonnell Douglas and Lockheed aircraft under a licensing agreement arrangement (*Wall Street Journal*, 18 May 1983, p. 35).

Areas of Conflict and Conflict Resolution

The series of negotiations between Boeing and CTDC for the establishment of a joint program pertaining to the 767 took place over a five-year period. Since this was a multibillion-dollar program that would involve cooperation over a twenty- to twenty-five-year period, numerous issues were negotiated. Only the key issues will be discussed here.

One crucial issue was the nature of the business agreement or the role to be played by the Japanese partner. At first the Japanese partner wanted a true joint venture, but Boeing was reluctant partly because it had never entered into such arrangements before and, in Thomas Bacher's words, was "not sure whether it was workable."

A second issue under negotiation was the percentage or extent of Japanese participation. Initially CTDC wanted a much larger share, as high as 50-percent involvement at one point. Boeing objected because it believed that the capabilities of the Japanese aircraft industry may still be limited.

The third key issue pertained to the specifics of the working arrangement and the pricing of the component. When would the Japanese partner get paid? What would the average unit price be? Which partner does what kind of work? What are the criteria for successful performance?

Of the three aforementioned issues, the nature of the business agreement and the percentage of participation were the most difficult to negotiate. The issue of extent of participation was resolved by logic. When Boeing gave the Japanese partner a better understanding of the kinds of facilities and the millions of dollars of investment that would be involved, Bacher believed that the Japanese readily "accepted a lesser role in recognition of their industrial capability as well as their commitments to other programs, including military. I would not say that they didn't want a little bit larger role. Fundamentally, the difference was between 50 percent, which was a kind of political role, and 15 percent, which is the airframe portion. Most of that was resolved by logical review of their capabilities in the industry in a time-frame reference, and they accepted it based on reason."

With regard to the nature of the business agreement, the discussions were on a broader basis. Initially the Japanese wanted a joint-venture arrangement; that is, they would make a general contribution proportionate to their equity-ownership position, and subsequently would share in the receipts or revenue based on some formula that would presumably include a special recognition for Boeing's contribution to the venture, which from a technological standpoint was significantly greater than that of the Japanese. One sensitive issue was the difference over special contribution—what the Japanese call *norendai*. The latter resembles a dowry; in this case the dowry was a special entry fee. This issue posed a major stumbling block in the early stages of the negotiations.

When the program began to progress from a market standpoint, Boeing changed its position and informed the Japanese that it would not accept a joint-venture arrangement. That posed a problem for both partners because of earlier indications that Boeing might agree. Boeing, however, believed that to accept both Japan and Italy as full partners in the program would create complex management problems that would not be worth its while. Consequently, Boeing's top management changed their earlier position and decided that a full partnership role for the Japanese would not be feasible. The Japanese accepted the change, though reluctantly: "But when they did, they accepted it in very good form."

It was interesting to see whether Boeing tried to accomodate the Japanese preference for avoiding direct confrontation on issues. Bacher indicated that Boeing never refrained from using direct confrontation: "We not only used the Western approach, but the West Coast approach. You might say we were very outspoken and very direct. But there were fundamental cultural differences between our negotiation approach and theirs. Most of the time the initiation of an alternative was taken by us, and they were the listener: 'So what else have you got?' We went along with that partly for cultural reasons but partly because of our experience in the leadership in this industry. We were the leading party in the negotiation. That was used as negotiating psychology: 'Well, what else have you got?'. " The acceptance of the U.S. method of direct confrontation, coupled with the concessions made on the terms of the agreement, show how accomodating the Japanese could be in areas where they have a vested interest, and which are vital to the national interest.

The actual negotiations took four to five years. Bacher explained that this lengthy process was not only "a combination of the problems of negotiating the arrangement, but was also related to the timing of the product introduction. In other words, the market was not ready for this product, at least not in the economic viability sense. Hence there weren't enough customers who wanted the aircraft at the rate that you have to produce them at the beginning. At that rate, we were not ready to authorize the program go-ahead. We were in what we call a preliminary development evaluation phase.'' The four- to five-year duration actually represented a combination of waiting for the market to develop and responding to the complexities of the negotiations. In Bacher's recollection, once Boeing decided the market was ready and it was prepared to proceed on the program, the negotiations picked up speed: ''There is only one point in these projects that a participant can come in, and that's at the beginning. You either do it, or you wait five to ten years before the next product. They realized that, and I would say both sides speeded up on the negotiation process.'' The number of civilian-aircraft production programs in any given decade is limited. In the 1960s, for instance, there were eight programs; in the 1970s the number increased to twelve; and in the 1980s it will probably be above twelve.

A second factor accounting for the lengthiness of the negotiation was the size and magnitude of the program. The project costs $25 to $30 billion and has a life expectancy of twenty to twenty-five years. Hence both sides felt justified in spending several years discussing the issues.

A third factor accounting for the long negotiations was the time it generally takes the Japanese to make decisions, particularly in projects involving government funds. In Bacher's opinion, ''it gave them a negotiating edge because the Japanese partner always have a 'they' in the picture: 'We agree, but MITI does not agree.' They use that technique, I think, quite consciously. Like a car salesman, the Japanese partner will say, 'I want to sell you this car at this price, but the sales manager does not approve.' So they use MITI—they will say 'Well, we agree, but we are not sure they (meaning MITI) would agree.' So you have a two-tier negotiating process with them.''

Given that the Japanese participant could call on the role of the Japanese government and MITI, and given the sensitive nature of the aerospace industry, it was interesting to see whether the U.S. government was involved in any way. In Bacher's opinion, the U.S. government was not involved except for the antitrust division of the Justice Department, which was briefed about the progress and outcome of the negotiations and was authorized to interfere from an antitrust standpoint: ''There was absolutely no U.S. government involvement except for this aspect and a recognition that certain technology that we are working with will need an export license. It was assumed to be available, and it did not enter into the negotiations.''

Over the four- to five-year period in which these negotiations took place, the two parties met six to eight times every year on the average. At first the site of the negotiations was equally distributed between the United States and Japan, although there was a tendency to hold more of the discussions in Seattle for reasons of physical proximity: Much of the data and reasearch-and-development activities were located in the United States. Bacher noted that ''there was no hang-up on either party to come to the other place—that never was an issue. Once we compromised on Hawaii.

After Hawaii, we decided that Hawaii was best.'' Thus the two parties literally met halfway.

Composition of the Negotiating Teams

The composition of Boeing's negotiating team changed several times over the five-year period, particularly during the preliminary phase. In the early stages the Boeing team was represented largely by the executive vice-president of the Commercial Airplane Division of the company, the entity that manufactures the airplanes. The executive vice-president, of course, represented corporate views, had corporate concurrence, and served as the chief negotiator of Boeing's negotiating team. The executive vice-president was assisted by Bacher, the director of international business. Consequently, the staff from the international business office was always present throughout the negotiations on business aspects. A program-management person at the director level from the technical and product-development side was also present in the negotiations.

Toward the end of the five-year period, when the negotiations became intense and time-limited because Boeing was operating against a deadline, the vice-president of finance, contract, and international business (the individual to whom Bacher reported at that time) took over as the chief negotiator. At all times the Boeing team comprised three other individuals, each representing a different functional area—engineering, finance, and operations. These people were present on the Boeing team *in addition* to the executive vice-president and the vice-president of finance, contract, and international business. Thus the Boeing team was fairly large. There was hardly a meeting, except where policy issues were discussed, that did not involve at least two to six individuals on Boeing's side. The attorneys came in toward the end of the negotiations. Boeing has in-house legal personnel. The head of the legal staff was involved throughout the negotiations more because of his educational background and stature in the company; he served in the capacity of a consultant rather than as a legal counselor. In Bacher's words, ''the legal role as such was partially involved but not too visible at the beginning, and was quite visible toward the end.''

There were generally four people on the Japanese negotiating team, consisting of the vice-chairman of CTDC and the managing directors of each of the aircraft divisions of the three companies that constituted the working entity of CTDC. These managing directors were the most senior people of the respective aircraft divisions. The vice-chairman of CTDC served on a rotating basis and was also the chairman of one of these companies. These four individuals were generally accompanied by people from the respective companies who had expertise in different functional areas.

The CTDC was managed by a managing director, of which this particular joint program was one part. His involvement in this project represented approximately 10-20 percent of his total effort. CTDC also had corporate involvement; these individuals were sometimes present at the negotiations. A courtesy-call approach was also adopted, whereby Boeing would periodically talk to the chairman of the three companies that made up the working entity of CTDC, and to some senior-ranking government officials, extending up to the ministerial level.

During the early phases of the negotiations, there was very little legal representation on the Japanese side. This appeared to be characteristic of their approach to contract negotiations, but Bacher was quick to add that "I would not want to say that they did not have a legal staff look over the writing."

Although CTDC was a quasi-government organization, and the Japanese partner indicated that they had to caucus with MITI frequently, no Japanese government officials were physically present in the negotiations; they were behind the scenes. Boeing had occasional contact with them, but it was never as intense and frequent as those with the individuals from the three companies and the vice-chairman and corporate staff from CTDC. On every second or third trip to Tokyo, Boeing would pay a courtesy call to the senior-ranking government officials who sponsored these negotiations. This helped to develop relations between the parties.

English was used throughout the negotiations. Language was seldom, if ever, a problem because Boeing always included at least one *nisei* (second-generation Japanese-American) employee on its negotiating team. The nisei's role was to assist and correct, or at least to deter the Japanese team from talking Japanese while the Boeing people could not understand them. The presence of the nisei deterred the Japanese team from whispering notes to each other about how to negotiate the next sentence. On the Japanese side there was one interpreter who also served as a negotiator and who was present throughout the five-year period. This individual was the assistant to the vice-chairman of CTDC. He spoke excellent English and displayed marked competence in technical terms and U.S. slang.

In general, Bacher felt that the Japanese interpreter and Boeing's nisei employees were able to translate technical terms and convey sentiments on most issues, although there were still some misunderstandings. In Bacher's opinion, it is difficult to tell whether such misunderstandings were linguistic or cultural. The subject of cultural difference will be discussed later.

Factors for Success

Bacher was asked to characterize the quality of Boeing's past negotiations with the Japanese. He indicated that if the factors that were unique to the aircraft industry (such as waiting for the market to develop, the technical complexity of the product, and the four-year time period associated with the development of a new airplane) were excluded as too cumbersome, "I would say that the negotiations were very productive, effective and cordial. Furthermore, the production of the 767 has proceeded smoothly, and the Japanese partner has done an excellent job in picking up the production technology." In fact, production progressed according to schedules established some three and a half years earlier, which was almost unprecedented in Boeing's history of aircraft production, except for its 757 program (*Boeing Annual Report*, 1981).

At the time of the interview in July 1982, Bacher indicated that they had already completed production of twenty-five to thirty-five airplanes, and the first deliveries were made in August 1982. Bacher indicated that Boeing "feels very comfortable with the Japanese performance and their ability to deliver their components, the fuselage section. So we don't foresee any major problems in implementing the program—we are happy with the arrangements. We are talking to them about another venture with a broader role this time. We are willing to repeat the thing and then some." The new venture that Bacher alluded to is the production of Boeing's YXX series, in which CTDC will assume a 25-percent share of the financial cost (*Japan Economic Journal*, 25 January 1983).

Although production has proceeded very smoothly and the relationships between the partners were cordial, the Japanese partner has already requested modifications to certain terms of the agreement because of major currency fluctuations and changes in the aircraft configuration. These requests for modification pertain to the rate of production and the like. Bacher was confident, however, that the Japanese will abide by the terms of the original agreement because Boeing was not prepared to make any modifications. In Bacher's opinion, "any changes that would be made would be minor ones—just 'fine-tuning' the contract."

Even though the negotiations were lengthy and the Japanese have already asked for some modifications in the terms of the agreement, the quality of the negotiations and the relationships between the U.S. and Japanese entities were characterized as highly satisfactory.

In Bacher's opinion, a foremost reason for success was that "both parties have underlying motivations to agree on a joint participation." The Japanese had a national interest, as discussed earlier. Furthermore, the individuals that made up the negotiating team on either side were technically competent; consequently, the negotiations could be conducted in a knowledgeable fashion. Unlike most European aircraft companies, which are owned by the government, such as France's Airbus, the three companies that made up the working entity of CTDC are privately owned. Consequently, both the U.S. and the Japanese partners were motivated by the same economic considerations of profitability, growth, and so on: "This made a mutually beneficial relationship a reality."

A closely related reason for the success of the negotiation was the fact that the Japanese needed the aerospace industry. Hence they were very accommodating on practically all matters, including acceptance of the U.S. mechanism for conflict resolution.

A third reason for the success, as perceived by Bacher, was the cultural awareness on the part of the Americans. Bacher believed that Americans "have a certain advantage over Europeans, particularly on the West Coast where we have many Japanese-Americans." Boeing had several capable management people who are native Japanese, including an employee who lived in Japan until the age of 19 and is thoroughly bilingual. "I think that gave us an advantage over possibly other nations, and they respect us for this multiracial quality."

Bacher was then asked to comment on some of the factors he perceived as responsible for the breakdown of negotiations between U.S. and Japanese entities that he may be aware of (these do not pertain to Boeing in particular).

A major reason for failure would be product characteristics. In Bacher's words, "any negotiation has what I call 'inherent' characteristics—each party wants this thing, how badly they want it, and so forth. That would be true with both Japanese and Americans." A second major reason for failure is impatience on the part of the Americans. In general, Bacher feels that Americans do not allow sufficient time to negotiate. They should recognize that language differences and the consensus style of decision making in Japan account for the longer time required in negotiating with the Japanese. In Bacher's opinion, "I think our failure is that we look back and see how good are the terms we got, and that maybe we could have topped them." Furthermore, many Americans do not fully understand the government-business relationship in Japan: "We don't appreciate the interplay, and probably put it in a U.S. perspective: an adversarial rather than a cooperative position."

Although the Japanese government presence is different from that in the United States, it does not overshadow the profit motive. Sooner or later a venture has to be profitable; that is the only basis on which the government is willing to support industry, and vice versa. Unlike some other countries where the government is willing to subsidize the industry consistently, the Japanese government is not prepared to do so in the long run. In Bacher's opinion, many Americans tend to distort the government-industry relationship in Japan: "They think that the government is buying into the business, they do it for other reasons besides profits. We, at least I personally, do not think so. Most people at Boeing don't accept it. They are going to make money on this venture, and they are going to do it by hard work and efficiency."

Bacher had the following advice for U.S. manufacturers on how to enter into collaborative agreements with the Japanese. The approach for selling would differ from that for a collaborative effort. In selling a product, Bacher emphasized the need to understand the nature of Japanese consumers, their buying habits, and the domestic and foreign competitors in the Japanese market. "If you are going to enter into it, you have to be ready to compete." Due to the lengthy decision-making process, a U.S. manufacturer should allow some extra time. A rule of thumb is: If a firm can sell in the United States in one year, it should count on two years in Japan. "You must allow time to get acquainted. It is a little harder to negotiate an agreement."

In a joint venture or other form of collaborative agreement, the U.S. manufacturer has to evaluate the capabilities and contribution of its Japanese partner, examine the implications of possible government involvement, and understand Japanese business practices such as consensus decision making. Bacher feels that Americans should not focus too much on the differences between the two countries or on the alleged superiority of the Japanese system. In his words, "On the positive side, don't overestimate them. They are human, they don't walk ten feet tall. They are motivated by the same economic factors as we are. There are a lot of common things too. The difference is their negotiating style, their national cohesiveness; but I think that once you have adjusted to the linguistic differences, approaching a potential Japanese partner should not be that different from approaching a potential U.S. partner."

With regard to the selection of a Japanese partner, Bacher suggested using the facilities offered by the trading companies in Japan because these have extensive knowledge of the industry and may provide invaluable services. Since it may not be easy for the neophyte firm to work with the government, the first point of contact should be a trading company. Bacher believed that it is acceptable to associate oneself with a number of trading companies before deciding on one. "There is nothing wrong with contacting several before you settle down with one. They have a tremendous insight into the workings of the Japanese industry and economy and so forth." This theme was echoed by Mr. Epstein, president of Anglo American Aviation Company, who had worked through several general trading companies and found that this mode of entry offered advantages over the establishment of a wholly owned subsidiary.

Salient Characteristics of the Negotiating Situation

In this section the salient characteristics of the negotiating situation between Boeing and CTDC for the formation of a joint program to produce Boeing's 767 will be examined. Some of these have been alluded to in previous sections and will be summarized here.

Lengthiness of Negotiations

As noted previously, the negotiations took four to five years. This could be attributed largely to the unique characteristics of the aircraft industry, the size of the investment involved, and the duration of cooperation between the two partners. Of course, the Japanese style of decision making and frequent caucusing with the government also prolonged the negotiations.

Role of the Japanese Government

Since CTDC is a quasi-government organization and the aerospace industry has been designated as one of Japan's growth industries, the government was naturally involved in the decision-making process, although officials from MITI were not physically present at the negotiations. The excuse of having to caucus with the government, or that the government might not agree, was used as a negotiating tactic and gave the Japanese partner an edge. Given the pervasive influence of the government throughout the negotiations, Bacher was asked to comment on the so-called phenomenon of Japan Incorporated. Bacher noted that he "does not like the term Japan Incorporated. I am the first to admit, as any Japanese would, that it is a cohesive nation. They live on an island, they hardly have any minorities, and they are efficient in getting along—that makes them a cohesive entity. I think their government-industry relationship is based on a business premise. They have certain leeway in their antitrust. In other words, it is acceptable under their law and customs to agree among companies who is going to bid on the work. That would not be acceptable legally nor customary here. Once you understand those differences, I don't think that there is a conspiracy against Americans or outsiders or anything else. I think they are, at least from an international-marketplace viewpoint, as international as any of us."

Even with the pervasiveness of the government in this particular negotiating situation, Mr. Bacher felt that there was no antiforeign conspiracy on the part of the Japanese government, as noted in chapters 1 and 2. Perhaps U.S. exporters or manufacturers should try to dispel this myth and instead try to understand and work within the unique framework that exists between industry and government in the Japanese context. More important, however, U.S. firms should focus on the factors that account for the success of other foreign manufacturers, and try to emulate such positive aspects.

Negotiating Tactics

Besides using the Japanese government as an excuse for delaying decisions or obtaining concessions on certain issues, another negotiating tactic perceived by Bacher was the frequent use of counterproposals by the Japanese partner. In Bacher's words, "We were annoyed with this often-used technique: 'Okay, let's not fight. What we have in mind is an alternative proposal.' I think we were a party to possibly too many counterproposals." In my opinion this tactic could stem partly from the Japanese tradition of resolving conflicts through compromise, wherein both parties would make certain concessions. Given the leading position taken by Boeing, however, the latter was generally unwilling to make too many concessions.

Since most of the members of the Japanese team understood English, it was interesting to see whether the Japanese used interpreters as a negotiating tactic to give them more time to think over the issues. Bacher did not believe so; in his opinion: "I don't think they need an excuse to wait. I think that they have problems with speaking the language even though they can understand." Often, however, the use of an interpreter would given an individual twice the amount of time to think of an appropriate response to a question, which could be a crucial advantage.

Cultural Differences

Although language, in general, did not pose a problem, there were some misunderstandings which could be attributed to either linguistic or cultural differences. Bacher was asked to comment on the most salient cultural differences between the U.S. and Japanese teams. A major difference, he responded, is that "the Japanese have an incredible ability to listen instead of talking; and the Westerner, by their standard, is a talkative individual." As mentioned in chapter 2, the Japanese dislike direct confrontation; a period of silence is generally used to give both sides an opportunity to rethink the issues. Because of the cosmopolitan nature of Boeing's negotiating team, some of its senior people were also very astute and said little. In Bacher's words, "I think our tone of conversation after a few people got into it was, 'Okay, you guys want to take twenty seconds to say nothing, well, we will just wait.' But I think the fundamental difference in negotiating psychology between Americans and Japanese is the amount of conversation versus silence. Silence in a meeting is incredibly awkward." As noted in an earlier chapter, the maxim that silence is golden is deep-rooted in Japanese society.

A second difference is that the Japanese like to use a let-us-consider-this approach. In contrast, Bacher indicated, the U.S. management style is typically "All right, given me three more alternatives, and I will choose among them today." This difference could be attributed to the Japanese preference for avoiding direct confrontation and saving face. Through the let-us-consider approach, the Japanese would not have to reject a proposal outright, and thus could save the face of everybody concerned.

A third difference is the consensus style of decision making, which is more time-consuming. Boeing accepted this because, although it might delay progress, decisions arrived at through the *ringi-sho* would be much easier to implement: "The consensus means that they have so coordinated their own views and approaches—not only the people in the room but also the people who work with them—that when they agree, they move very rapidly and effectively to implement what they agreed to." Given these cultural differences, the relationship between the two entities has been excellent: "The outcome of their performance and their working relationship with us are very, very good," which could account for Boeing's willingness to cooperate with CTDC on the YXX series, with a larger Japanese involvement the second time around.

Bacher noted that although cultural differences may be great, they were by no means insurmountable. Both sides should focus on the commonalities that exist between them. Both Americans and Japanese are motivated by economic considerations, which should serve as a major unifying force.

Litigation

In general, the role of attorneys in this situation conformed to conventional wisdom in that it was downplayed, particularly in the early stages of the negotiating process.

In terms of method of conflict resolution, however, the Boeing team never refrained from direct confrontation on issues. This accommodation on the part of the Japanese team could be attributed to the fact that they needed the aerospace industry.

Socializing

Contrary to the popular view that important decisions were made after hours while the partners were socializing, Bacher indicated that most of the decisions were made during office hours, which were "very productive, effective and cordial." Bacher stated that he "would not want to push it over into the evenings." Since the U.S. partner had the upper hand in this instance, the Japanese were naturally very accommodating. Furthermore, since the negotiations were extended over a four- to five-year period with approximately six to eight meetings per year, the two sides had ample time to get acquainted and develop good working relationships. Moreover, the courtesy-call approach used by Boeing, whereby its people would call on and confer with the senior-ranking government officials who sponsored the negotiations, helped promote good working relations between the two entities.

Time Perspective

A number of Americans see differences in objectives between U.S. and Japanese firms as a reason for failure. In general, the Japanese tend to have a longer-range perspective and to view matters in terms of market share and growth. The Americans, on the other hand, are generally more concerned about bottom-line figures for every quarter or year. This was not the case here because of the unique product line. The product life cycles of aircrafts are long. For example, the Boeing 707 has now been in production for twenty-two years. In Bacher's opinion, "When you deal with a product life cycle of twenty plus years and a developmental time of five years, and a break-even point halfway over the life cycle of the product, if anything, we are longer-range planners by the nature of our business than anybody in the world. The Japanese, I think, were no different. If anything, we were looking farther ahead than they were." Hence time perspective did not pose a problem here.

Concluding Remarks

In the negotiation of this joint program, although there were common factors in the success, such as cultural awareness and product characteristics, there were also significant differences between this and other situations presented in this book. In this case the Japanese partner was more accommodating, accepted the terms of the U.S. partner, and adjusted to the U.S. way of doing business and of conflict resolution. This could be attributed mainly to the fact that the aerospace industry has been designated by the Japanese government as a growth industry for the rest of the twentieth century.

The working relationships between the two entities have progressed smoothly, so much so that Boeing was willing to enter into a subsequent joint agreement with CTDC for the production of its YXX series. Although both sides were reluctant to discuss the specifics of this second agreement so early in the production program, it was reported that originally CTDC wanted a 20-percent share of the financial cost, but accepted Boeing's terms of 25 percent. This again showed that Boeing's technological edge in the aircraft industry, permitted it to dictate terms that the Japanese more or less accepted without objection (*Japan Economic Journal,* 25 February 1983).

Although this type of cooperative agreement is conducive to the development of friendly ties and relationships between entities from either country, and may alleviate trade tensions in the short run, concern has been raised from several quarters about the possible long-term implications of such collaboration. The argument is that since the aerospace industry is one of the last fields in which U.S. manufacturers still have a technological edge over their Japanese counterparts, these collaborative efforts may enable the Japanese to catch up rapidly, as they did in other sectors. Consequently, these collaborative arrangements may generate dangerous competition for U.S. manufacturers in the long run.

Although this possibility certainly exists, only time will tell whether this event will actually materialize. In the meantime, however, these cooperative agreements at least serve to promote better ties between U.S. and Japanese industrial concerns, which are greatly needed in this time of highly strained trade relations between the two countries. Through prolonged cooperation among major industrial concerns from the two nations, perhaps both sides will discover commonalities that may serve to build a solid foundation for long-term industrial and economic coexistence and collaboration.

6 A Tale of Two Pharmaceutical Joint Ventures

The Japanese pharmaceutical industry is interesting from several perspectives. First, there is significant foreign presence in the industry, which is characterized by many producers (Abegglen et al. 1980). Consequently, there is tremendous competition from both domestic and foreign manufacturers. Second, the distribution system in the Japanese pharmaceutical market is unique. Ethical pharmaceuticals are sold through physicians and hospitals rather than drugstores. This increases the layers in the distribution channel and implies that the sales pitch has to be directed at the professional level. Each detail man calls on physicians on a one-on-one basis and could average eight to ten calls per day. With approximately 150,000 physicians in the country, the size of the detail force has to be very large.

Furthermore, the Ministry of Health and Welfare in Japan (the equivalent of the Food and Drug Administration in the United States) imposes strict laboratory-testing and product standards pertaining to the safety and efficacy of ethical drugs sold in the Japanese market. Such standards have often been cited by foreign manufacturers as a nontariff barrier to trade, as discussed in chapter 1. In March 1983 the Nakasone government repealed the practice of requiring foreign pharmaceutical manufacturers to obtain new product approvals each time they changed import agents (*Wall Street Journal*, 25 March 1983, p. 26). In May 1983 Parliament enacted legislation allowing foreign manufacturers to use the results of laboratory tests conducted in their home countries for product-certification purposes (*Wall Street Journal*, 19 May 1983, p. 38).

The unique characteristics of the distribution system in the Japanese pharmaceutical industry and the often rigid standards of the Japanese Ministry of Health and Welfare pose tremendous problems for foreign manufacturers. It would be interesting to see how some successful companies have overcome these problems. A third factor that makes the pharmaceutical industry interesting for study is that the Japanese ethical-drugs market is the second largest in the noncommunist world. Consequently, any pharmaceutical company that hopes to capture a substantial share of the world market cannot ignore the potential of selling its drugs in Japan.

In this chapter the cases of three joint ventures between U.S. and Japanese pharmaceutical entities will be examined. Two of these involved reciprocal arrangements between SmithKline and Fujisawa for the establishment of two separate joint ventures, one in the United States and the other in Japan. Since the same partners were involved, for analysis purposes these two joint ventures will be examined in the same section. The other joint venture examined in this chapter is the one formed between Merck Sharp and Dohme International and Banyu Pharmaceutical Company in 1954.

The cases of Merck Sharp and Dohme and SmithKline could be viewed as complementary in that the former deals with a joint-venture company that was established 29 years ago, whereas the latter focuses on two joint ventures concluded within the past six years. Consequently, in the case of Merck Sharp and Dohme the focus will be on the implementation of a joint-venture arrangement; in the case of SmithKline the focus will be on the negotiations for the actual establishment of the joint ventures. The SmithKline-Fujisawa joint venture in Japan was established in 1977, and the agreement on the reciprocal joint-venture arrangement in the United States was signed in 1981. Thus the two cases capture different dynamics of the cooperative arrangements between U.S. and Japanese entities in the industry.

The Case of Merck & Co., Inc.

In 1981 the sales of Merck & Co., Inc. exceeded $2.92 billion. With its shares trading at 15 times earnings and a return on equity exceeding 25 percent over the past several years, it is one of the most profitable pharmaceutical companies in the United States (*Forbes*, 22 November 1982, p. 14). Besides pharmaceuticals and health-care products, Merck & Co. is also involved in the production of specialty chemical and environmental products, such as evaporative condensers and granular activated carbon (*Merck, Annual Report*, 1981). The manufacturing and marketing of the company's pharmaceutical and health-care products outside North America are handled by its wholly owned subsidiary, Merck Sharp and Dohme International Division (MSDI). In 1980 approximately 50 percent of the company's sales came from international business.

Shortly after the end of World War II, Merck & Co. foresaw the potential for profit in the Japanese market. In those days, however, there were restrictions on the extent of foreign-equity ownership. The pharmaceutical industry was not completely liberalized until the 1970s; in the fifth round of liberalization, which went into effect on May 1, 1973, pharmaceuticals was one of the 17 industries completely liberalized within the next three years to allow for 100-percent foreign ownership (Yoshino 1975). Because of this restriction on equity ownership and the differences in distribution in Japan, MSDI formed a joint venture with an indigenous company called Banyu Pharmaceutical Company. The name of the joint-venture company is Nippon Merck Banyu.

Banyu Pharmaceutical Company is a medium-size family-managed company that was established in 1915. Besides the 50.5-49.5 joint venture with Merck as the majority partner, Banyu had entered into a 50-50 equity arrangement with Bristol Myers in 1973 and has joint research facilities with other foreign concerns. The information presented in this case was obtained from an interview with P. Reed Maurer, vice-president-Japan, Merck Sharp and Dohme International. Maurer is highly qualified to comment on the subject because he lived in Japan from 1970 to 1979. Although he is now stationed at the company's headquarters in Rahway, New Jersey, his staff is located in Japan, and he makes frequent extended business trips to the country.

History

The relationship between Merck and Banyu started shortly after World War II. Merck had developed streptomycin, the first cure for tuberculosis, which was a major problem in Japan after the war because of poverty and unsanitary conditions. The Banyu Pharmaceutical Company was manufacturing antibiotics; because of this affinity, it became a customer of Merck, first for streptomycin and later for cortisone.

The formal relationship with Banyu Pharmaceutical Company began some 30 years ago with Banyu importing Merck's cortisone. Cortisone represented a major medical breakthrough at the time, and this led to the establishment of the joint venture in 1954. Since then essentially the entire line of Merck's drugs and pharmaceutical products has been introduced into Japan through the joint venture. Originally the Japanese partner had a 49-percent equity share, Merck had 50 percent, and an individual held the remaining 1 percent. In 1976 the individual with the 1-percent equity sold out to the two major shareholders, which accounts for the present split of 50.5-49.5, with Merck as the majority partner. The joint venture is a privately held company with only two shareholders.

Between 1970 and 1975 the joint-venture company grew at a compounded annual rate of 10 percent; since 1976 it has expanded at a compounded rate of 14 percent per annum. In 1982 its sales reached 30 billion yen ($122 million at the exchange rate of 245 yen to the dollar), representing approximately half the total sales of the Japanese parent company. The company now employs 1,250 people, 535 of whom are detail men. The joint venture has fully integrated manufacturing and research-and-development facilities, and sales operations in Japan. In the fall of 1982 the joint-venture company completed construction of a new production or finishing facility, where imported bulk drugs can be processed into tablets or capsules. A year before that the joint-venture company built a research laboratory on the same site, bringing the value of the new project to around $65 million.

Since the joint venture was established shortly after the war, there was some reluctance by a number of Merck's board members to collaborate with their former enemy. Much of this opposition was overcome by the foresight of some of Merck's board members, who realized that Japan would eventually become a center of growth, and particularly by the efforts of Huskel Ekaireb, a Merck executive then in charge of the geographic region extending from Japan to India. Ekaireb later rose to the position of executive vice-president of Merck and Company and subsequently became a board member. He retired in mid-1982. He was very committed to the project and was so persuasive that he convinced the rest of Merck's management people at the time of the merits of establishing a joint venture in Japan.

The U.S. side took the initiative and approached its Japanese customer about a possible joint venture. Although Merck had other customers, in Maurer's words: "I don't think there is any other explanation except that the man from Merck and the man from Banyu just hit if off very well."

Merck was then a small company; Ekaireb was virtually on his own, with "whatever support he got back at headquarters." Maurer had no personal knowledge of the major issues under negotiation 30 years ago, but he believed there was no issue that proved very difficult to negotiate—not even extent of equity ownership. This is surprising since even today, when the industry is completely liberalized, percentage of equity ownership can still pose a major problem. This may reflect the importance the Japanese attached to Merck's products at the time. The original agreement was to establish a manufacturing operation to import cortisone in a semifinished form, with final processing to be conducted in Japan.

Historically, the products manufactured and marketed by the joint-venture company have come from the U.S. parent company. In recent years Japan changed its patent laws from a process patent system to one of substance-and-matter patent; incentives are provided in the pricing of drugs under the health-insurance scheme that reward the innovator and penalize the me-too manufacturer to a certain extent. These changes have led to a greater emphasis on discovery than on development. In Maurer's opinion, Nippon Merck Banyu has now reached the stage where the Japanese partner could also contribute to product development: "I think you can categorize the Japanese vis-à-vis the American approach in the following way: If a machine or a drug does not give the desired results, the Japanese approach is most often to improve that machine. The American approach is more toward throwing out the machine and coming up with a new or better one. Both processes may end up at the same spot. Let's take R&D, for instance. R is the new idea in the American approach, where we are stronger; D is the development, where the Japanese approach has more strength. What we are trying to do is combine these two approaches. If we can combine them, then I think we have something better than either one of us had singly."

This is one of the reasons for the formation of a joint venture to which presumably both partners will be able to contribute and generate synergy of results through their combined efforts. Although this is a desired goal of a joint-venture operation, if a joint venture becomes too successful, it may pose a threat to either one or both parent companies. This issue will be examined later on.

Management and Control

The management of the joint venture has always been Japanese. In the early years the Japanese parent provided some personnel to work at Nippon Merck Banyu, but they have not placed any people in the joint-venture company in the past 26 years. The management has been remarkably stable. The chairman of the joint venture originally came from Banyu and has served in that capacity for the past 27 years.

Given the commitment of Japanese personnel to their company, it is interesting to examine whether the employees that originally came from Banyu were divided in their loyalty. In Maurer's opinions, this was never a problem. Furthermore, many of them are close to retirement age now; hence most of the employees that now make up the joint-venture company were hired by Nippon Merck Banyu. At the time of the formation of the joint venture, the president came from Merck; he served until five years ago and has now been replaced by a Nippon Merck Banyu recruit. The joint-venture company is Japanese, but that does not imply that it is Banyu's. The Japanese employed by the joint venture feel that they are working for Nippon Merck Banyu, not for either Banyu or Merck. Practically all the Japanese employed by the joint-venture company are college graduates who chose to join Nippon Merck Banyu, not Banyu itself; they are not people who worked for Banyu before.

Merck works with the joint-venture staff and is closely involved in all strategic issues but generally stays away from personnel matters. The joint-venture company has more interaction with the Japanese parent company on these matters. This does not mean that the personnel system at Nippon Merck Banyu is the same as that of the Japanese parent company. The joint venture has its own personnel system. In Maurer's words, "When we say the management is Japanese, that doesn't mean it is not Merck's. Sometimes it is one and the same."

In all the years that Maurer has been associated with the Japanese operation, he has never made a personnel decision because of his conviction that Murphy's Law will always operate in this regard. According to Murphy's Law, anything that can go wrong will go wrong: "If a foreigner can make a wrong personnel decision, he will, because it is difficult to know what characteristics make a good employee in Japan. I think we can go to England, Germany, or France and say 'He's a good man,' and our instincts often will be right. In Japan the same instincts aren't right—they are wrong, and so personnel selection is a difficult area. I think Americans should defer such decisions to the Japanese partner."

When asked why Americans tend to make the wrong personnel decisions in Japan, Maurer explained that this could be attributed largely to cultural differences: "In the United States, it is important to stand out—we like outstanding people. In Japan it is important to stand in line; that makes a good person." As the Japanese maxim goes, "The nail that stands out will get hit with the hammer." Thus the outstanding individual may not be suitable for the Japanese organization.

Maurer continued: "Americans tend to believe that if a person can conceptualize about a business, even if he had no experience, he could run the show. In Japan everything comes from experience; you have to experience it to know how to run it. That's why in Japan production is so important, and many people in the top management ranks have come from production. In the United States top management tends to come from marketing. Marketing is conceptual, and production is real."

Although the joint venture hires its own personnel, Merck has placed some of its people in staff positions. Merck currently has ten expatriate families stationed in Tokyo. Not all of them work in the joint venture; Merck has another wholly owned subsidiary in Tokyo, with a staff including both Japanese and foreigners, some of them American. The president of the wholly owned subsidiary is an Englishman, who maintains constant contact with the Japanese partner. Maurer is the chairman of the wholly owned subsidiary. Rather than maintaining only periodic contacts with the Japanese partner through regularly scheduled visits, Merck's staff in the wholly owned subsidiary stays in constant touch with the Japanese partner.

Besides these contacts, Merck actually puts its people into the joint venture as needed. For example, their two expatriates are currently involved in the construction and operation of the new factory. In the summer of 1982 another expatriate was dispatched to Japan to help install computers in the new facilities.

Constant contact between the parent company and the Japanese partner and subsidiary is crucial to the effective operation of a joint venture. In a subsequent chapter discussing the dissolution of a joint venture, it is seen that a reason for failure may be that the U.S. company maintained only periodic contact with the joint venture and hence lost touch with its operations to a certain extent. Maurer indicated that Merck "does not conceptually treat NMB [Nippon Merck Banyu] any differently than any subsidiary of Merck with regard to home-office interaction. The difference comes on what I call strategic issues. Obviously, here we must and do interact with our Japanese partner. On operating issues we operate no differently than anywhere else in the world. The local managing director has a great deal of discretion in the allocation of local resources."

Constant communication and interaction, however, are not synonyous with control. Maurer indicated that many U.S. firms are concerned about the issue of control in a joint venture with a foreign partner. In his opinion, "control is a word I try to avoid over there."

There are seven directors on the board, with the U.S. partner having four. This does not mean domination by the U.S. partner, however, because in the past twenty-nine years of operation no issue had been decided by vote at the board level. In Maurer's words, "If it came to a vote, you would probably be declaring war."

Since the products sold by the joint-venture company are Merck products, obviously the U.S. parent company exercises strict control in the development and manufacturing phases. These are normal procedures in the pharmaceutical industry, however, and do not involve control or domination in the management of the joint venture.

Problems of Implementing the Joint Venture

Although the joint venture has been very successful, it has encountered problems. The most salient ones are as follows.

Personnel Recruitment

A previous chapter discussed the difficulty for foreign firms in recruiting competent Japanese college graduates. Maurer believes it is because such problems exist that Banyu put its own people into the joint venture in its early years. Even 29 years later, the joint venture still has some difficulty in recruiting. In recent years the joint-venture company has been successful in hiring approximately a hundred new college graduates a year, although it is still unable to attract any from the imperial universities, such as Tokyo University. A major reason for the improvement is that both parent companies have given the employees of Nippon Merck Banyu a real opportunity to rise in the ranks of the organization, although barriers still remain at the board level.

Problems of Maturation

A second problem encountered is not unique to Nippon Merck Banyu, but occurs in joint ventures in general. In Maurer's opinion, a joint venture is like a human being who grows and must change: "There are certain things that you must do for a baby—he can't feed himself, and so on. I think probably our joint venture now has become a young man. It has gone through the teens, has had a lot of education, and so on. So it has got to change. It can't be the same as it was yesterday, and it is going to be different tomorrow. This causes stress and strain as it does in the family situation. We can't keep the child tied to the apron strings. Those kinds of issues probably are difficult."

For example, representation at the board level has to be expanded to include members of management in the joint venture. The fact that Nippon Merck Banyu has not done so has now become an issue. Other pharmaceutical joint ventures in Japan have done so because that is the ultimate post to which a college graduate joining the firm can aspire. If these positions are not open, the company is in effect telling the college graduates not to enter the joint venture but to join either Merck or Banyu. When the joint venture was first established, of course, there was no one at Nippon Merck Banyu to fill that capacity. Now that the joint venture has matured, some of its employees can take over these positions. Both parent companies must accommodate their aspirations.

Coping with Success

A closely related problem is that once a joint venture becomes very successful, it may pose a threat to the parent companies. The sales of Nippon Merck Banyu reached 30 billion yen in 1982, approximately half the gross sales of the Japanese parent company. Since the sales of Merck and Company are not broken down according to individual operations, it is impossible to come up with a similar percentage.

Maurer sees this kind of problem brewing for the Japanese partner. In his opinion, the success of the joint venture could become a threat to the Japanese parent company, but not for Merck: "It is like the threat that children give parents when they are 19 versus when they are 6, and some people can't handle that. There are Japanese companies that cannot cope with it because they try their best to keep the joint venture a small baby. You can't do that. If you do, then the joint venture is going nowhere and it will never be a success." In Maurer's opinion, the problem is beginning to surface now and may reach a crisis level within the next two years, although he would not comment on the possible outcome.

Besides the aforementioned issue, Maurer does not think the joint venture experienced any serious problems in terms of its operations over the past 29 years; he believes that most of the issues encountered were simply the normal problems of running a business. In his words: "I hate to single this out as being different from running any other kind of business. Every time we want to put a plant somewhere, there is always discussion within the company as to whether it is wise or not. We have had those kinds of discussions, but I don't think that can be categorized as being any different from what one would find within our own company on any capital item. With regard to management, the board of directors really restricts itself to the level of management reporting to the president. Everything below that is really the management of the joint venture's decision."

Differences between U.S. and Japanese Practices

In this section Maurer was asked to comment on some of the salient differences between U.S. and Japanese business practices.

Decision Making

Maurer believes there is a general myth that all decisions in Japan are made by a bottom-up approach. He believes that senior executives like Mr. Honda, Mr. Matsushita, and Mr. Morita from Sony—individuals with whom he is familiar—do not make decisions in that manner. Rather, they use the one-screech-of-the-crane mechanism described in chapter 2.

In Merck's case, the U.S. partner keeps in constant touch with the management of the Japanese partner, and there are regularly scheduled meetings. The board meeting is a formality in the sense that the U.S partner will never raise any issue at that level that would be a total surprise to the Japanese partner. The same is true in the U.S. context, however; the Merck board of directors would not bring up an issue that had not been previously discussed by the chairman with the board members. Since the management of the joint venture are in charge of the day-to-day operations of Nippon Merck Banyu, they are constantly encouraged to bring matters to the attention of both parents, and they do. Consequently, the board meetings themselves are, "rather, confirmation of actions which have already been decided on by both partners."

Maurer believes there is another myth about excessive delays in decision making in Japan. In his opinion, although Americans pride themselves on the speed with which they make decisions, implementation is much slower; the converse is true in Japan. Maurer was asked to comment on the average length of time it takes to reach a decision in the joint-venture company. In his opinion the decisions that take most time are those relating to senior executive appointments and to position succession planning. Even in these instances, "We are talking about months, not years."

In his opinion the biggest difference in decision-making styles between the Japanese and U.S. partners is the heightened sensitivity in Japan about the possible impact a decision may have on a wide audience. "If the decision could have a serious impact on someone or some group, then I think they tend to move quite carefully in Japan. In the United States, if we have 51 percent of the people, we expect the other 49 percent to come along. So I think the difference that is probably the greatest in Japan is that we tend to look more at the overall 'soft' or human impact versus the quantitative numerical impact on the business."

Negotiation Tactics

Maurer believes that the Japanese are more persistent: "On the U.S. side we have a feeling of what we basically want to get. If the decision looks like it is basically what we want, we will tend to say, 'Okay, that's it. We have to get on a plane and go home.' The Japanese are probably better businessmen—they keep trying to get this, that, and the other thing. They will work a little harder at their homework and really try to get all they can, and I don't fault them for that. I think we have become a little too soft here. We tend to give up and say, 'Enough is enough; take what I have and go.' There are times when I think that you have to hit the Japanese over the head and say, 'That's it, no more.' We do it; it is a kind of a shock approach. But this is not unlike what Japanese managers will do in their companies. They will say, 'We have this major threat to our business, and we all have to pull together now. We have to work from eight o'clock in the morning until eight at night, on Saturdays and Sundays, and we are all going to do this.' Often, the Japanese manager himself will devise this kind of shock approach. So there are times that I think the U.S. side should simply say, 'That's enough, finish, this is the deal, we are walking away'."

This kind of approach has been used quite often by U.S. companies, as in the case of TRW's negotiations with Fujitsu reported in chapter 4, and in the SmithKline-Fujisawa negotiations described subsequently.

Attitude toward Litigation

Again, Maurer believes there are myths in this area: "When you are on the other side of the table bringing something in, I think the Japanese can get just as legalistic." He concedes, however, that attorneys are seldom part of the Japanese negotiating team, primarily because the Japanese do not like to include people "who are not part of the business, or who don't have experience in the business." This explains why, in labor negotiations in

Japan, management and the personnel department negotiate with each other, rather than the latter with the union leader.

Maurer further acknowledges that Americans in general are more legalistic; he has tried to explain to the Japanese why that is necessary: "I think that overall, with the exception of antitrust and tax laws, we are successful. We are absolutely having problems in those two areas because the concepts of antitrust and why certain things are necessary in our agreements because of our antitrust and tax laws are quite incomprehensible to the Japanese."

To get around these problems, the U.S. partner has tried to do several things, including offering detailed explanations and asking the Japanese partner to consult outside U.S. attorneys to help them understand that it is not just Merck's policy, but a requirement of the U.S. government. The problem, of course, is that in the United States attorneys often have differing opinions on issues; it really "comes down to the unwritten matter of trust." In most of Merck's contractual agreements with the Japanese partner, there is a clause at the end stipulating that "if anything in the agreement causes some kind of problem to either party, we will negotiate it in good faith."

Maurer admitted that the operation of any joint venture is "never really smooth." There are always issues that require discussion, some more extensive than others and involving major compromises on both sides. Where issues cannot be resolved, the joint venture will simply cease to exist. Fortunately, this has not happened in the case of Nippon Merck Banyu. Maurer noted that he had closed a joint venture in Japan (not Nippon Merck Banyu) "because of an issue we could not resolve—the way we were operating was just not economic, and the only alternative was simply to stop." Ultimately, the successful cooperation between two partners hinges on the bottom-line figure. If a joint venture is unprofitable, then neither party will have an interest in salvaging the relationship. In chapter 8, which examines the dissolution of a joint venture, this was the key factor responsible for the breakup between the two partners.

Time Perspective

Although differences in time perspectives may pose a problem in some joint operations between U.S. and Japanese entities, it was not the case in the pharmaceutical industry, where the typical development time frame for new drugs is ten years from test tube to market. The U.S. parent company is conditioned to think in long-range terms. Furthermore, both parties are concerned about the bottom line—profitability. This opinion is similar in many ways to the one expressed by Bacher in the case of Boeing Commercial Airplane Company. In the case of SmithKline and Fujisawa, this perceived difference in time perspective initially posed a major stumbling block to the progress of the negotiations.

Language

Language may pose a problem in some joint efforts, but it was never an issue in the case of Nippon Merck Banyu to the best of Maurer's recollection. Maurer understands spoken Japanese but does not use it in business. In his opinion, communication problems may arise when a U.S. parent company tries to run the Japanese operation from the United States: "I don't think they can do that. You have to be there on the scene, and you need to have Japanese help you. That doesn't mean interpreters."

Because of the relatively low status accorded interpreters in Japan, Maurer believes that an American should not rely on an interpreter to conduct the negotiations. To overcome the communication problem, he believes it is important to have a Japanese staff who understand what the U.S. partner wants. To accomplish this, the Japanese staff have to be brought to corporate headquarters to become acquainted with Merck's operations. If the Japanese staff members "understand what you want to do, then they are going to say that in their own words, not just the words that you say. Indeed, that is the way I operate. I try to have my Japanese staff understand what we want to do and we agree on that. Then when I go into a meeting with another party, whether it be the parent or someone else, I don't need to say anything except the formalities."

Cultural Differences

In Maurer's opinion, the biggest cultural difference lies in the notion of the individual versus the group: "It is so built into U.S. culture that the individual is the important thing—we attach qualifications to our person. In fact, if you ask children in the United States what their father does, they will say plumber, minister, lawyer, and so on. In Japan they say he works for a particular company. So the person's qualifications are attached to the company, not to him, the individual."

In the United States, if a person lacks the qualifications for a job, he is dismissed. In Japan there is a greater tendency to find some way in which this individual can contribute: "It may be very minor, but at least he is not in the way anymore." A U.S. partner must understand and accommodate this difference in staffing and personnel policies.

Maurer postulates another reason that cultural differences may create a problem. When foreigners visit Japan and see skyscrapers and people in

Western-style suits and dresses, they perceive that Japan is changing: "When we say Japan is changing, we think it is getting Westernized. That's not true; it is changing, but it is Japanese. We get into a little trouble because we think it is really a Western model. So again I think it is very important to get behind the facade" in order to discover the underlying reasons the Japanese have for doing things: "Japan's cultural heritage leads to quite a different conclusion when looking at the same thing. That doesn't mean they are wrong or right." Consequently, it is important to have an adequate understanding of the Japanese mentality, their rationale for doing things, and the way such matters are implemented.

Face-Saving

Maurer believes that face-saving is a very important cultural difference. Although face-saving is important in any country, the difference is in the level of sensitivity and the ability to cope with it. Maurer feels that the Japanese are more sensitive in this area and are less capable of coping with affronts than the average American. In the United States, if someone says "'Come on Harry, that's stupid,' well, I rock back in my chair and think, 'How will Harry feel?'" We are able to handle that a lot better than the Japanese. But I think we all have a feeling of self-worth—as soon as anyone touches that, then we have a problem." Sensitivities are often difficult to understand and have to be fine-tuned in a given cultural context. Often the foreigner in Japan is at an advantage because the Japanese do not expect him to know these customs, so he can afford to make mistakes.

Role of the Government

In Maurer's opinion, the only way in which the government exercised strong influence in the pharmaceutical industry in the early years was through restrictions in foreign-equity ownership, which have since been removed. Although the joint-venture company does have problems with the development and registration of drugs, these are no different from those encountered with the Food and Drug Administration (FDA) in the United States. This perception is essentially the same in the case of SmithKline. Maurer does not believe that the Ministry of Health and Welfare (*Koseisho* in Japanese) is any more pervasive than its counterpart in the United States. "The FDA is changing, and the Ministry of Health and Welfare changes. But no one is telling us how to run our business."

Factors Responsible for Success

Since 1970 the joint-venture company has grown at a compounded annual rate of 10 percent and later at a rate of 14 percent. Maurer was asked to comment on some of the factors he feels were responsible for the success of the operation.

Willingness to Nurture the Joint Venture

Maurer saw the willingness of both parent companies to nurture the joint venture company as a key to success. On the Japanese side, although they are now experiencing problems of coping with the maturation of the joint venture, there has always been a willingness to allow it to grow and develop from infancy through adolescence. It was not viewed as a side activity of the Japanese parent company, or merely as a means to acquire technology and products.

   Conversely, a major reason for the failure of some joint-venture operations is the lack of commitment on the part of the parent companies. Often the activities of a U.S. multinational may be highly diversified. Consequently, they may not be willing to devote adequate resources and time to nurture the kind of relationships necessary in the effective operation of a joint venture.

To Be Inside Japan

On Merck's part, there has been a sincere desire to understand the Japanese way of doing business and to be "truly inside Japan, rather than in New York or outside Japan. When you are truly inside Japan, then it becomes a very nice place to be. When you are outside Japan, it is terrible." Maurer was asked to elaborate on what he meant by being "truly inside Japan." He responded: "It means you have friends. It means that you have people whom you can talk to, and they will say, 'That's really nonsense,' and not just sit back and say, 'Yes, that is a good idea' and really mean it is not. Get to the inside behind the 'Hai'—you have to be behind that. Unfortunately, a lot of people never get beyond that; they never do market research or understand why certain systems are what they are. There is often a very good reason that things are done a certain way. To be truly inside, I think first of all you need friends; you need to be a part of the local scene there; you need to have a long-term commitment to the business there—all those things that people often tend not to get behind, and then they run off complaining that it is a closed market. They never really got underneath the skin of Japan, and it is not difficult to do so. Frankly, I think there are many people in Japan—retired businessmen and government officials, people from academia—who are indeed willing to help if they are only asked to do so.'' To illustrate this willingness on the part of influential Japanese to help a foreign company, he cited the example of the executive advisory committee at Nippon Merck Banyu. The committee is composed of many distinguished Japanese, including business and professional people.

Maurer noted that perhaps U.S. companies have been afraid to ask for assistance in Japan, but that they should overcome this fear. When the Japanese establish operations in the United States, they know how to use consultants and influential members of the community. For example, when Kikkoman, a major Japanese manufacturer of soy sauce and other food products, established a plant in Wisconsin, it formed an advisory council that included the governor of the state of Wisconsin, the mayor of the local town, a local lawyer, a prominent local businessman, and a distinguished professor from the University of Wisconsin. ''I am not sure U.S. companies are doing enough of that, and there are people that are willing to offer that kind of help. That's what I mean by being inside.''

Product Adaptation

Knowledgeable local people could assist a foreign company by pointing out possible problems. For example one of Merck's latest pharmaceutical products—'Blocadren,' has been proved effective in significantly lowering the incidence of a second fatal heart attack among people who have survived a previous one. Merck planned to introduce 'Blocadren' in Japan, highlighting this important product feature. A member of the advisory committee, however, who was the head of a cardiovascular unit in a major Japanese hospital, indicated that the incidence of heart attacks in Japan is very low. Consequently, instead of introducing the product as preventing further heart attacks, 'Blocadren' should be advertised as an effective medicine for treating hypertension, which is a major problem in Japan.

Similarly, the Japanese have aversions to certain colors of tablets or capsules. For example, SmithKline discovered that the Japanese dislike green and purple tablets and capsules. The company has had to modify the colors accordingly (*Keys to Success*, 1980).

Hard Work

Since there are many manufacturers of pharmaceutical products in Japan, the environment is extremely competitive. Success in the Japanese market requires a lot of hard work. In Maurer's words: ''You have to be prepared to work hard. That sounds so simple, but people come to Japan expecting that the world has been waiting for them to come there; that's not the case anymore, if it ever was. It might have been for certain products, but it is not the case in the pharmaceutical industry."

Foreign manufacturers tend to complain about nontariff barriers to trade. Although there are problems in this area, perhaps the single greatest obstacle to trade is the reluctance of the foreign firm to commit its resources to make the venture a success. Procter and Gamble, for instance, has invested millions of dollars and has been successful. 'Pampers' helped them, of course. In Maurer's words, foreign firms have been "successful despite what everyone hears about nontariff barriers—people are going in and they are being successful. So I tend to discount some of these generalizations about nontariff trade barriers." Maurer's assertion supports the findings of the U.S.-Japan Study Group that U.S. penetration in the Japanese market is more prevalent than generally assumed.

Patience

Because of the consensus style of decision making and the different time perspective of the Japanese, things do not progress quickly in Japan. Patience is a necessity in doing business there. Maurer told a Japanese folk story to illustrate why patience is considered a cardinal virtue in Japan. During the bloody civil war between rival warlords in the fifteenth century, the Japanese emperor summoned the three major warlords and told them that who would rule the entire country would be determined by their answer to a single question: "If you had a nightingale in your hand and it wouldn't sing, what would you do?" The first said he would kill the bird because it was useless. The second said he would force it to sing. The third one, reputed to be Tokugawa, who later became the shogun and whose family ruled Japan in peace and harmony for over two hundred years, replied, "I would wait for it to sing." The moral for the foreign firm, in Maurer's words, is that "there are certain instances when you must wait for things to happen. If you are not prepared to do that, then you are going to get into some trouble."

Staffing of the Operation

Given the tremendous cultural differences between Japan and the United States, although it is important to have Japanese staff, it may be necessary to have some expatriates in the overseas operation to communicate with U.S. corporate headquarters. In Maurer's words: "If you try to Japanize your operation, then the Japanese will have a great deal of trouble with the home office. As effective as the Japanese can be in their country, they can be ineffective relating to the home office. The foreigner will have a hard time dealing in Japan but may be better able to cope with the home office. So we can combine them; that is why I don't like working with all Japanese or all foreigners. I like to have that combination." The kind of dilemma mentioned here is very common among U.S. multinationals.

In terms of staffing Merck's wholly owned subsidiary, the company has been geocentric in its approach. The head of the subsidiary is an Englishman who was chosen because he was most suited for the position. The Englishman had not worked for Merck before but had had 12 years of experience with another company in Japan. When that company wanted to transfer him to the United States, he decided to remain in Japan and took the position with Merck.

The Englishman shares the responsibilty of running the wholly owned subsidiary with a Japanese. The former is the president, the later the vice-chairman. The president is in charge of the day-to-day operations; the Japanese vice-chairman is responsible for strategic issues. The marketing operation of the wholly owned subsidiary is headed by a Japanese, while marketing operations of the joint venture are headed by a French national who has been with Merck for a long time. In staffing the wholly owned subsidiary, Merck makes hiring decisions on the basis of a person's qualifications rather than nationality.

Since Americans have to work alongside Japanese, it is interesting to see whether there were tensions. Maurer observed that some initial problems have largely been overcome, and that the American production engineer now works side by side with the Japanese: "They argue, of course, but they are building that plant and it will probably be the best one in the Merck world." Of the ten expatriates in Japan, two are in marketing; the rest are either technical people or medical doctors.

Besides the aforementioned factors in the success of the joint-venture operation, Maurer was asked to give some advice to the neophyte foreign firm that wants to penetrate the Japanese market. Maurer noted: "First of all, I would say nothing is impossible. You have to get behind the myths. In the past there were things that were impossible—it was impossible to have a wholly owned subsidiary; it is not impossible today." The firm has to decide on the mode of market entry with which it will be most comfortable. "There are companies that have a mentality that no matter what, they just can't work with a partner. They are better off going 100 percent because no matter what they do, not matter how much Japanese they learn, no matter how many books they read, they are not going to be successful. It is not their style of management to deal with a partner. When you have a partner, that means you have to make joint decisions." In chapter 8, which examines a joint venture that failed, this is cited as a major reason for the breakdown in the relationship. The U.S. company was more comfortable with a 100-percent ownership arrangement, rather than working with a partner.

Factors in Failure

Maurer was then asked to comment on some of the reasons for the failure of joint ventures that he may know of (*note:* these do not pertain to Nippon Merck Banyu per se). In Maurer's opinion, a major reason for failure is the reluctance of the parent company to let the joint venture grow and take on its own identity. Other factors include poor selection of personnel to staff the joint-venture operation, capital requirements beyond the capability or willingness of both parent companies to contribute, and technological obsolescence.

Postscript

In August 1983, Merck & Co. acquired 51-percent equity interest in Banyu Pharmaceutical Co., its Japanese partner. The transaction was valued at $313.5 million.

The Case of SmithKline Corporation

In recent years SmithKline Corporation (now SmithKline Beckman Corporation), a Philadelphia-based pharmaceutical company, has emerged as an industry leader in profitability. Within a six-year period the company's revenues quadrupled, from $700 million in 1976 to approximately $3 billion in 1982, making its ethical-pharmaceutical division the twelfth largest in the world. Much of this rapid growth could be attributed to the phenomenal success of 'Tagamet,' which has been proved effective in curing peptic ulcers. The product was first introduced in 1976 and is currently marketed in 122 countries. The company is pursuing an aggressive research-and-development program, and its objective is to attain sales level in the $4-billion range by the mid-1980s (SmithKline, *Annual Report*, 1981).

Prior to the 1950s SmithKline distributed its products to overseas markets primarily through direct exporting or licensing agreements. Throughout the 1950s and 1960s, in order to realize greater profits in the overseas markets and to exercise tighter control over its products, the company adopted a policy of establishing wholly owned subsidiaries in a number of countries in Europe, Latin America, and former British Commonwealth nations. In 1981 approximately 47 percent of the company's revenues were derived from international business. Despite its rapid expansion in overseas business, until the mid-1970s SmithKline had no equity presence in the Japanese market for ethical pharmaceuticals, which had emerged as the second largest in the Free World. Faced with this situation and recognizing the potential for substantial profits in the Japanese market, the company decided to establish a more visible presence in Japan.

After considering various market entry modes, SmithKline decided that a joint-venture arrangement with an indigenous Japanese pharmaceutical company would be most suitable for carrying out the firm's objectives. After nearly four years of negotiations, an agreement was finally reached to form a 50-50 joint venture with Fujisawa Pharmaceutical Co., Ltd., the third-largest pharmaceutical firm in Japan in terms of net sales and the second largest in terms of net income. The agreement for the joint-venture company in Japan, known as SmithKline·Fujisawa K.K., was signed in 1977. 'Tagamet' was introduced to Japanese physicians in January 1982.

Soon after the conclusion of the joint-venture agreement for operation in Japan, SmithKline entered into subsequent negotiations with Fujisawa to form a reciprocal joint venture for marketing Fujisawa's products in the United States. The agreement on the second joint venture, known as Fujisawa SmithKline Corporation, was signed in 1981. The first product to be marketed by the U.S. joint venture is Fujisawa's third-generation cephalosporin antibiotic, known as ceftizoxime ('Cefizox') (Fujisawa, *Prospectus*, 1981).

As distinguished from the Merck & Co. case, the discussion here will focus on the negotiations for the establishment of the two joint-venture operations. The information presented here was obtained from interviews with Quincy N. Williams, vice-president of business planning and development, Smith Kline & French Laboratories, a division of SmithKline Beckman Corporation; Peter Sears, vice-president, corporate development, SmithKline Beckman Corporation; and Gary L. Snable, vice-president and chief operating officer of Fujisawa SmithKline. Besides serving as vice-president of business planning and development of Smith Kline & French Laboratories, Williams is also a vice-president of Fujisawa SmithKline. In his words, he serves "as a 'window' to SmithKline for the U.S. joint venture, and as a 'translator' in both directions." These gentlemen are highly qualified to comment on the establishment of the two joint ventures. The information obtained through the in-depth interview was supplemented with materials presented in a course project by two groups of students whom I taught at The Wharton School. I would like to acknowledge the contribution of Robert Canning, Daniel Chesterman, Mathias Chikaonda, Hans Fredericks, and Robert Donald Green in the graduate class; and Michael Corso, Andrew Blatter, Wendy Sarrett, John O'Neill, and Chin Hock Low in the undergraduate class for some of the supplementary information on the two joint ventures. The students conducted interviews with Messrs. J.P. Young, director, agreements, Smith Kline & French Laboratories; and Warren Hauser, vice-president, legal affairs, Smith Kline & French Laboratories International.

History

SmithKline's products were introduced in Japan in the 1960s. These were primarily proprietary drugs—products that did not require a prescription. The first major product introduced was 'Contac' cold capsules, an over-the-counter medicine. In those days SmithKline had no appropriate line of ethical pharmaceuticals to sell in Japan because many of the company's largest-selling items were either unsuitable for the Japanese market or were licensed from European pharmaceutical companies under agreements that did not include Japan in their territory. SmithKline therefore had to wait for new product developments that would be large enough and also suitable for the Japanese market.

This opportunity came with the development of 'Tagamet', the result of a 12-year research program on H2 antagonist receptors carried out in SmithKline's United Kingdom division. In 951 clinical studies conducted in some 50 countries, 'Tagamet' was found to be effective in curing duodenal ulcers. Furthermore, it was proved that continued use of the product could significantly reduce the relapse rate among ulcer sufferers. This product appeared suitable for the Japanese market because of the high rate of gastrointestinal disease, particularly gastric ulcer, in Japan (SmithKline, *Annual Report*, 1981). With the potential for huge profits in Japan, SmithKline decided to explore the possibility of establishing a presence there. Three alternative modes of entry were possible: licensing, the establishment of a wholly owned subsidiary, or the establishment of a joint-venture agreement with an indigenous Japanese pharmaceutical company.

Licensing was inappropriate because it would not result in equity ownership. As for the establishment of a wholly owned subsidiary, there appeared to be formidable barriers to entry. When asked to comment on the difficulties of this second strategy, Williams noted that the decision to explore business opportunities in Japan was made some ten years ago, when conditions there were quite different from those prevailing today. He indicated that although several foreign pharmaceutical firms have successfully established wholly owned subsidiaries in Japan, these generally had long-standing relationships with indigenous partners. Williams believed that if SmithKline had been doing business in Japan since the 1940s or 1950s, it might have cultivated the necessary relationships to establish a wholly owned subsidiary in the 1970s. Since the company was not very internationally oriented in the 1940s, however, "When we faced the problem in the mid-1970s, the start-up from scratch faced too many obstacles in too little time."

Some major obstacles to establishing a wholly owned subsidiary in Japan included, first, the complex distribution system in the Japanese pharmaceutical industry, discussed previously. The multiple layers of the distribution system plus the practice of making one-to-one sales calls on physicians require the effective pharmaceutical company to have a very large detail force. The second problem is that of recruiting such a sizable detail force. The problems of recruiting competent Japanese to work for foreign companies were also discussed earlier; it is virtually impossible for a foreign firm that is relatively unknown in Japan to hire qualified personnel. In Williams's words, "If one were interested in merely getting by or could endure having a mediocre sales force, I suppose it could be done. We, however, are not that kind of a company. As a matter of fact, the better companies in our industry, both in Japan and in the United States, would not follow such an approach at the cost of mediocrity."

A third problem is the relationship a pharmaceutical company, whether foreign or indigenous, must have with the regulatory agency. This is similar in many ways to the kind of goodwill that U.S. pharmaceutical firms must cultivate with the FDA. Again, it would be very difficult for a foreign pharmaceutical company that had no significant prior presence in Japan to recruit pharmaceutical development personnel who had the necessary working relationships with the Japanese Ministry of Health and Welfare (*Koseisho*). A fourth barrier relates to the difficulty of recruiting capable Japanese medical investigators, who are generally more independent than their U.S. counterparts. To compete with indigenous and foreign pharmaceutical firms for the recruitment of high-caliber investigators, the company has to be "a first-class outfit, a well-known outfit. Investigators want to work with the most exciting companies, with the most attractive compounds. Smith Kline & French as a name meant very little in Japan in the early 1970s."

Although 'Contac' was and is a successful product, the channels of distribution and marketing for a proprietary medicine are different from those for an ethical-pharmaceutical product. As an over-the-counter product, 'Contac' is advertised to consumers, whereas ethical pharmaceuticals are promoted not to the consumers directly but to the physicians or hospitals that dispense and sell them. Consequently, the channel of distribution and marketing organization developed for 'Contac' had limited utility for an ethical-pharmaceutical product line. Furthermore, an over-the-counter product did not require relationships with physicians and hospitals on the one hand or with regulatory agencies on the other.

Given these constraints, SmithKline recognized the problems that would be inherent in the establishment of a wholly owned subsidiary to distribute its ethical pharmaceuticals. SmithKline believed that the best course of action was to seek an appropriate Japanese partner with whom it could form a joint-venture arrangement.

SmithKline initially contacted several of the largest Japanese pharmaceutical companies; it quickly narrowed the list of prospective candidates to two, Sumitomo and Fujisawa. In the mid-1960s SmithKline had entered into a licensing agreement with Sumitomo for manufacturing some of the former's over-the-counter drugs in Japan. This agreement was still in effect in 1973. At that time, however, Sumitomo already had a joint-venture agreement with UpJohn, another U.S. pharmaceutical company. This last factor led SmithKline to believe that Fujisawa would be a more appropriate candidate for a joint-venture arrangement.

Fujisawa was established by Tomokichi Fujisawa in 1894 and is engaged in the manufacture and distribution of ethical pharmaceuticals, over-the-counter drugs, household sanitary products, and industrial chemicals. In the fiscal year ended March 31, 1981, the sale of ethical-pharmaceutical products accounted for over 80 percent of the company's revenues. Like SmithKline, the Japanese partner had experienced very rapid growth over the past decade, much of it attributable to the success of its cephalosporin antibiotic, Cefazolin ('Cefamezin'), which is currently marketed in some sixty countries around the world.

As noted previously, Fujisawa is the third largest pharmaceutical company in Japan in net sales and the second largest in net income. SmithKline was particularly impressed with Fujisawa's sales and distribution network in Japan. In 1981 the company had nine branch offices and fifty sales offices, and employed approximately thirteen hundred detail men. In addition, Fujisawa possessed comprehensive laboratory facilities suitable for product testing. Although Fujisawa also pursued an aggressive marketing strategy overseas until the early 1970s, this was confined to licensing agreements with foreign firms such as Eli Lilly and Bristol Myers in the United States, Farmitalia Carlo Erba in Italy, and Boehringer Mannheim in West Germany (Fujisawa, *Prospectus,* 1981).

SmithKline's contacts with Fujisawa prior to the negotiations for the joint venture were primarily in two areas. In the 1960s, when 'Contac' was first introduced in Japan, Dr. Fujisawa provided support for the then general manager of the business, Henry Wendt (now president of SmithKline Beckman Corporation), by testifying to the Japanese distribution system that SmithKline was a respectable and solid company.

A second and more significant relationship was formed between the two companies through the licensing agreement signed in 1971 whereby SmithKline obtained the exclusive right to distribute Fujisawa's cefazolin in the United States. This licensing agreement proved profitable and provided a welcome boost to SmithKline's sales in the United States. This licensing agreement further strengthened the business relationships between the two companies. It was against this backdrop that SmithKline approached Fujisawa for the possible formation of a joint venture to market 'Tagamet', a drug that could potentially be very profitable in the Japanese market.

Negotiating Team

The formal negotiations for the possible formation of a joint venture in Japan between SmithKline and Fujisawa began in 1974. Peter Sears was then stationed in Tokyo as general manager of the company's Japanese operations; consequently, most of the negotiations were undertaken by him. In Sears's recollection, for three years (1973-1976) he "breathed, ate and slept the prospect of a joint venture with Fujisawa." During this period he engaged in extensive after-hours socializing with the Fujisawa people. These efforts bore fruit; in his opinion, substantial progress was made during these informal discussions conducted in a more relaxed and congenial environment. This lends support to the thesis that important business transactions in Japan are discussed and consummated during after-hours socializing, although this is not always the case, as is evident from some of the other negotiating situations presented in the book.

Other members of the SmithKline negotiating team included Warren Hauser, the attorney involved in the negotiations, and Alan Dalby, then president of the International Division and currently president of Smith Kline & French Laboratories. Dalby was the senior management person represented in the negotiations.

Another SmithKline employee, J.P. Young, provided invaluable input into the negotiations. He had been commuting between the United States and Japan since the late 1960s, and by 1974 had approximately five years of experience in visiting Japan. According to Williams, "Mr. Young is uniquely qualified to be a consultant on SmithKline's side because he had made a study of Japanese history, business, and culture, and he has from his first visit appreciated and respected the differences between our cultures and societies." Although Sears conducted most of the exploratory negotiations, he was supported by top management from SmithKline who visited Japan when key issues were discussed.

On the Japanese side the negotiating team consisted of senior management personnel, including board members from Fujisawa. Toguchi, a director of Fujisawa, served as the chief negotiator for the Japanese side and developed close personal relationships with Sears over the years of negotiating with him. Toguchi was assisted through most of the negotiations by Aoki, the company counsel.

The first set of negotiations for the formation of the SmithKline·Fujisawa K.K. joint venture in Japan began in 1974 and ended in 1977; the second set of negotiations for the establishment of the reciprocal joint venture in the United States began in 1979 and ended in 1981. The negotiators for Fujisawa were the same in both events, although Aoki had a far more active role in the second case. On SmithKline's side the actual members of the negotiating teams for both joint ventures changed, although Young served as a consultant throughout both sets of negotiations. A second common link was provided in the person of Warren Hauser; in Williams's opinion, however, he was "involved really in a legal, rather than a business sense," whereas the chief negotiator for Fujisawa throughout the two sets of negotiations was involved in all aspects of the formation of both joint ventures.

The negotiations for the first joint venture took place in Japan. This was reasonable, in Williams's opinion, since SmithKline was the party that was interested in entering the Japanese market. Conversely, when Fujisawa wanted to establish a joint-venture operation in the United States, most of the discussions occurred in Philadelphia.

Issues under Negotiation

The major issue under negotiation was the form of cooperative agreement between the two companies. This proved to be the most difficult issue to negotiate, and certainly the most time-consuming. Once this issue was resolved, other matters—percentage of equity ownership, management of the joint venture, and the name of the joint venture enterprise—were resolved more expeditiously. Each of these issues will be examined.

Form of Cooperative Agreement

When Sears approached Fujisawa about the possibility of forming a joint venture, the initial reaction of the Japanese partner was one of "puzzlement and skepticism." Fujisawa wanted to license SmithKline's products, not enter into a joint venture. Although Fujisawa had licensing agreements with other foreign pharmaceutical companies, it had never formed a joint venture with a foreign entity and hence was not sure that this was operational. In Sears's opinion, Fujisawa was skeptical about the profitability of a joint venture because of the lackluster performance of some of SmithKline's products in the Japanese market theretofore. SmithKline's Japanese operations had incurred substantial losses prior to 1975 in the over-the-counter field.

A second possible reason for Fujisawa's reluctance was that although SmithKline marketed Fujisawa's product in the United States under a licensing agreement, a reciprocal arrangement should involve precisely that—a licensing agreement in Japan—and no more. SmithKline, however, persisted in the idea of a joint venture because of its corporate objectives pertaining to the Japanese market. One goal was to launch 'Tagamet' in Japan, the second-largest pharmaceutical market in the world; a second was to establish a visible presence in Japan. Because of this initial difference over the form of cooperative agreement, SmithKline was prepared to negotiate with Fujisawa for a long time. This accounted in the main for the lengthiness of the negotiations.

Sears, who does not speak Japanese and had never lived or worked in Japan, found these prolonged negotiations extremely stressful. He was, however, constantly reassured by Young, the company's in-house Japanese expert, that matters proceed slowly in Japan. In retrospect, Sears described his three-year stay in Tokyo as a "tense time" and indicated that if he were to relive the situation, he would definitely attempt to be more relaxed. This highlights the importance of being able to adjust to cultural differences in a foreign country. Young explained that the key to understanding this phenomenon is to use the judo metaphor: "You see, it is just like judo. The Japanese will rest on their haunches, waiting for their opponent to make his move, anticipating it and finally turning it to their advantage." In fact, this approach may be more deep-rooted than the sport of judo itself. This was precisely the technique preached by Miyamoto Mushashi, a samurai of the sixteenth century, whose advice on how to gain the upper hand in any kind of combat is contained in his collection of writings entitled *The Book of Five Rings,* which is still widely read by Japanese. From Fujisawa's perspective, prolonging the negotiations might lead SmithKline ultimately to agree to a licensing agreement rather than a joint venture.

Frustrated by the procrastination and inaction on the part of Fujisawa, Sears issued an apparent ultimatum to the Japanese that if they would not agree to a joint venture, then SmithKline would establish its own independent operation in Japan to market 'Tagamet'. By this time 'Tagamet' was very close to its initial launching date in the United Kingdom, and preliminary laboratory results all pointed to its efficacy—and hence profitability. This shock approach worked, and Fujisawa finally agreed to proceed with negotiations for the formation of a joint venture.

Since the second joint venture formed in the United States was to be on a reciprocal basis, the issue of form of cooperative agreement did not pose a problem.

Percentage of Equity Ownership

After the two parties agreed to form a joint venture, a second issue under negotiation was the percentage of equity ownership. Fujisawa proposed a

50-50 equity-share basis, whereas SmithKline's management was divided on the issue. In general, the financial people within SmithKline insisted on a 51-percent equity share for purposes of consolidation of income statement from the Japanese operation. According to U.S. accounting practices, the consolidation of sales of a foreign operation is permitted only when the U.S. partner has the majority ownership. This is the reason that in the case of W.R. Grace, presented in chapter 7, the U.S. partner insisted on and obtained a 51-percent equity share. In the case of W.R. Grace, however, this issue was raised at the beginning of the negotiations. In the case of SmithKline it was reported that the vice-president of finance of Smith Kline & French International arrived in Japan very late in the negotiation process and nearly blocked the consummation of the joint venture by insisting on a 51-percent share. Henry Wendt, J.P. Young, and Peter Sears, however, were more compromising and agreed in principle to a 50-50 joint venture. In their opinion Fujisawa had already made a major concession by agreeing to a joint venture instead of insisting on a licensing agreement. Hence, from Fujisawa's perspective, "They had already given away 50 percent, if you will." Furthermore, top management at SmithKline felt that a change coming very late in the negotiations might constitute a breach of trust that was essential to the smooth functioning of a joint venture.

Given the emphasis on trust and honor in Japanese society, described in an earlier chapter, SmithKline's decision to abide by what was originally agreed to in principle appeared to be a wise move. Had SmithKline reneged on its original principle, it might possibly have had devastating ramifications for the long-term operations of the company. In addition, since the Koseisho requires very extensive testing of the product before introduction in the Japanese market, time was of the essence; SmithKline could not afford to prolong the negotiations by insisting on 51-percent ownership. In Williams's words, "SmithKline, in the interest of moving ahead with the development and ultimately the launch of 'Tagamet', was willing to give in on a number of minor issues—minor relative to the importance of the major issue of joint venture versus licensing. We gave in for the short term in order to achieve the rapid development of our asset." This was largely justified. For instance, although the joint-venture agreement was signed in 1977, 'Tagamet' had to undergo elaborate testing for another four years in Japanese laboratories before it was approved in December 1981 for distribution in January 1982. Some two thousand patients and eighty leading clinical investigators were involved in the elaborate testing procedures—which included replications of many preclinical and clinical studies previously conducted in other nations—to satisfy the requirements of the Japanese Ministry of Health and Welfare. Consequently, in the interest of time and of principle, SmithKline agreed to a 50-50 equity share.

Although some factions within SmithKline still feel that their company sacrificed majority ownership for expediency, it is important to note that the equity position may change in the long run. In both cases the intention is for the offshore partner eventually to take the majority position in the long run; that is, in the case of Smith Kline·Fujisawa K.K., SmithKline would eventually be the majority partner in the Japanese joint venture; in the case of Fujisawa SmithKline, Fujisawa would eventually acquire majority ownership. In the opinion of Snable (vice-president of the U.S. joint venture), one reason behind SmithKline's willingness to form the second joint venture in the United States, besides the issue of reciprocity, is the implicit understanding that the equity position will change in the future. Hence the short-term arrangement of a 50-50 joint venture is viewed as a vehicle for assisting either partner to gain entry into the other's market. As Snable perceives it, "SmithKline wants to gain control over the business in Japan, and the quickest way to do it is to help Fujisawa have a profitable and dynamic business in the United States, and have Fujisawa gain control in the United States. Then, quid pro quo, SmithKline allows Fujisawa to take operational control of the U.S. business, while maintaining a minority investment position. At the same time, SmithKline gets operational control in Japan."

Williams was asked to project what the future equity positions in the two joint ventures will be; he responded: "I think we feel philosophically that the minority partner ought to have enough of a share so that when it gets its dividend cheque, it gets a significant amount." Therefore, when the equity position changes, the minority partner would probably retain a quarter ownership or perhaps slightly more.

Since the second joint venture formed in the United States was to be on a reciprocal basis, the issue of percentage of equity ownership did not pose a problem.

Management of the Ventures

The differences pertaining to management practices or operational details were minor relative to the aforementioned issues. It was agreed that in the initial years of the operation of the Japanese joint venture, SmithKline will be responsible for marketing, personnel, administration, and finance; Fujisawa will be responsible for development, manufacturing, and regulatory affairs, and will provide appropriate marketing, sales, and distribution support. After all, one of the major reasons for SmithKline's decision to choose a joint-venture mode of entry was to overcome the barriers associated with distribution and lack of working relationships with the regulatory agencies. Although SmithKline is responsible for personnel and marketing, given the problems of recruiting a sizable and competent detail force by a foreign firm, the joint venture will use Fujisawa's sales force to market its products initially.

Somewhat different arrangements apply in the U.S. joint venture. Initially, for example, in the case of Fujisawa SmithKline, the U.S. partner is doing virtually all the work. Given the implicit understanding that the equity position will change in the future, however, this arrangement will evolve to mirror that in Japan. Eventually the SmithKline·Fujisawa K.K. joint venture in Japan will become a predominantly SmithKline business; and the Fujisawa SmithKline joint venture in the United States will ultimately become a predominantly Fujisawa business.

Name of the Japanese Joint Venture

Another minor issue under negotiation in the first joint venture in Japan involved the proposed name for the venture. It has been the policy of Smith-Kline Beckman Corporation to use the name *Smith Kline* as two separate words in its foreign operations, with the one-word name *SmithKline* reserved for use by the parent company only. A senior Fujisawa official vehemently objected to the use of *Smith Kline* as two words because *Fujisawa* was only one word; this might connote SmithKline's dominance in the venture. This issue was brought up at the eleventh hour in the negotiations and was resolved to Fujisawa's satisfaction. In the second joint venture in the United States, the one-word SmithKline name was used also.

Product and Perceived Differences in Objectives

There were a number of issues specific to the second joint venture in the United States, one of them real and the other perceived. Although ceftizoxime is a profitable item for Fujisawa in Japan, it cannot match the magnitude and potentials for huge profits of 'Tagamet'. When both parties discussed the possibilities of forming a reciprocal joint venture in the United States and of its future growth after the marketing of Fujisawa's first product, it became apparent that the second joint venture would not initially be able to generate as great profits as the first joint venture in Japan.

In Snable's opinion, this is where a perceived problem came into the picture, at least in the first year of the negotiation. Recognizing the traditional differences in objectives between U.S. and Japanese firms, SmithKline perceived that Fujisawa, in its pursuit of market share in the United States, might need to operate in the red for a number of years. That might result in substantial losses that SmithKline, as a 50-percent partner, would not be willing to absorb. In Snable's opinion, "SmithKline was worried that Fujisawa's main objective of establishing a presence in the U.S. would take precedence over short-term profits to the extent that Fujisawa would be willing to accept what to SmithKline would be unreasonable losses."

Although this perception was erroneous, it took some time and a lot of convincing before SmithKline "got a clear picture in their mind as to what Fujisawa's plans really were, and became convinced that Fujisawa is also managed by very sensible, profit-minded business managers, and that though the long-term goal remains the same (building an independent, viable, and fully integrated pharmaceutical here in the United States, controlled by Fujisawa), how soon that goal is achieved still depends on the practicalities of the marketplace."

Perhaps SmithKline could not be blamed entirely for harboring this misperception because when Fujisawa first approached the U.S. partner for the formation of a joint venture in the United States, the Japanese indicated their desire to "establish a presence in the American market." SmithKline was not sure what the Fujisawa people meant by *presence* and what that would translate into in terms of market share. SmithKline had to question its Japanese partner closely about the true nature of their objectives and what they meant by the word *presence*. In Williams's opinion, "This took a long time because they did not like the direct questions that we asked." It took approximately six months before Fujisawa defined *presence* as a majority-owned business that would account for 1-2 percent of the U.S. market in the long run—that is, twenty or more years hence. Williams believed that had it not been for the presence of Snable, an American on the Fujisawa negotiating team, SmithKline might not have obtained a definitive explanation of the term *presence* for another six months or a year. In his opinion, "It was only because we had good communications and because Mr. Snable spoke the same cultural English, that we were able to establish a rapport that was necessary in order to finally understand what they wanted."

This incident illustrates three important points in international business negotiations. The first is the significance of cultural differences. Because of the Japanese preference for vagueness on issues, it took them six months to articulate a specific objective. Second, the incident highlights the value of including a member who can bridge cultural gaps on one's negotiating team. Had it not been for the presence of Snable, who is an American and therefore able to communicate with the SmithKline team, this issue might have caused further delay. Third, the incident illustrates the importance of perceptions, real or not, in influencing the progress and outcome of negotiations. In the framework of international business negotiations, Kapoor (1975) emphasizes the need not only to examine the perspectives of each party to a negotiation, but also to study the perceptions each partner may have of the other. Since perceptions are not generally revealed to the other party, this may be a major stumbling block in negotiations because the other partner may not even recognize the existence of a problem. In this case Fujisawa did not recognize this as a problem at first. Only after the Japanese recognized this as an issue could the matter be directly addressed and discussed between the two parties. This misperception may account in part for the prolonged negotiations in the second joint venture. It took two years for the two parties to reach consensus on the second agreement.

Implementation and Conflict Resolution

The first joint venture has been operating since 1977; although there have been some problems, none of these could be attributed to the 50-50 equity basis. In Williams's opinion, both parties "have scrupulously avoided taking positions that had to be resolved by a vote of the board or shareholders." It would be embarrassing if any issue were brought to a vote and resulted in a tie. In Williams's words, "If we have to vote, a tie is a negative vote, or at least, it is a lack of an affirmative vote, and that would cause stress. I don't foresee having tie votes like that." Furthermore, as is evident from the case of Merck & Co., even when the U.S. firm is the majority partner, in Merck's twenty-nine years of operation with Banyu Pharmaceutical Company not one issue has been brought to a vote because that would signal the collapse of the joint venture. In both joint ventures between SmithKline and Fujisawa, issues are resolved by consensus and through compromise. In Snable's terms, the "issues are discussed and when people realize that everybody is in general agreement, then the resolution is passed."

To date the operation of both joint ventures has been smooth. Williams believed that perhaps the difficulties experienced in implementing the joint ventures so far should not be viewed as problems but should be described as "frustrations." In his opinion, the frustrations have been similar for both offshore partners—SmithKline in Japan and Fujisawa in the United States. These frustrations generally center on "how to integrate a small joint venture with the mammoth local organization and make the small joint venture an influential factor in the decision-making structure."

Snable indicated that the second joint venture has not encountered any problem in the United States from an operational standpoint. As of May 1983 Fujisawa SmithKline had had four board meetings; both sides have so far concurred on all issues. Thus the second joint venture is operating very smoothly. Snable acknowledges, however, that as the joint venture develops, there may be problems relating to the recruitment of more people and the demand for greater autonomy. In his words, "How does a small group of, say, ten to fifteen people have an impact on the thousands of people of SmithKline here? That is going to be a very tricky problem." These, however, are really just growing-up pains—similar in a way to those mentioned by Maurer in the case of Nippon Merck Banyu, which is currently in its twenty-ninth year of operation. In the case of Merck, both parent companies have to cope with the growing independence of the joint venture; Banyu Pharmaceutical Company (Merck's Japanese partner) has problems adapting to this change.

Given the Japanese dislike for open confrontation, it is interesting to examine how differences were resolved between the parties. Recognizing the Japanese emphasis on face-saving, both parties have avoided direct confrontation. In Williams's words, "Perhaps it would be better to say that we did not affirmatively agree than to say that we disagreed." Williams believed that in time any issue could be resolved: "I don't think we have encountered issues in either joint venture that were not resolvable by compromise, and we have the joint ventures as proof of it."

SmithKline has operated on several guiding principles with respect to these joint ventures, one of which is reciprocity. SmithKline recognized that each party was interested in establishing a business in the other's country; and to make this operational, both sides (particularly the onshore partner) would have to make concessions. In the initial stages of the joint venture, the onshore partner has to provide assistance. As the joint venture evolves, however, the onshore partner may be required to relinquish some of its control, either from a management or from an equity standpoint. There is an implicit understanding that whatever concessions Fujisawa makes in Japan, SmithKline will reciprocate in kind in the United States, and vice versa.

Cultural Differences as They Bear on International Business Negotiations

This section examines some of the salient cultural differences that influenced the progress and outcome of the negotiations leading to the formation of the two joint ventures. Some of these were alluded to previously, but will be summarized here.

Consensus Decision Making

Although there are exceptions to the consensus decision-making process in Japan, in the case of Fujisawa Pharmaceutical Co., Ltd., most of the decisions were arrived at through consensus; the Japanese negotiators frequently had to caucus with their headquarters about the courses of action to pursue. As an American working for a Japanese organization, Snable indicated that perhaps a major difference betweeen U.S. and Japanese negotiating teams was the level at which decisions were made: "Maybe this is where we talk about consensus management. I found that when I worked at Fujisawa in New York under the previous management, almost no decisions were made directly in New York. They were always sent back to Japan and circulated there, and their response would come back. If it was in the affirmative, we would go ahead." By contrast, most managers in U.S. firms tend "to make big decisions at a lower level on their own. Japanese managers just don't do that. They always send it back and then have a number of people look at it. If nobody disagrees, then you can go ahead."

Consequently, in Japan it generally takes longer to make decisions, which may account in part for the nearly four years it took to arrive at an agreement on the first joint venture, and the two years to conclude the negotiations on the second one. Implementing decisions is easier, however, because any decision has already received the endorsement and understanding of everyone who will be involved. By contrast, the negotiators on the SmithKline team were authorized to make important decisions on behalf of the company.

There were variations in how the U.S. employees of Fujisawa's U.S. operations were involved in the decision-making process. In Williams's opinion, these U.S. nationals were hired to assess the U.S. market and therefore were sometimes quite independent in their orientation. For example, in one instance during the negotiations for the second joint venture in the United States, the two negotiating teams met in New York just before Christmas of 1979. SmithKline thought that agreement had been reached with the Japanese team until the lead negotiator on the Japanese team disagreed with his associates and the two sides had to start afresh.

Snable was then asked to comment on his role as an American in a Japanese organization. In his words, the Japanese company "looked to me to lend expertise about the U.S. market, and I definitely contributed to the decision-making process where market-information input was important." Snable was further asked to comment on his involvement in decision making in the Japanese parent company; in response he noted that if the Japanese were in agreement and he was the only one that dissented, "then it ran counter to their culture to just override me, if they knew I felt strongly about it. I think this is true when you have a really sticky issue—what happens is that no decision is made. The negotiations go into a frenzy, in a nice way. When both parties realize that the point cannot be agreed on, the issue will be dropped until the next meeting, knowing full well that the two sides are too far apart to reach an agreement. The same thing happened with me. We would discuss situations, and often I would not know whether a decision had been made until I went back to Japan.

"The consensus is really at the management level. When they say they have to go back to the board, it is really true. Even the top Japanese negotiator would go to the board and say that this is the way we now see it, this is what we recommend. The board would pick at it at their operational meetings, which they have monthly and sometimes more often, where they get together and discuss these issues in very significant detail. Once they arrived at a consensus, the negotiator would then come back and tell us what the Fujisawa position was.''

Differences in Time Perspectives

One distinguishing characteristic between U.S. and Japanese firms is the difference in time perspectives. In general, U.S. companies tend to have more of a short-term outlook and to display a greater concern for quarterly and annual profits; Japanese firms have a longer-term orientation and are more concerned with market share. As noted previously, this perceived difference was a major stumbling block in the negotiations for the second joint venture in the United States. In Williams's opinion, the Japanese tend to look ahead twenty to thirty years, which may explain why Fujisawa indicated that their desire to establish a ''presence'' in the U.S. pharmaceutical market involved a 1-2-percent market share twenty or more years hence.

This longer-term orientation does not imply that the Japanese are not concerned about bottom-line figures. As noted earlier, ultimately the joint venture has to be profitable or there is no incentive for either partner to continue the relationship. In Williams's words, ''They are; however, they are more interested in the bottom line relative to the budget or plan that they have created, rather than the bottom line as perceived by Wall Street or financial analysts or competition. Therefore, their concern is to achieve the level of performance that they themselves have set internally, rather than the level of performance anticipated by some outside influence.'' This difference may be attributed to the kinds of investors in each country. In Japan investors are primarily institutional, (for example, banks); they can afford to develop a longer-term orientation toward their investments.

Thoroughness in Preparation

Besides the aforementioned differences, Williams indicated that the Japanese appeared to be more thorough in their preparations for the negotiation. Williams contended, however, that this may be only a facade; he did not believe there were substantial differences in terms of depth and breadth of knowledge between U.S. and Japanese negotiators. The Japanese always appear to have ''mounds of notes, briefcases filled with papers, and they can dive in and find anything at a moment's notice,'' whereas Americans

are generally more "accustomed to winging it. If you cannot find the particular reference, you take a ball-park guess." This difference may be largely
cultural.

The meticulous preparation on the part of the Japanese negotiating
team may also be attributed to the fact that where the Japanese parent company is not as highly diversified in its activities as is the U.S. counterpart,
the top management of the former may be able to devote more attention to
the operations of the joint venture. The latter reason may not apply here but
certainly has been a source of friction in the operation of some joint ventures between U.S. and Japanese entities.

Continuity

Another reason that the Fujisawa team may appear to be more knowledeable
and to possess comprehensive documentation on matters that transpired between the two parties may be that the senior executive and the chief negotiator for the Fujisawa team were the same in both sets of negotiations;
whereas the composition of the SmithKline negotiating teams changed. The
only common links on SmithKline's side were Young, who served as a consultant, and Warren Hauser, the lawyer. The latter's involvement was
primarily confined to the legal aspects, however. In Williams's opinion, this
lack of continuity in the composition of the negotiating teams frequently
placed SmithKline at a disadvantage "from the point of view of lack of
knowledge of what had happened before."

This Japanese preference for continuity was demonstrated not only in
the composition of the negotiating team, but also in other aspects of the
business. For example, the Fujisawa management team and board of directors that are currently involved in the operation of the Japanese joint venture were associated with some aspects of the venture six years ago; whereas
most of the SmithKline people who were in Japan in 1977 have moved onto
other projects of the company and are no longer engaged in the Japanese
joint venture.

As pointed out in chapter 1, the Japanese have a marked preference for
continuity in personal relationships. Consequently, the frequent changes in
SmithKline personnel may not only hamper the U.S. partner's ability to
recollect incidents that transpired before, but may also pose a barrier to the
development of the close personal ties that are fundamental to the smooth
operation of joint cooperative arrangements. Once friendly ties were established between the companies, they have been continued. These were
generally modeled after the friendship between the top executives of the two
companies from the early 1970s, which has persisted to this day.

Attitude toward Change

Snable believed that another salient difference between Americans and Japanese is that the latter rarely change positions unless there have been some fundamental change in the environment. He recalled an instance when Smith-Kline raised an issue late in the negotiating process because somebody in the company had seen the agreement and felt that it might not be in the latter's best interest or that it might infringe on certain U.S. government regulations—for example, an antitrust problem. This last-minute change posed problems because in the Japanese view an expert on the matter should have been "involved earlier in the management consensus process." In Snable's opinion, this may be precisely the reason that Fujisawa objected to the raising of the 51-percent issue late in the negotiations for the formation of the Japanese joint venture, since SmithKline had originally agreed in principle to an equal partnership. From SmithKline's standpoint, the request for change may be justified for a business reason. It is SmithKline's practice to circulate the draft contracts to its functional experts, such as accounting and legal staff, after the business arrangements have been concluded. From the Japanese perspective, however, this request was unfounded because there had been no fundamental change in the situation. In Snable's opinion, the Japanese response was: "Why are you changing your mind now? What has happened? What is different? If nothing is different, except that somebody else is looking at it, that doesn't count. Something fundamental has to change, such as a government regulation, and so on. The Japanese feel that you should have known about it beforehand; their feeling is that you didn't do your homework. Therefore, you shouldn't be changing your mind at such a late point in the negotiations."

The Japanese are reasonable to a certain extent in their expectations in this regard. According to the framework of international business negotiations presented by Kapoor (1975), the negotiating team should consist of members from the various functional areas. Where this is not possible, the chief negotiator should exercise considerable caution to include team members who have expertise in the various functional areas of accounting, finance, marketing, production, law, and so on. After all, the formation and implementation of a joint venture between two entities require consensus on all these aspects.

The Japanese aversion to a change in position unless the business environment has been significantly altered may explain their deliberate lack of clarity on certain issues, which was identified as one of the salient cultural characteristics of Japanese businesses. This may account for the Japanese reluctance to pinpoint what they meant by establishing a *presence* in the U.S. market in the negotiations for the second joint venture.

Negotiating Tactics

Earlier, Young's use of the judo metaphor to describe the Japanese negotiating tactic was cited. Williams believed that this was an overgeneralization because, in his opinion, both sides have used time to their advantage, and the more eager partner in either case usually had to wait. In the formation of the first joint venture, when SmithKline was clearly more eager, Fujisawa could afford to procrastinate and wait for further information on the performance of 'Tagamet'. In the second joint venture the reverse was true. Thus, although in general the Japanese tend to progress at a more leisurely pace, it depends to a certain extent on the urgency of the matter. In the formation of the two joint ventures, both sides have used time to their advantage, depending on which was more eager in a given situation.

A second noticeable negotiating step was the issuing of an apparent ultimatum by Peter Sears to the Fujisawa people in 1976 that he had had enough and would proceed to establish an independent SmithKline operation in Japan. Sears was sincere in his belief that further negotiations would not lead to an agreement; hence the use of the apparent ultimatum was not merely a negotiating ploy. Nevertheless, this shock approach worked; the Japanese relented, and henceforth matters progressed more rapidly.

This tactic is similar to the one used by TRW in its negotiations with Fujitsu for the formation of the joint venture described in chapter 4. The entire TRW team walked out in the negotiations; thereafter, the Japanese was more conciliatory. A word of caution should be noted, however. This negotiating tactic may work only where the joint venture is perceived to be very important and where the other party is very desirous of establishing such an agreement because of the benefits to be reaped from its consummation. In this case, by 1976, although the sales figures in the United Kingdom had not yet been released, preclinical and clinical studies on 'Tagamet' showed the product to be highly effective in curing ulcers, a major problem in Japan. Consequently, Fujisawa did not want to lose out on an arrangement that could potentially be very profitable.

Language

All the negotiations were conducted in English because none of the Americans spoke Japanese. According to Williams, the Americans had a certain advantage because they were speaking in their native tongue, whereas the Japanese had to use an acquired language, which may have limited their ability to express themselves fully. Misunderstandings resulting from language differences did arise during the negotiations. In one negotiating session the two parties discussed matters for a full four hours. At the conclusion of each issue, the chief negotiator for Fujisawa would punctuate the statement with the question, "Do you understand?" Williams would respond in the affirmative. Just before lunch, SmithKline's team discovered that when the Japanese negotiator inquired, "Do you understand?" he really meant, "Do you agree?" When he heard affirmative answers, he naturally assumed that agreement had been reached on the nine to ten issues covered that morning. In fact, SmithKline had not agreed to a single item. They had merely indicated that they understood the issues. Consequently, after lunch the two parties had to start all over again and renegotiate each issue.

Williams indicated that in the second set of negotiations interpreters were not used because in general the Japanese team had a good command of English. After SmithKline discovered that there were minor language difficulties, they exercised greater caution in explaining matters and reiterated points several times to ensure that there was no misunderstanding. Williams felt that the use of interpreters "slows the process down by at least 50 percent, and makes it more impersonal." This delay, coupled with the longer time it generally takes the Japanese to make decisions plus the wait-and-see negotiating tactic, would unduly prolong the negotiations. Williams believed that on occasion it may be appropriate to use interpreters; he recalled his own experience in using interpreters in negotiating another deal in Japan. In general, he was not enthusiastic about the use of interpreters because he was "never quite sure what his interpreter said until I saw it in writing." This also depends on the interpreter's language skills, which can vary considerably. In China, for instance, I found that the language skills of the interpreters varied. I encountered one interpreter who constantly confused the term *pre* with *post*; she used to describe how bad things were "post-1949," when what she really meant was "pre-1949."

Conduct of the Negotiations

As noted in the case of Boeing Commercial Airplane Company, a major difference between a U.S. and a Japanese negotiating team is the amount of time the Americans speak and the observance of long silences on the part of the Japanese. Furthermore, the chief negotiator on the Japanese team would do most of the talking; the others are generally silent observers. In the case of SmithKline and Fujisawa, the latter observation held true. In Williams's opinion, Americans "tend to give the floor to whoever the expert is. If we are talking about an antibiotics marketing problem, and if we had a person with experience in that field on our team, he would take the leadership in the discussions. If it was a legal issue, the lawyer would handle the matter. If it was financial, the financial person would handle it. So we had many people that might be taking a lead position at any point in time.

This did not occur in the Fujisawa team, with the exception that Mr. Snable would behave like an American and occasionally take command, from a language point of view at least, in explaining a position. It might be explaining to his colleagues something that SmithKline had said, or it might be exlaining to SmithKline something that his colleagues had said. The rest of the Japanese team members, other than the chief negotiator, were basically silent. They witnessed." Although the Japanese team would occasionally caucus among themselves, the chief negotiator clearly took the leadership role.

Although Snable is not bilingual, he acknowledged that his daily contacts with his Japanese colleagues have considerably improved his ability to "understand their English." Consequently, he was in a better position to explain the situation to his Japanese colleagues in a manner that they could easily comprehend. This again points up the importance of having a bilingual member on one's negotiating team. Although the individual may not be involved in the actual interpretation of statements, given the knowlede of the other culture, he may be able to provide a better reading of the situation to his team, and thus may help smooth misundertandings that arise from cultural or language differences.

One of the principal negotiators of the Fujisawa team was trained as an attorney; this is atypical given the traditional Japanese distaste for litigation and the fact that attorneys are seldom present in the negotiating team. Snable contended that "Fujisawa is somewhat different in this regard," which supports my earlier assertion that there are always exceptions. Furthermore, there are some general misconceptions about the use of legal personnel in Japanese companies. In the case of Stanley Epstein of Anglo American Aviation Company, it was noted that one of his Japanese partners was in fact more litigious than its U.S. counterpart where the use of litigation was clearly to the former's advantage.

Role of the Government

The restrictive practices of the Japanese Ministry of Health and Welfare with respect to product testing in the area of pharmaceuticals and cosmetics have often been cited as a nontariff barrier to trade. Williams, however, did not believe that Japanese government regulations or the interface between government and industry posed a greater barrier to entry into the Japanese market than did the Food and Drug Administration in the United States. Williams believed that just as there is no governmental-industry interface in the United States, such interface in the Japanese pharmaceutical industry has been minimal until very recently. In the negotiations for the establishment of the first joint venture in Japan, the Japanese government was not a significant factor. In Williams's opinion, "The barriers to entry into Japan are cultural and the distribution system. There are equally formidable barriers to entry to the U.S. market for a Japanese pharmaceutical company. Just the sheer size of the critical mass and the scope required to cover the U.S. market effectively in themselves pose tremendous barriers. To think that you have to go out and hire three hundred representatives and then go through the regulatory process is a horrendous task indeed. The Japanese regulatory authorities are a little more stringent in that they do not permit foreign data to be used for clearance of a product, whereas our FDA recently has permitted the inclusion of foreign data in registration applications."

This supports the contention in chapters 1 and 2 that many of the alleged nontariff barriers to trade may be culture-based and hence cannot be construed as a part of a xenophobic conspiracy on the part of the Japanese. Successful penetration of the Japanese market may depend to some extent on the willingness and ability of the foreign firm to understand and work within the cultural constraints of the Japanese system. Furthermore, the Japanese Parliament enacted legislation in May 1983 allowing foreign data to be used for purposes of product certification. This brings us to the factors responsible for the successful formation of the two joint ventures, which are the focus of the following section.

Factors for Success

A number of factors that were responsible for the successful establishment of the joint ventures were alluded to previously. These will be summarized as follows.

Product

Clearly, a key to Fujisawa's concession to a joint venture over a licensing agreement could be attributed to the anticipation of the phenomenal success of the product 'Tagamet'. In Williams's words, "The successful establishment of both joint ventures is a function of new product development—that is, the discovery of new compounds with commercial potential. This is the bottom line." Conversely, the lack of a significant product may be a major factor in the failure of negotiations. In Snable's opinion, a major reason that some propositions by other foreign pharmaceutical companies to Fujisawa have fallen through or have been postponed is that "the asset on which the foreign company had based its negotiations was not of significant or sufficient value to warrant Fujisawa giving up whatever advantage it had. For example, it might already be distributing a product, and the company comes to Fujisawa and says, 'We want to form a joint venture.' If the product is not big enough, it really does not pay Fujisawa to do that. So the best thing to do is delay. You do not want to alienate people, but you do not want to give up your business either. SmithKline, on the other hand, had a product that had a profit potential. Consequently, Fujisawa was willing to make a major concession in forming a joint venture rather than taking a license.''

Although Fujisawa's third-generation antibiotic could not parallel 'Tagamet's' success, ceftizoxime is a "good drug in a therapeutic area of interest to SmithKline.'' Furthermore, Fujisawa is the third-largest pharmaceutical company in Japan and has a strong research orientation. Consequently, in Snable's opinion, the "past and expected future productivity of Fujisawa's research'' also played a role in the formation of the second joint venture.

Complementarity of Needs

The objective of both companies was to establish a presence in each other's market. At the time of entry, however, both companies lacked the capability to start out on their own, given the problems of product testing, recruiting a sizable detail force, and distributing their products. Fujisawa, being an industry leader in Japan, was able to provide that kind of assistance to SmithKline in the Japanese market, and vice versa. Furthermore, it was implicitly understood that the equity participation would change in the future to allow eventually for a majority position by the offshore partner—SmithKline in Japan and Fujisawa in the United States. Consequently, although there are still factions within SmithKline who feel that their company sacrificed initial majority ownership for expediency, this equity distribution is not permanent and may change in the future.

Close Relationships

The friendly ties between Mr. Wendt and Dr. Fujisawa dated back to the 1960s. Similarly, Sears developed a close working relationship with Toguchi, the chief negotiator for Fujisawa during the three years of negotiations for the first joint venture. These relationships were further strengthened during the negotiations for the second joint venture, even though the composition of the SmithKline team was largely different from the one that negotiated the first joint venture.

Cultural Understanding

Although the U.S. negotiating-team members did not speak Japanese, they demonstrated a genuine respect for Japanese culture, behavior, and busiiness objectives. This respect was mutual, and both sides made concessions. Furthermore, although Young was not an active member of the SmithKline negotiating team, he was the in-house Japanese expert and provided invaluable advice and assistance to his colleagues. Similarly, although Snable did not speak Japanese, his presence on the Fujisawa team helped promote understanding on issues because he could explain to his colleagues about U.S. perceptions and attitudes on certain matters and the U.S. way of doing business.

In Williams's opinion, both SmithKline and Fujisawa have attained their initial corporate objectives of forming a pair of joint ventures that would allow either partner to penetrate the other's country. Both companies have succeeded in their short-term objectives. It is still too early, however, to predict the future success in implementation of the joint ventures. The SmithKline·Fujisawa K.K. joint venture introduced 'Tagamet' in the Japanese market in January 1982, and all early indications appear to be in the affirmative. 'Cefizox', Fujisawa's product, was awaiting FDA approval as of mid-1983. Williams is optimistic and indicated that "one has to be very sanguine because of the history of success thus far." Despite the cultural differences, both companies share many common elements: the desire for profits, commitment to research and development of new products, and a genuine willingness to compromise on issues through a process of conciliation.

Both parties were relatively free of other obligations that could affect the creation of the joint ventures. Williams acknowledged, however, that the issue of multiple joint ventures may pose a problem in the future, particularly if it involves a competitive product. If a company has too many joint ventures in its country, the partner may question whether adequate resources and attention are devoted to a specific joint venture. In the case of SmithKline, the U.S. partner will rely on its Japanese partner for efficient distribution and marketing of 'Tagamet'. In his words, "If we felt that 'Tagamet' could not get a sufficient share of their field force time or a sufficient share of their promotional spending because Fujisawa was also handling products from half a dozen European or American pharmaceutical companies, I think that could be a future concern." Similarly, he feels that Fujisawa would not like SmithKline to enter into joint-venture arrangements with several other Japanese companies for fear that the partner may be overextending or overcommiting itself, and hence may not be able to meet effectively the objectives of the other partner and the joint venture as a whole. Fortunately, at the moment, this is not an issue in the relationship between SmithKline and Fujisawa.

Concluding Remarks

Despite the highly competitive environment in the Japanese pharmaceutical industry and the formidable barriers to product testing and distribution in

Japan, both Merck & Co. and SmithKline Beckman Corporation have been very successful to date. Merck and Co.'s joint venture has been in operation for twenty-nine years and has been highly profitable. SmithKline has achieved its short-term goal of penetrating the Japanese market. The two case studies capture different dynamics of the cooperative process between U.S. and Japanese entities. The case of SmithKline provided an in-depth review of the negotiating phase for the establishment of the joint ventures, whereas the Merck & Co. case examined the implementation of a joint venture over the past three decades.

7

The Case of
Automotive Chemicals

In 1980 Japan overtook the United States as the world's largest manufacturer of automobiles. To support the continued growth of the Japanese automotive industry, new technology is constantly being introduced to ensure a better-quality end product. This includes automotive chemicals and sound-absorbent systems. The latter are particularly important in smaller cars, which are the strong point of the Japanese automotive industry. In smaller cars the engine noise tends to be more audible, and the use of a sound-absorbent system to keep it out of the vehicle is an important design feature.

This chapter examines negotiations for the formation of a 51-49 joint venture in the field of automotive chemicals between a giant U.S. multinational, W.R. Grace, and Inoue M.P.T., a privately owned Japanese company, with the U.S. partner as the majority owner. The joint-venture agreement was concluded after six years of negotiations. The joint-venture company, Teroson K.K., began operation in Japan on October 1, 1982. The information presented in this case was obtained through an interview with W.M. Kinch, executive vice-president-operations, Pacific-Interamerican Division, W.R. Grace and Company.

The Partners

W.R. Grace (hereafter referred to as Grace) was established in 1854 by the ancestor of J. Peter Grace, the current chairman and chief executive officer of the corporation. In 1981 the company's sales exceeded $6.5 billion. The company is highly diversified and has interests ranging from specialty chemicals to natural resources, retailing, and the restaurant business. Grace manufactures over eighty-five major specialty-chemical products and is the leading specialty-chemical concern in the world and the fifth-largest chemical company in the United States (Grace, *Annual Report,* 1981). In all its overseas operations, Grace prefers the establishment of wholly owned subsidiaries where possible. Licensing is the least preferred mode of entry into a foreign market, and joint ventures with foreign entities are entered into only when necessary.

The Japanese partner, Inoue M.P.T., is newer and smaller than W.R. Grace. The company was established as a small bicycle-tire concern before

World War II by the father of the current president and owner, Mr. Soichi Inoue. After the war the company shifted to the production of automobile tires. The company underwent very rapid expansion when the present Mr. Inoue took over some twenty years ago. After Inoue completed engineering school, he went to Germany, where he learned about polyurethane—foam technology, which he later introduced into his company. Under his auspices the company concentrated its efforts in this area, and by the 1970s the company was well-established in the field of polyurethane-foam products such as dashboards and had established a reputation as an important supplier of automotive products to the major Japanese car manufacturers. The company now has 35 percent of the market share for automotive products of which it is a supplier. Its annual sales average between $400 and $500 million. As its name suggests, Inoue M.P.T. is a privately held concern, with ownership concentrated in the hands of the Inoue family.

History

In 1960 Grace established a wholly owned subsidiary in Japan. Kinch indicated that his company was one of the earliest U.S. companies to be authorized by the Japanese government to establish a wholly owned subsidiary in Japan. The subsidiary sold Grace's basic line of chemical products, including can-sealing compounds. Since the automobile industry was then designated as a strategic industry targeted for growth, the Japanese government needed technology in this area and consequently permitted Grace to establish the subsidiary company on a 100-percent basis. As with Boeing Commercial Airplane Company, this points to the fact that the Japanese government was and still is very accommodating when it comes to industries that fulfill national needs.

In 1963 Grace acquired a German company by the name of Teroson Gmbh, which had a very strong technology in the field of automotive chemicals, such as underbody coatings, seam sealers for doors, adhesives, and anti-corrosion materials. Today this German subsidiary is one of Grace's largest single operations. In Kinch's opinion, Teroson's technology in the area of anticorrosion materials is one of the most advanced in the world, far superior to that in Japan or the United States.

Besides automotive chemicals, Teroson also specialized in the manufacture of sound-absorbent materials used inside automobiles. Since European cars are generally smaller, engine noise is more audible, hence the importance of such materials. This sound-absorbent technology was subsequently transferred from Grace's German division to its operations in other parts of Europe and the United States. When the Japanese automobile industry began to take off in the 1960s, the demand for automotive components naturally increased, and Grace saw the potential for marketing these products in the largest automobile market in the world.

Grace's wholly owned subsidiary, however, like many other foreign firms, experienced difficulties in recruiting competent Japanese to work for the company. It had trouble working within the complexities of the Japanese framework of customer-supplier relationship, which are unique. Given the distinguishing characteristics of the Japanese automobile industry, a supplier has to locate a manufacturing plant in the country to meet the needs of its consumers, the automobile manufacturers.

The Japanese automobile industry operates on a combine system, first introduced by Toyota. All suppliers have to be located within a minimum distance from the plants of the automobile manufacturers so that the latter could maintain a just-in-time inventory system. To reduce operating costs, an automobile manufacturer would typically store only three to four hours' inventory on the premises. Consequently, prompt and efficient delivery of components and parts is crucial to the smooth operation of this system.

Kinch approached the company's board of directors with the hope of changing their attitude toward the establishment of joint-venture operations in Japan. His reasons were primarily twofold. First, given the complexities of the customer-supplier relationship and the difficulty of recruiting capable Japanese employees, it is imperative to tie up with an indigenous firm that has a well-established position in the market that Grace seeks to enter. Second, the automobile market in Japan is large enough to justify the creation of a separate company. The board at Grace conceded to a joint venture but insisted on majority ownership—that is, a 51-percent equity share. There were two reasons for this insistence: (1) it would be easier to transfer technology to a company in which Grace had majority ownership and hence could exercise tighter control; (2) 51-percent ownership would permit greater control over the management of the company, which is very important from Grace's perspective.

Grace initially approached the automotive-products business and made some headway with the smaller companies but not with the larger concerns like Nissan and Toyota. The U.S. partner sought a company that already had an established business in the automotive-products field. Grace had to be careful in selecting a partner because in Japan it is common for automobile manufacturers to have some equity interest in their supplier companies. Any link with such supplier companies could greatly restrict Grace's activities in Japan. For example, if Nissan Corporation owned the company in which Grace was interested, the only manufacturer this supplier could sell to would be Nissan, which would limit the market for its products. The same principle would apply to the other major automobile manufacturers.

After much investigation, Grace finally decided on a Nagoya-based company owned by an internationally oriented Japanese, Mr. Inoue. As noted previously, this firm was already well established in the field of polyurethane-foam products and, before the formal negotiations for the establishment of the joint venture in 1976, already had two years of prior experience with Grace in the area of foaming technology.

Inoue first approached Grace because of his interest in a unique polyurethane foam that the U.S. company had developed but "quite honestly, had never matured." This initial contact provided an opportunity for the two parties to work together; and hence, get to know each other. This points to the need to develop long-term relationships in the Japanese business context. Besides complementarity of needs, Grace was further attracted to Inoue because of two other factors: (1) Inoue had no ownership by any of the automobile companies; this meant that there should not be any restrictions on whom the company might sell to; (2) in Kinch's opinion, Inoue is a "very capable businessman, and he is very international in his thinking." Even though Grace had contacts with several prospective partners, Kinch always came back to Inoue as his preference.

From the beginning Grace tried to convince Inoue of the benefits of entering into a joint-venture arrangement with it. In typical Japanese fashion, Inoue wanted to take time to study more closely the U.S. partner's products and operations. He made a thorough investigation of Grace's operation in Japan and analyzed some of the problems the U.S. company had been facing. Inoue discovered that a basic problem with Grace's Japanese operation thus far was that the latter did not understand the purchasing habits of the Japanese automobile manufacturers or their system of favorite suppliers.

After extensive negotiations spanning a six-year period, the two entities agreed to the establishment of a 51-49 joint venture with Grace as the majority partner. Through the establishment of the joint venture, Grace transferred approximately $1 million of existing Teroson business previously sold through Grace K.K. (Grace's wholly owned subsidiary) to the new joint venture at no cost to the latter. This is an interesting contrast to the case presented in chapter 8 of the dissolution of a joint venture. In the latter case the U.S. partner bought out the capital of the joint venture and merged that with its wholly owned Japanese subsidiary. In the case of Grace the reverse was true: The business of the wholly owned business was transferred to the joint venture.

Both partners would contribute to the technology used in the joint venture. Grace's contribution was in acoustics. In Kinch's words, "This is a new area where we have superior technology in analyzing the problem, but have had great difficulty in designing the product to fit the problem. We chose Inoue because the best sound barrier that could be put in the car would be a polyurethane product,'' which is the Japanese partner's area of expertise. Under the joint-venture agreement the Japanese partner was expected to help develop the product and modify it to fit the needs of the local market.

The board of the joint venture consists of five members, three from Grace and two from Inoue. As noted previously, one of the reasons for Grace's insistence on majority ownership is that the company is very concerned about how its operations are managed. Therefore, Grace will provide the management in the joint venture. The general manager of the joint-venture operation, who will be responsible for the day-to-day activities of the company, will come from Grace. This is in sharp contrast to the practice mentioned in most of the other cases presented in the book, where management is generally left to the Japanese partner. In the area of management, Inoue's contribution will primarily be in providing sales contacts for the venture because he has access to the buyers. In Kinch's words, Inoue "has got the sales contacts at all levels. So what we expect from him is to put these contacts in.''

The name of the joint venture is Teroson K.K. Unlike the case of Smith-Kline and Fujisawa, where both parties were concerned about the use of their names, neither partner in this case deemed it appropriate to include the parent company's name in the venture. Teroson is the name of the German company acquired by Grace, and the name has never been changed because Teroson is a highly regarded trademark in the automobile industry throughout the world. Since the products were to be distributed worldwide, Grace wanted to identify heavily with the Teroson name. In Kinch's words: "We developed a trademark that automobile manufacturers throughout the world can rely on, whether it be in Japan, Germany, or the States. This would be a tremendous advantage to our company.'' The Japanese partner agreed that the trademark name would be an asset; consequently, neither the Grace nor the Inoue name was included in the joint venture.

The joint venture will start out on a small scale with minimal capitalization and only four employees. Both parties disliked the idea of high initial capitalization (which is common among Japanese firms) because they agreed that this would be associated with a longer payoff period. In general, the more capital put into a new business, the longer it takes before the business can make a profit. In Kinch's opinion, although Inoue is "100-percent Japanese, his management philosophy is similar'' to that of Grace. Unlike most Japanese companies, Inoue M.P.T. is concerned with bottom-line figures for every quarter and year. In Kinch's view, Inoue "is very concerned, for instance, that when his own reports are published, his customers see how much money he is making, even though these are 100-percent-held companies and are not public. He is very bottom-line oriented. The projects that he personally is involved in are ones that concern his company's investments, and he is interested in a payoff within a reasonable period of time. He does, however, look for growth or businesses that can sustain themselves. That's the reason he is interested in starting these up on a small scale so they will not have the heavy pressures of lack of profit." This unconventional trait stems primarily from the fact that the company is a privately held concern, and hence Inoue's personal fortune is at stake. To compensate for the low initial capitalization, both parent companies will help by absorbing some of the operating costs.

Besides the general manager, who will come from Grace, Inoue will provide some of the personnel for the joint venture at first. Inoue has a company with 3,000-4,000 employees, whereas Grace K.K. has only 150. Inoue was big enough to attract bright young people. Thus the joint venture will rely on the Japanese parent company for staffing in its early phases. Although Kinch acknowledged that this initial dependence on the Japanese partner for recruitment needs may lead to problems of divided loyalty, he hopes that will not happen. When the joint venture becomes well established, it should be able to hire its own people.

Issues under Negotiation

There were essentially two major issues under negotiation. One pertained to the distribution of equity ownership between the partners, and the other related to Inoue's reservations about Grace's "ability to supply the technical input necessary to be successful." Each of these will be examined in greater detail.

Equity Position

From the beginning Grace had insisted on 51-percent ownership. At the time Grace believed that there would be no serious objection because the primary technology would come from the U.S. side. The Japanese, however, wanted an equal partnership. In William Kinch's opinion, Inoue's reluctance arose primarily from the fact that under the Japanese *ringi* system, he would have to explain to—not simply tell—his employees why he would consent to a 49-percent equity share when his other joint ventures were on a 50-50 basis. Inoue M.P.T. had previously entered into two joint ventures with German entities and another with a U.S. building-products firm. Consequently, the onus fell on Grace to explain why it needed a controlling interest.

The reasons for Grace's insistence on majority ownership were, first, for consolidation purposes. According to U.S. accounting practices, the consolidation of profit-and-loss statements would be permitted only if the U.S. corporation had a controlling interest in the company. Given Grace's extensive worldwide operations, this was certainly an important consideration. A second reason pertained to the transfer of technology. Since the technology was to come from Grace's sister company in Germany, majority ownership would facilitate technological transfer and the flow of information. According to Kinch, "I don't want to say that our German sister was distrusting, however many countries do not trust the Japanese. In international business, you must work around nationalities. You can never tear down those barriers. They will always be there. I think it would be easier to transfer the technology if they knew that we owned the majority of this business." In Kinch's opinion, the percentage of equity ownership "became not an issue, but a point that never seemed to be resolved until the latter part of the discussion." Since a joint-venture arrangement would involve cooperation between the partners, Kinch never tried to force the issue. Rather, at a certain point in the negotiations, Kinch simply told Inoue, "If this presents a problem, please tell me and I will withdraw my request and bring it to a 50-50 joint venture." Thus Kinch gave the Japanese partner every opportunity to say that it could not accept anything other than 50-50. Grace would have given in, though reluctantly, because Kinch wanted the Japanese to concur with the decision.

Kinch also emphasized that 51-percent ownership does not mean overriding the Japanese partner's wishes and decisions. Although voting privileges were 3 to 2 in Grace's favor, Kinch did not foresee any issue coming to a vote. This is in line with the practice of other U.S. companies that have entered into collaborative arrangements with the Japanese. Kinch sought to reassure his Japanese partner on this issue by trying to arrange for equal representation on the board and equal vote, with Grace casting the deciding vote only if there was a tie. This practice was prohibited under Japanese law, however, and in Kinch's words was "unfortunate because then it makes it like a true 50-50 joint venture, but I like the consolidation privileges of the 51." Under Japanese law, the board could not be structured to allow for equal representation in numbers and the 51-percent shareholder cast the deciding vote in case of a tie. Japanese legislation prescribes that the board must be structured so that the majority partner has more seats.

Inoue's Reservations

A second major stumbling block in the negotiations pertained to Inoue's "serious reservations" about Grace's ability to provide the technical input necessary to make the venture successful. Most of the negotiations were conducted on a one-on-one basis between Kinch and Inoue. Given his cosmopolitan outlook, Inoue was very open with Kinch. This was helpful because many foreign firms are unable to gauge a Japanese partner's thoughts on particular issues.

Although Inoue was frank and open, he would not get to the point of insulting the U.S. partner. As noted earlier, face-saving is important in any culture, but more so in eastern societies. Inoue's frankness, coupled with a genuine desire not to affront others, created a comfortable atmosphere for the entire negotiating situation. Given Grace's less-than-spectacular performance in Japan up to that point, Inoue was afraid that the venture might not receive the kind of support and input from U.S. headquarters necessary to make it successful. He tried to procrastinate by asking Kinch for more time to study the proposal and ferret out more information in the field. In Kinch's words, "It wasn't until the last two years that the discussions were accelerated to the stage of what can we do, are you interested or not?"

This delay is reminiscent of the strategy adopted by Fujisawa Pharmaceutical Co., Ltd., in its negotiations with SmithKline Corporation. In that case the Japanese partner wanted to wait for the performance figures of 'Tagamet' in the United Kingdom before making a final decision. In this case the onus fell on Kinch to convince Inoue that both top management in New York and the German subsidiary were committed to the project and would stand solidly behind it. In Kinch's opinion: "One of the reasons we initially encountered trouble when we introduced these products through our own company in Japan is that the Japanese come back with a hundred questions. In Japan it does not matter how insignificant the questions are; you must respond. This is particularly true in the automobile industry. Our response time was bad because the New York side, which has the only capable people for responding, did not truly feel it was necessary, so the response was nonexistent in some areas and slow in others."

This points to differences in business practices between the United States and Japan. As noted earlier, the Japanese want detailed information on all matters. The Americans, on the other hand, may consider some of this information unnecessary and hence may be reluctant to respond promptly to such queries. Japanese customers often react negatively to this kind of attitude. To operate successfully in Japan, a U.S. firm must develop enough patience to respond to all inquiries from the prospective local partner and customers, however trivial or unreasonable they may appear from the U.S. perspective.

Another reason Inoue was hesitant was that since he is the owner-operator of the company, his personal fortune, goodwill, and reputation were at stake if he agreed to the joint venture. As Kinch indicated, Inoue's "reputation is on the line. He is part of that company, so he has a moral commitment to them. He was somewhat concerned that we would be unable to back this company with technical help. This was his basic concern all along for declining our offer.'' Given the relatively small size of the venture compared with Grace's mammouth organization worldwide, Inoue was wary that Grace might not be able and willing to devote adequate attention and resources to this project.

This reservation was not wholly unjustified. Many giant multinationals with highly diversified operations may be unable to devote adequate attention to a relatively minor joint venture in a particular country. The interests of such giant multinationals may be diverted from project to project throughout their various operations worldwide, whereas the Japanese partner, which is fairly limited in its overseas operations, could concentrate full time on the joint venture. Perhaps Inoue was concerned that this might be the case in a joint venture with Grace, whose overseas operations are highly diversified.

To allay Inoue's concerns, Kinch took him to New York to meet Grace's top management. He also took Inoue to visit Grace's sister company in Germany, "where the heart of the technology exists." Inoue visited the German division on several occasions, and these visits were supplemented by reciprocal visits to Japan of management and technical personnel from the German division, who toured all the Japanese automobile manufacturers and gave presentations on the applicability of the product in the local market. In Kinch's opinion: "I guess it was his fear, knowing the business and the demands that the automobile companies put on their suppliers. There was doubt in his mind that we might not be willing to provide the kind of support to enable this joint venture to be successful. That was his constant objection or reservation." It took a lot of convincing before Inoue finally agreed to participate in the joint venture. Although Inoue had entered into joint ventures with other foreign entities, the proposed arrangement with Grace was "in an area with which he is most familiar, and he had to assure himself that the backup would be there." Furthermore, his reputation with the major automobile manufacturers, which were his principal clients, was at stake. Consequently, he had to resolve all his doubts before consenting to the joint venture with Grace.

Besides these two main issues, another subject that was discussed extensively between the parties pertained to whether the German technology could be adapted to the automobile industry in Japan. In Kinch's words, the question was: "Do we really have something unique?" This was of great concern to Inoue. As noted in chapters 1 and 2, a foreign firm could not hope to be successful by introducing a mediocre or unoriginal product. To penetrate the Japanese market, a foreign company must introduce a product or technology that is truly innovative and unique. Consequently, this issue was discussed extensively. Besides these major issues, all the other points under negotiation were relatively minor and easily resolved.

Composition of Negotiating Teams

The composition of the negotiating teams was simple. On the U.S. side there were only two individuals, Kinch and Shojiro Makino, the president of Grace's wholly owned Japanese subsidiary. On the Japanese side, Inoue was usually accompanied only by his top technical men. There was no legal representation on either side until the contractual agreements had to be drafted. Kinch believed that the use of lawyers in all the negotiations would unnecessarily prolong matters; hence attorneys were only brought in separately toward the end for drafting purposes. Kinch noted that the legal issue was fairly easily addressed because Inoue asked him to draft all the agreements. Kinch indicated that he would "certainly pass these through my lawyers; but when we asked him for a letter of intent or any legal document, we would put that on his desk, and he would read and sign it. He is a very capable, uncomplicated man." Inoue, of course, had his own legal counsel, who would then go through the documents.

All legal documents signed by Grace have to be approved by its legal office in New York. Kinch felt, however, that given the differences in legal systems between the United States and Japan, it would be prudent to engage the services of a legal counsel in Japan who would give him an accurate reading on how the U.S. legal document would fit under Japanese law. Kinch noted that Grace was fortunate to engage the services of an excellent law firm in Japan—Logan, Okumora, and Takashima—which in his words "has some of the best lawyers I have ever dealt with, either Japanese or American." The attorney Grace used was Bob Takashima, who is Japanese-born and received his legal training at the Harvard Law School. Consequently, he was fluent in English and had a thorough understanding of the legal aspects of both U.S. and Japanese societies.

Most of the agreements were in English with a Japanese translation. Since Inoue asked the U.S. partner to draft the legal documents, Kinch generally adhered to the following procedure: The boilerplate part of the agreement would be drafted by Grace's legal staff in New York. This document was then transmitted to its legal counsel in Japan for review and revision, and then finally turned over to the Japanese partner. Kinch felt that things were done more expeditiously in this manner because, had the Japanese partner drafted the document, it would have had to go through two sets of lawyers on Grace's side, the legal staff in New York, and legal counsel in Japan. In his words: "It takes twice as long to approve somebody else's draft than to approve the revision of your own draft. We have learned that through bitter experience."

The agreement establishing the joint venture was comprehensive and included provisions for the dissolution of the venture should the relationship between the partners deteriorate. As in most of Grace's joint venture agreements, it is written into the contract that if either party cannot resolve a situation for whatever reasons, "then either partner has the right to buy out the other." In the subsequent case of the dissolution of a joint venture, such a provision saved a lot of haggling over issues when the relationships between the partners were fairly strained at the time of dissolution.

All the negotiations were conducted in English. Inoue speaks fluent English, so very little interpretation was required. When an item did need further clarification, Mr. Shojiro Makino (the president of Grace's wholly owned subsidiary in Japan) would translate to make sure that Inoue fully understood the matter. In Kinch's opinion, language never posed a serious problem. Occasionally, however, Kinch detected that a question had never really been answered. On such occasions he would raise the issue again and explain in greater depth why a certain thing had to be done in a given manner. This detailed explanation was necessary because the Japanese partner had to provide reasons to his employees that a certain course of action was taken.

In Kinch's recollection, the negotiations were prolonged but very amicable "because it was really a negotiation between two old friends." As noted previously, Kinch had worked with Mr. Inoue for two years on foam technology before the formal negotiations for establishment of the joint venture began in 1976. Consequently, there existed the mutual understanding and trust that are absolute requisites to a successful international business negotiation. In Kinch's opinion, the negotiations went smoothly because of Inoue's "experience, background, ability, and good business sense." Furthermore, since Inoue is the owner of a privately held company, "he did not have to speak for a board. He spoke for the company." Kinch could not do this; consequently, he felt the Americans were at a slight disadvantage. Given these factors, Kinch felt that Inoue was an "ideal partner to have negotiations with."

Differences in Negotiating Styles and Business Practices

Kinch was asked to comment on the most salient differences between Americans and Japanese in business practices and negotiating styles. The following is a summary of his perceptions.

Decision Making

As mentioned in chapter 2, 90 percent of the decisions made at the middle- and lower-management levels in Japanese organizations are arrived at through consensus (*Doing Business,* 1982). Some decisions at the top-management level are made through the mechanism described as one screech of the crane, whereby the chief executive officer, who is usually the owner and founder of the company, uses a top-down approach. In Kinch's observations, almost all the decisions were made by Inoue personally. He is the owner of a family-held business which was established by his father and which did not undergo significant expansion until he took over. Although he did not consult with his staff in terms of decision making, he did feel an obligation to explain to them the rationale behind his actions. For this reason, Inoue was greatly concerned about the minority equity position of the Japanese partner. He felt it would be difficult to justify his acceptance of a 49-percent equity in this instance since all his other joint ventures were on an equal-partnership basis. Grace had to provide adequate reasons why they wanted 51 percent, so that Inoue could in turn relate these to his employees.

Time Perspective

As noted earlier, Inoue was truly international in his orientation; this was one of the features that attracted him to Grace as a prospective partner. As the owner-entrepreneur, Inoue was more oriented to the short term than the typical Japanese firm; he was more concerned about the bottom-line figure in the immediate future. This may partly explain his reservations about a joint venture with Grace; he was apprehensive that the U.S. partner would not provide adequate support to make the operation a success.

Although Inoue placed heavy emphasis on short-term results, he demonstrated the more traditional Japanese concern with carefully examining and analyzing matters before reaching a final decision. For example, when Grace proposed the formation of a 51-49 joint venture in the U.S. partner's favor, Inoue's typical response was that he needed further information and time to research the matter thoroughly. This cautiousness may have stemmed from his awareness of Grace's limitations in the Japanese market theretofore and the fact that if he were to form a joint venture with Grace, his personal fortune and reputation would be at stake. Although it took him nearly six years to agree to a joint-venture arrangement with Grace, in Kinch's opinion Inoue never used time as a negotiating ploy.

All the negotiations took place in Japan except when Inoue visited the United States to pay courtesy calls to his U.S. partner. These visits were largely social. Nierenberg (1973) discusses the benefits associated with conducting negotiations in one's home country, one of which is home-court advantage. Other advantages include the time factor and nondisruption of the circadian rhythm. Although Kinch recognized these advantages, he felt that "quite honestly, one cannot negotiate in the United States for anything in Japan" for two reasons. First, even though the Japanese company may have a subsidiary in the United States that appears to be staffed by very senior people, the latter are usually not authorized to make decisions but constantly have to relay matters and receive instructions from headquarters in Japan. This is time-consuming and may lead to communication errors. In the case of Inoue M.P.T., Inoue personally makes all the important decisions; there is no overseas representative who could speak for him. Second, given the management practices of Japan whereby most decisions are reached through consensus and frequent caucusing is common, the only place a foreign firm can get all the people assembled in one spot is Japan.

This second reason may not have been too important in this case because Inoue made all the decisions himself. Since the plant was to be built in Japan, however, and Mr. Inoue felt an obligation to explain his decisions to his employees, the most logical place to conduct the negotiations would appear to be Japan. Furthermore, Makino, who helped clarify certain issues to Inoue in Japanese throughout the six years of negotiations, is stationed in Japan, where he serves as the president of Grace's wholly owned Japanese subsidiary.

Socializing

In an earlier chapter it was noted that after-hours socializing can promote closer personal ties between prospective partners that are fundamental to business relations in Japan. This theme was echoed by members of U.S. negotiating teams in some of the previous cases. Although a number of Americans noted that important decisions were made during the after-hours socializing, this was not universally true (see the cases of Boeing and Merck). Similarly, Kinch noted that since he already had fifteen years of experience in traveling to Japan, with an average of six to seven trips per year, he no longer "had to put up with the typical after-hours socializing". He maintained, however, that it is important to socialize with his Japanese partners over a relaxed dinner. On every trip he had dinner with Inoue either the night before or the night after the negotiations: "This entails only a lovely dinner at a tempura or a French restaurant. It was almost like a friendly dinner, never going out to the Ginza and places like that. I haven't had to do that in years. Quite honestly, I don't miss it. But I do enjoy the camaraderie of dinners that I have had with my joint-venture partners."

Kinch follows essentially the same protocol with another of Grace's joint-venture partners in Osaka. The board meetings in Osaka would always be followed with a lovely dinner, but there was no pub crawling. Nevertheless, in the United States there appears to be a general misconception that all important decisions in Japan are made in bars and restaurants. The Japanese do place a high premium on the need to develop friendly social relations among partners in a variety of social settings. The Japanese are not unique in this regard; Kinch found that the same principle holds true in most of the other countries he deals with in the Pacific Basin. For example, in the official dinner after a negotiation in China, "many times you find out what the nuances are or if there are any problems or what the true feelings of the people are." This observation is echoed by most other Americans who have negotiated with the Chinese (Tung 1982a).

Cultural Differences

Although Inoue is internationally oriented and shares a basic philosophy with his U.S. counterpart, Kinch acknowledged that there were cultural differences that had a bearing on the negotiations themselves. One major difference pertained to the primary concerns of either party. Inoue's foremost concern was his arrangements with his customers: He would never make a decision that would negatively affect the relationship he had carefully cultivated with his clients over the years. Although Inoue was global in his orientation toward business opportunities—which explains why he approached Grace in the first place about a possible collaboration between the two companies, and as evidenced by the joint ventures he had entered into with other foreign entities—his underlying major concern was that the joint venture should not jeopardize or upset his existing relationship with his Japanese clients. This may arise from the unique supplier-customer arrangement in Japan.

Grace's concern, on the other hand, was to establish a strong position in Japan because it assumed that, first, the relationship between the supplier and the consumer will be predicated on that, and second, the arrangement will persist as long as either party can derive benefits from it. This assumption was accurate to some extent because ultimately any business agreement has to be premised on sound economic principles, as seen in chapter 8, which examines the dissolution of a joint venture where the unprofitability of the operation was a principal factor in the breakup. In Japan, however, this assumption must be modified to take into consideration the importance of personal relationships, which are fundamental to the establishment and continuation of any business arrangement. This explains Inoue's overriding concern with maintaining existing relationships with his Japanese clients.

Grace was more concerned with the technical aspects of running the business and making a profit; its principal goal in a joint venture with Inoue was to establish a worldwide product-line operation. Since Japan is the leading automobile manufacturer in the world, and Grace had so far not established a presence in the automotive-chemicals and sound-absorbent-systems markets, the link with Inoue was perceived as crucial to attaining this goal. Thus the primary concerns of the two partners were different.

Besides its cultural root, this difference in concern could be attributed to the fact that Grace is a well-established multinational corporation with global operations. Hence its primary concern is to develop its product lines on a worldwide basis. Inoue, on the other hand, is an international firm whose primary focus is still in the Japanese market, although it actively seeks worldwide opportunities. This difference in the stage of internationalization affects the company's organizational structure and its orientation and objectives, which is apparently the case here (Robinson 1978; Robock and Simmonds 1983).

Although the primary interests of the two partners differed, their secondary concerns were similar. Kinch shared Inoue's concern that the reputations of both companies were at stake, and hence perceived the need to make the venture successful. Although Grace's initial investment was minimal, Kinch felt that Grace's "exposure is big because we too are concerned that if this thing were to fail, not only Mr. Inoue's reputation would be harmed but ours as well. In Japan, we try to think as a Japanese company. In other words, I am always very concerned about anything that is done by some of our sister groups in Japan because they can harm the reputation of our company, which is the major Grace operation in that country. We are Grace in Japan, whether it is our particular business or a restaurant business. We are the Grace entity in Japan, and keeping our reputation whole and unblemished is one of our first and foremost responsibilities. That is an unwritten law that I have to cope with myself."

Kinch's secondary concern bridged the differences between the two parties and cemented the relationship between them by emphasizing the commonalities among them.

Face-Saving

In line with popular opinion, Kinch believes that face-saving is very important in Japan. As noted previously, Inoue had reservations about the proposed joint venture because his reputation was at stake if he teamed up with Grace and the venture failed. Kinch, however, believes that face-saving is important in any culture, a point made in chapter 1. Kinch noted that he would sometimes use the need to save face to his advantage, too: "If I get into a position where I have made a commitment to my board here based on what somebody has told me in Japan [although he has never done so in this particular negotiation], and they in turn say they would try to change this a little bit, I would use the Japanese tactic of saying that you really can't do this because I will lose face, which I will. I have no qualms about that, and I don't think I am using the system against them. I just feel that everything is on a par. If commitments are made, I happen to agree that you do have your reputation on the line. If you back off, even for good, valid business reasons, there is some loss of face. Face loss in any language is not good."

Factors for Success

Kinch was asked to identify some of the factors responsible for the success of the negotiations. These will be examined in this section.

Willingness to Cooperate

Kinch indicated that both partners were willing to enter into a joint venture. In his opinion this was the primary factor responsible for the success of the negotiations. Although the primary objectives of the two parties differed, both shared the desire to make a profit within a reasonably short period of time and an overall concern with the respective parent company's reputation. Furthermore, the product lines and technological capabilities of both partners were complementary.

Understanding

Besides the willingness to cooperate, both parties must genuinely understand and accommodate the desires and requirements of each other. In Kinch's opinion, a major factor responsible for the breakdown of a joint-venture relationship after it has been established is that the partners have never arrived at "a complete understanding" in the first place. "We have learned through experience that if somebody says, 'Fine, you don't have to worry about this, we will address this until the joint venture is formed,' it is a very poor thing to do. Even though it may be between friends, my attitude has always been that you negotiate on the basis that the friendship or personalities in the future will not be involved. So you must set the joint venture up almost on an arms-length basis so the joint venture can run without me or Mr. Inoue because we may decide to leave and do something else, and this thing has to go on, we hope, forever. I think most of the joint ventures have difficulties because the U.S. partner does not truly understand the requirements of the Japanese partner."

This assertion brings up an interesting debate between those U.S. firms that believe that, given the Japanese distaste for law, a contractual agreement in Japan must be a living, organic document that could evolve with changing conditions. Hence there is no need to spell out all details or provide for all contingencies. On the other hand, some U.S. firms prefer to be as specific as possible and insist that a contractual agreement should include provisions for all possible contingencies that may arise in a collaborative arrangement, including the dissolution of the venture. Given changing conditions and the Japanese emphasis on human relations, it is clearly impossible for a contractual agreement to cover all possible contingencies that may arise over the life of the venture; if the agreement is left too loose and unstructured, however, it may be subject to differences in interpretation and lead to subsequent conflict. In case of major disputes and in the event of dissolution of a contractual agreement, these specific provisions would come in handy and save both parties a lot of haggling over issues.

A lack of understanding could also contribute to the breakdown of the actual negotiations. Misunderstanding may arise from inadequate preparation, closed-mindedness and a concomitant inability to view matters from a different cultural perspective, or impatience. In Japan the inability to recognize what is important from the Japanese perspective could prove detrimental, even though such matters may appear trivial from the U.S. standpoint. For example, Kinch understood that although Inoue personally made all the important decisions, under the *ringi* system he had to justify his actions to his employees. Consequently, although Inoue was not personally concerned with his own minority share in the proposed venture, he had to explain to his staff why he had accepted a 49-percent equity position. Because Kinch understood this need, he was prepared to explain to Inoue why Grace had to have a majority position. Furthermore, Kinch did not pressure his Japanese partner to accept the minority position. Rather than debate this delicate issue, he gave Inoue ample opportunity to think it over because he wanted Inoue to be comfortable with the decision. This helps explain why the negotiations took so long.

Cultural differences are peculiar; what may be trivial from one cultural standpoint may be paramount from another. Consequently, it is necessary to recognize what are considered sensitive issues in another country and to avoid them where possible or to work around them.

Mutual Trust

Both parties trusted each other. In Kinch's opinion: "The trust has to be there. If there is no trust, then I don't think you can make any agreement with the Japanese." This mutual trust between the two parties was developed eight years earlier when they first worked on foam technology in Japan, and was cemented over the six years of negotiations for the establishment of the joint venture.

Patience

Kinch indicated that if there was one single lesson that he learned from all his years of doing business in the Orient, it was patience. Consequently, he was willing to wait six years while Inoue made up his mind about the proposal. He noted that most Americans have a "tendency to analyze situations and push for an answer. I have learned not to do that. You can sense when you come to a stumbling block, and to pursue it any further is going to do you more harm than good. So you just call a halt to the discussions. Be patient, and try to understand even though some of the requests seem nonsensical to Americans." In his fifteen years of doing business in the Orient, Kinch has developed the patience to wait for matters to develop rather than pressuring the other party into a decision. If inordinate pressure is applied when the other side still has reservations on the issue, the latter may have no recourse but to turn down the proposal, effectively terminating the negotiations.

Given his extensive experience in doing business in Japan, Kinch was asked for advice on penetrating the Japanese market. First, he believes that U.S. banks could be invaluable sources of information on which individuals and agencies to contact in Japan. Second, he advises the firm to spend some time in Japan to talk to people about the industry it seeks to enter. These individuals can put the firm in touch with entities that may be interested in doing business with the U.S. firm. Although Kinch has not used the services of the U.S. government or of the commercial attaché in the U.S. Consulate, he has no reservations about using them.

The key is to develop as many personal contacts as possible so that one can gain plenty of information. The Japanese trading companies can also provide valuable assistance. It is important, however, to know which trading company has expertise in the particular line of business one seeks to enter. Here again the U.S. banks can provide useful input. If a U.S. firm decides on a particular trading company, it should try to establish high-level contacts with the firm. Kinch cautioned that people below the level of director are usually not authorized to make decisions and hence may prolong matters. Third, Kinch reiterates the need for the U.S. firm to be patient. Things will not happen overnight. Fourth, Kinch emphasized the need to understand Japanese business practices and the industry one seeks to enter. Given the vast cultural differences between the two countries, it is important to remember "that no successful Japanese company is ever run as an overseas arm of a U.S. corporation. You can't treat it like a branch office or an offshoot of a Peoria, Illinois, sales office. It has to be run very differently, and you must bend your rules to meet Japanese market requirements because they are definitely not going to change." This is where open-mindedness, flexibility, and patience come in.

Implementation

Kinch acknowledged that although the relationships between the two partners are very cordial, he does anticipate some problems in implementing the
joint venture. These potential problems can be summarized as follows.

Recruitment of Employees

Kinch anticipates difficulty in recruiting competent young Japanese to work
for the joint venture. Since Inoue is a well-established firm with 3,000-4,000
employees, he expects the Japanese parent company to help staff the operation at first. This may lead to problems of divided loyalty if the individuals
who work for Teroson K.K. still see themselves as employees of Inoue
M.P.T. Kinch recognizes that Inoue would probably have to guarantee
those employees who are on loan to the joint venture the right to return to
the Japanese parent company if they wish.

In the subsequent case of the dissolution of a joint venture, this posed a
key problem. Even after the dissolution of the joint venture, when some of
the staff of the joint venture chose to go with the U.S. parent company, the
Japanese partner guaranteed them the right to return to the Japanese parent
firm after a two-year trial period. Kinch hopes that when the joint venture
company is well established, it can become independent in this regard. He
believes that if he can make the joint venture attractive enough, some of the
staff provided by the Japanese parent firm may choose to remain with the
joint venture. Furthermore, he hopes that since Grace is a well-establihsed
multinational corporation, the joint venture will soon acquire a reputation
in Japan and be able to attract internationally oriented people to work for
the firm.

Kinch plans to recruit employees through a mixed Japanese-U.S. system,
rather than in the pure Japanese fashion. The latter would refer to the
system whereby workers are inducted straight from college, after which they
undergo extensive in-house training. Some Japanese who dislike this route
may prefer to leave the company to acquire an advanced degree from a U.S.
university. After completing this advanced degree, a Japanese who wants to
return to his country of national origin may have difficulty in being accepted by the large, well-established Japanese companies. (These Japanese
should *not* be confused with those who are sent by their companies to study
in the United States. In the latter instance the company pays for all the tui-
tion and expenses, and the individual is guaranteed a position in the company on completion of the program.)

In Kinch's opinion, these Japanese would be ideal candidates for the
joint-venture operation for at least three reasons. First, they know English.

Since all of Grace's interdivisional correspondence is in English, language skill is an absolute requisite. Second, a major reason for these individuals' dissatisfaction with the traditional system is that they are usually mavericks who want to move up the organizational ladder more rapidly than is permitted under the Japanese system. Third, they are familiar with both U.S. and Japanese business practices. The Grace-Inoue joint venture has so far hired one such graduate of the University of South Carolina, who has turned out to be an excellent recruit. Incidentally, some well-established Japanese companies are also looking to this alternative source of manpower to staff their overseas operations. Nomura Securities International Inc., for instance, has adopted this practice fairly recently (Tung 1984).

Differences in Philosophy

Although Inoue's basic philosophy is similar to that of Grace, there are still some fundamental differences in outlook between the U.S. and Japanese partners. For instance, Grace has established a high return-on-investment criterion on all its operations, far above that for Japanese companies. Kinch believes that to compete effectively against indigenous Japanese firms, the U.S. parent company must adjust this return criterion to an acceptable level so that the joint-venture operation can compete in Japan.

Another potential problem is the overidentification of the Japanese partner with its customers. As noted earlier, this was Inoue's principal concern; it is characteristic of the relationship between supplier and customer in the country. In Japan it is common to overextend oneself to get a customer, even at the expense of losing money initially. Kinch believes that since Inoue is very bottom-line oriented, he will probably not resort to such extremes; but the possibility is there. In Kinch's words: "These are things that we both go into knowing full well that these are potential problems that we will have to solve when they arise. I don't anticipate any serious problems, but I expect minor ones. We have to learn to deal with these differences." A joint venture is similar to a marriage wherein both partners have to learn to accommodate each other's interests, although relations may be turbulent at times.

Although conflicts may arise, Kinch does not believe that matters will ever reach a crisis level, because he is on the board and will not allow matters to deteriorate that far. In his words: "I understand enough about Japanese business to be somewhat flexible. I think Mr. Inoue, on the other side, is also flexible enough to reach a decision based on a meeting of the minds a lot quicker than we could in some other joint ventures."

Although the voting privileges are 3 to 2 in Grace's favor, Kinch does not foresee that any issue will ever be brought to a vote because this would be embarrassing for the Japanese partner since it does not have an equal vote. As Maurer of Merck & Co. indicated, when an issue has to be voted on, that is tantamount to warfare, and the dissolution of the venture is then imminent. Instead, Kinch believes that both partners would try to iron out any differences that may arise through mutual discussions. In his words: "It is really up to us to work these out as problems arise, which is typical in a Japanese company. It goes back to the *ringi* system. It is not black and white. You can't say 'This is it,' and walk away." Because of this aversion to using legalistic means to resolve conflicts, Kinch emphasized the need to understand each other and the genuine willingness to accommodate each other's demands and desires in order to make the venture successful.

8 When the Chips Fall

The previous chapters have dealt with negotiations for the formation or continued operation of joint cooperative agreements between U.S. and Japanese entities, and the factors responsible for the success of these arrangements. This chapter examines the events leading to the dissolution of a twelve-year-old joint venture between a U.S. and a Japanese company. Since the U.S. partner has other operations in Japan besides the one that has been dissolved, the name of the company will be disguised for confidentiality. The U.S. entity will be referred to as ABC Corporation and its former Japanese partner as XYZ Company. Furthermore, since the products manufactured by ABC Corporation are unique, to ensure anonymity, their exact nature will also be disguised. They will be referred to simply as industrial equipment and instruments.

The information presented in this case was obtained through an indepth interview with Mr. A, vice-president, international, ABC Corporation. It is important to emphasize three major points. First, although Mr. A has characterized the overall negotiations for the dissolution of the joint venture as "amicable," there were certain bad feelings between the partners over the operations of the joint venture both before and after its dissolution. Consequently, although Mr. A has tried to be objective in describing the events and assessing the situation, this perspective is one-sided; that is, only the views and perceptions of the U.S. partner are presented. This should be taken into consideration in reviewing the material presented here.

Second, although the use of anonymity may hinder analysis of the case, it is still worthwhile to examine the factors responsible for the breakdown in relations between the two partners, and the dynamics of the negotiations for the dissolution of a joint venture. Although many firms are willing to discuss their successes in operating in Japan, only a few are prepared to talk about a venture that failed. I am grateful to Mr. A for sharing his company's experiences and providing interesting insights into a cooperative agreement that had broken down beyond compromise.

Third, although the joint-venture agreement has been dissolved, both the U.S. and Japanese parent firms are highly successful, profitable companies on their own; the capital of the former joint venture has now been absorbed by the American partner into its existing wholly owned subsidiary operation in Japan.

History

ABC Corporation is a manufacturer of industrial products with sales of over $300 million in 1981, representing a 6-percent increase over the 1980 level. In the past five years the sales and earnings of the company have increased substantially. Although ABC's customers are diversified, the corporation's objectives are focused primarily on one aspect of industrial activity. The company was established some seventy years ago and is run largely as a family-held concern. This may explain in part why ABC prefers to operate wholly owned subsidiaries elsewhere in the world.

The company has operations in various parts of Europe, South America, Africa, Southeast Asia, and the Indian subcontinent. All the operations are on a wholly owned basis except for three joint ventures, two in Japan and the other elsewhere in Asia. One of the joint ventures in Japan was terminated several years ago; the second (the focus of this case) was dissolved in 1981. Consequently, the company now has only one joint-venture operation in its entire overseas business.

The Japanese partner, XYZ Company, is a leading manufacturer of industrial instruments in Japan. It is fairly large, though not an industrial giant. The company is involved in general process-control instrumentation. Coincidentally, the company was also formed some seventy years ago by the father of the current president. Although XYZ's shares are publicly traded on the Tokyo Stock Exchange, it is fair to assume that the company was largely operated and managed as a family-held concern.

Although XYZ has overseas operations in two countries, these are either on a wholly owned or on a majority-partnership basis. Although the company is both a licensee and a licensor of a number of technical agreements with foreign companies, it has entered into only one joint venture with a foreign entity—the one with ABC that has now been dissolved. XYZ has a strong research orientation and manufactures a diverse range of products.

In 1969 ABC Corporation and XYZ Company entered into a 50-50 joint venture (designated ANX Company) for the production of industrial equipment, most of which was sold in Japan and part of which was marketed in other countries in Asia. None of these products were shipped back and sold in the U.S. market. The initial capitalization of the joint venture was 100 million yen. In Mr. A's opinion, the joint venture company "had always been marginal." The company's income has oscillated sharply over the years; it made profits in some years and operated at a loss in others. Although the company had made certain benchmarks, in Mr. A's words, "The underlying business was doing poorly." In 1979 the company underwent a major restructuring in the hopes of bringing it around. Despite these efforts, matters took a dramatic downturn in 1980, when performance was dismal.

In early 1980 there was a major shake-up in top management of the joint-venture company, involving the replacement of its most senior man. There were no other personnel changes. When asked about the reason for the management changeover, Mr. A responded: "We will never know the real reason why there was a management change. Basically, our partner came to us and said that so and so had to go. We thought that some of their reasons were not expressed to us. The other things they presented to us were such that under the circumstances we could not object to the change. Finally, in a joint venture the manager must have the confidence of both partners. If he does not have it, it really won't work."

The management of the joint-venture company was provided by XYZ Company and had always been Japanese. Over the years, although ANX recruited a number of Japanese on its own, the management was largely on loan from the Japanese parent company. ABC never played an active role in the management and administration of the joint-venture company. The manager for ABC in Asia, an American, used to visit the joint-venture company once every quarter to review strategies and basic decisions jointly. Besides these regularly scheduled quarterly review sessions, most communication with the Japanese parent and joint-venture companies was through correspondence, telex, and occasional phone calls where the U.S. parent company would review the results. ABC basically adopted a hands-off management approach; in Mr. A's words, the joint venture was run as an "over-the-counter kind of business." In Mr. A's opinion this approach had worked "exceptionally well" in the other subsidiaries, and is highly effective when the individual in charge of such an operation demonstrates "strength and has an entrepreneurial flair."

Under the arrangement, the U.S. parent company provided most of the technological and product know-how; the management, marketing, and other support activities were entirely relegated to the Japanese partner. This is in sharp contrast to the Merck & Co. case, where the U.S. parent company was in constant contact with its Japanese partner, Banyu Pharmaceutical Company, and the joint-venture operation, Nippon Merck Banyu. Hence the U.S. parent company would be immediately apprised of any developments. This allowed Merck to respond to situations before they got out of hand.

Initially, ABC thought that the reorganization in 1980 would turn things around and expected to see some improvement in the company's financial situation by 1981. In the first quarter of 1981 there was indeed some improvement. For a variety of reasons, however, the joint venture had never solidly entrenched itself in the Japanese market and had never become highly profitable.

Against this backdrop, the ABC executives, during their visit to Japan in the spring of 1981, casually mentioned to their Japanese partner their overall frustrations and "discouragement that this venture had never really taken hold." To the U.S. partner's surprise, the Japanese seized this opportunity to express their doubts about the joint operation. The U.S. partner was surprised since they had always thought the joint venture was "a prestigious thing" to the Japanese partner, because, through the joint venture, the Japanese partner had acquired formal contractual relationships "with a well-regarded international company in a field relating to theirs."

After this incident Mr. A and another executive from the U.S. parent company went to Japan in April 1981 to inquire more fully about the reasons for the Japanese partner's misgivings. In this set of meetings the Japanese side stated bluntly: "Look, there are two reasons for having a subsidiary—One, to make a lot of money, and two, to fit the rest of our business. Really this subsidiary is not doing either. It is not making any money, and it is becoming less and less of a fit with our business."

Since ABC could not disagree with its Japanese partner on either count, the two parent companies had drifted apart. ABC's new product developpoint would be to dissolve the operation. Over the years the objectives of the two parent companies had drifted part. ABC's new product developments were becoming more concentrated in one aspect of industrial activity, whereas the Japanese partner was more oriented toward process-control instrumentation. Despite considerable overlap between the two areas, the Japanese were dissatisfied with ABC's product developments in the area in which they were interested; ABC, on the other hand, was disappointed with XYZ's marketing efforts in those areas in which ABC felt they had the greatest competitive edge.

Thus one of the factors that had brought the partners together more than a decade before—complementarity of needs and fit in business between the two companies—had dissipated over time. Over the years both parties had moved in different directions, to the point where each felt that the other company could no longer complement its needs. In Mr. A's words: "Over the years we have been getting more and more spread apart, and finally they recognized that our efforts were not going to be in the area that would be of greatest interest to them. In addition, I think they could see that we are having problems with their entire group, so it behooves them to clean up marginal subsidiaries."

The negotiations on the dissolution and an analysis of the factors that led to the dissolution of the joint venture will be examined in the subsequent section.

Dissolution

In the dissolution of the joint-venture operation, ANX was basically divided between the two parent companies. ABC Corporation purchased the capital of the company, which meant that the U.S. parent company purchased all the working capital plus fixed assets. There was disagreement over the pricing of the inventory. Since fixed assets such as land and buildings were minimal, these did not pose a problem. The U.S. company purchased all rights to the former joint-venture operation. Many of the employees of the joint venture who came from XYZ Company reverted back to the Japanese parent. Furthermore, XYZ would continue to function as an original equipment manufacturer (OEM) distributor of ABC Corporation in the Japanese market. The corporate structure of the former joint venture and some of its key personnel would merge with ABC's existing wholly owned subsidiary in Japan and would continue to operate in those areas that are of interest to the U.S. parent company. The wholly owned subsidiary was established in 1977 and will be merged with the former joint venture as soon as the dissolution proceedings have been completed.

The purchase of the capital by ABC did not pose a problem because the original agreement to establish a joint venture specifically provided a formulation for settling share prices in the event of dissolution. This incident brings to light an interesting ongoing debate between those practitioners who advocate that the terms of a contractual agreement should be as specific as possible and should cover all possible contingencies, including provisions for dissolution, and those who argue that a contract should be a living, organic agreement between two parties, in which it may not be necessary or possible to spell out all the terms and conditions. This second approach is favored by many practitioners who enter into contractual agreements in Japan given the traditional Japanese distaste for lengthy legal documents. In the event of a dissolution, the former approach may well appear more appropriate.

Although Mr. A characterized the overall negotiations for the dissolution of the joint venture as "amicable," there were certain thorny issues. In Mr. A's opinion, the negotiations "got a little nasty when we discovered that near the end of the venture, many jobs had been accepted that were going to lose money. Some of the inventories were questionable. Making provisions for that has turned out to be a difficult thing, and there are some aspects that still are not settled" as of June 1982, a full year after the beginning of proceedings for dissolution.

The basic transactions for the dissolution of the joint venture have been completed, however. ABC has purchased the shares of the company, and the money has been transferred. Mr. A was in Japan in March 1982 and signed all the final papers dissolving the joint venture. As soon as the outstanding issue of the order that was accepted by the joint venture prior to dissolution could be resolved, the merger of the former joint venture company with ABC's wholly owned subsidiary in Japan could occur. The major items pertaining to the dissolution of the joint venture will be examined in detail.

The thorniest issue pertained to the ongoing business—that is, business entered into by ANX when it was still a joint venture. Much of this business turned out to be highly unprofitable. A major item under negotiation related to an order that had been accepted by the joint venture at inordinately low prices and that would involve losses on execution. A major conflict arose over the cost of fulfilling the order. The Japanese partner offered to carry out the contract for a certain sum, and the U.S. partner agreed. The issue turned into an "absolute mess," however, and the order was not invoiced until mid-1982. This has proved to be the most difficult issue to negotiate, and as of June 1982 the ex-partners had not resolved the matter. Mr. A indicated that both sides "were still basically fighting over that job."

Furthermore, some aspects of the business changed dramatically during the course of the year-long negotiations. In Mr. A's words, "It was a problem that we went into thinking things were a certain way, and found that they really weren't that way." In the six months immediately before the transition, the portion of the business to be taken over by the U.S. partner "suddenly collapsed," and the segment of the operation to be assumed by the Japanese partner "suddenly greatly improved." At the time of the negotiations there was no way ABC Corporation could have detected this problem until the final closing of the firm in early 1982. By then it was too late for the U.S. partner to remedy the situation.

Mr. A indicated that this situation could not be attributed to its partner's "cooking the books" because these were essentially kept straight. He blamed this situation on the internal "dissension within the ranks of management in the company, and overall mismanagement of the joint venture." In Mr. A's opinion, the situation could be likened to the kinds of issues raised by Senator Howard Baker in the investigation into the Watergate affair: "Who knew?" "What did they know?" and "When did they know?" Mr. A indicated that the U.S. partner tended to believe that XYZ might not be fully aware of the "severity of the problem at the time, and chances are it was something that all concerned muddled into." Subsequently, the two chief executives of the joint-venture company who chose to join the U.S. parent firm resigned. The U.S. parent will never be able to unravel the extent to which its Japanese partner knew about the situation beforehand.

Other issues under negotiation pertained to space and rental of existing facilities. Essentially, ABC would continue to rent facilities from XYZ. The negotiations relating to personnel were generally amicable; XYZ had offered certain people who chose to join the U.S. partner the opportunity to return to the Japanese parent company after a two-year trial period, if they found that the U.S. subsidiary was not to their liking. The Japanese partner also assisted by lending some of its staff to help the former joint venture (which has now been absorbed by ABC) with some of the day-to-day work.

In Mr. A's opinion, this was a "very gentlemanly" gesture on the part of XYZ, and ABC clearly appreciated the Japanese generosity in this respect because of the difficulties frequently encountered by foreign firms in recruiting competent Japanese. Mr. A considered the difficulty in recruiting Japanese workers to be the "ultimate nontariff barrier." In his opinion, it was not only difficult for a foreign firm to recruit the graduates from elite universities, but also hard for "anybody to work for a foreign firm."

On the whole, Mr. A characterized the negotiations at the top level as amicable. ABC Corporation essentially got what it wanted. "There was no antagonism nor animosity," although there were some hostilities at the operational level over differences in opinion, particularly between Japanese personnel from either parent company. At the time of the negotiations, however, the goals of both partners were compatible. The Japanese wanted and gained access to the U.S. partner's products by serving as its OEM distributor so that it could continue to support its end of the business. The U.S. partner wanted and obtained control over the marketing and manufacturing operations and was henceforward able to direct the joint venture (which has now been absorbed into its wholly owned subsidiary) to pursue activities in those areas in which it had a competitive edge. Furthermore, through the dissolution the U.S. company was able to divest itself of those segments of the market that were not very profitable. Thus the overall goals of the two partners were fairly compatible, and most of the demands of both parties were accommodated in the dissolution agreement.

When the negotiations were over, however, and ABC actually took over the operation of the company, Mr. A indicated that they "weren't very happy, to say the least, with what they got." Mr. A noted that the situation was perhaps analogous to the purchase of a used car: "After we had some very good negotiations with the car dealer over this used car and we paid the money, when we drove the vehicle out of the lot down the street, the engine broke down."

To their dismay, ABC's executives discovered that the joint-venture company had been grossly mismanaged, especially in the six months immediately preceding the transition. The U.S. company discovered severe problems in how operational decisions were made, such as how pricing policies were determined and the way orders were accepted. In short, ABC concluded that "good judgment" in decision making had clearly been lacking. This mismanagement could be attributed in part to the fact that toward the end the Japanese partner realized that it did not have to "live with this business very much longer"; consequently, it did not care much about what would happen to it eventually. When the former joint venture is merged with the wholly owned subsidiary, the U.S. parent company will exercise tighter control over its operations.

Although the negotiations were turbulent at times, neither side resorted to arbitration or sued the other. This may reflect the negative attitude toward litigation in Japanese society. There were instances in which questions of fact were put to an independent auditor; these questions, however, pertained primarily to accounting and to how the agreement was to be interpreted under the present circumstances. There was no problem in selecting an independent auditor because the same accounting firm represented both companies. In Mr. A's words: "These were all very friendly arbitrations because we were just determining questions of fact. In general, we were able to agree. The negotiations were hard, but we really did not have to bring outsiders in at all."

It was interesting to see whether there were attorneys on either negotiating team. Mr. A indicated that for ABC, the executives from the U.S. company conducted all the negotiations and made all the basic decisions that led to the final signing of the agreement. These executives occasionally traveled to Tokyo. Some of the negotiations were done through correspondence, others in person. The U.S. side was assisted by an attorney who would then contact his Japanese counterpart. In Mr. A's opinion: "In general, our executives and theirs made agreements in principle. Then it was turned over to their in-house lawyer and maybe some outside counsel, who would then get in touch and send drafts to our attorney. Our counsel would periodically ask us what was important and what he should do. We gave him instructions. Then he completed the legal work in the negotiations. But he was not a decision maker, just an advisor."

The Japanese manager of ABC's wholly owned subsidiary, who would take over the management of the joint-venture operation, was not involved in the negotiations because the retired president of ABC felt that, given the past conflict this manager had with some of the executives from ANX and XYZ, his presence might complicate matters, even though ABC understood the nature and reason of these disputes. A second reason for not involving the Japanese manager was that the retired president of ABC "felt more comfortable simplifying the negotiations by making them come *entirely* from the American head office" [emphasis added].

The negotiations were conducted in both lanaguages. A key executive from XYZ had worked in the United States before and hence was fluent in English. He basically acted as the interpreter for both sides. Sometimes ABC brought along its own Japanese employees, who were also bilingual; but the individual from XYZ did most of the interpretation. There were no language problems because the key executive from XYZ was very fluent and had an excellent command of English, including business and technical terms. Furthermore, given his position in the company, he was authorized to make important decisions, although he occasionally had to consult with his management. At times, however, the Americans from corporate headquarters felt frustrated because the Japanese from either company would "go flying off arguing" in their native tongue, and what transpired was never fully translated into English. Consequently, the Americans "felt left out" in some instances. Other than this frustration, Mr. A felt that the translation was adequate and that they were able to convey their sentiments on all issues.

Reasons for Dissolution

Some of the reasons leading to the breakdown of the joint venture between the U.S. and Japanese will be summarized and anlayzed in this section.

Financial Situation

Although the joint venture turned in a profit in certain years, it had failed to establish itself as a financially sound and profitable company, nor was it "big enough to be able to cover all its overhead." In Mr. A's opinion, "It is the kind of operation that is probably suited to be the division of a bigger corporate entity." Ultimately, a joint operation has to be profitable, or there is little or no incentive for either partner to continue the relationship. In this case XYZ was an atypical Japanese company in that it appeared to be more concerned about the short-term profitability of the company than was its U.S. counterpart. In Mr. A's words, "At the very end, it came to a point where they were squeezed on the short-term bottom line, and they had to do something to help it out." XYZ Company was under tremendous profit pressures at the time, and the focus of its operation was drifting further and further away from its core business. In Mr. A's opinion, "Ironically, the Japanese were looking for the short-term benefits, and we, the Americans, were aiming at long-term market development." ABC Corporation preferred to reinvest its profits in the company for purposes of developing market share.

Diverging Interests

The partners were initially brought together by a complementarity of needs and interests. When ABC's efforts became more concentrated in a particular aspect of industrial activity, whereas XYZ was more heavily involved in general process instrumentation, the original objective was gone. When both sides felt that there were no further benefits to be had from the establishment of the joint venture, the only alternative was dissolution. Although cultural differences estranged the two partners, they were not responsible for this divergence of interest. In Mr. A's words: "The kinds of problems we experienced could have happened if our partners were Americans. We were just basically going in different directions."

Inadequate Control

Although ANX was a 50-50 partnership between ABC Corporation and XYZ Company, equity ownership did not necessarily mean equal control over management and operations of the venture. When asked whether the failure of the joint venture could be attributed in part to the fact that the U.S. partner did not exercise sufficient control over the operations of the venture, Mr. A responded: "Although we always look back over life and see what we would do differently, I would say that was not a basic problem. After all, we are a long distance away." He did admit that the joint venture "somewhat lacked control and was run on a generally informal basis."

The U.S. company was primarily responsible for providing the technological and product know-how, but the actual management of the joint venture was left entirely in the hands of the Japanese partner. The U.S. parent essentially ran the company as an over-the-counter kind of business, with only quarterly visits by the company's Asian manager to review performance over the past three months and discuss plans for the future. As evident from the previous cases, this approach may be inadequate and may partially account for the fact that the U.S. parent was not fully informed about the reasons for the reorganization of top management in 1980, and was generally kept in the dark about how operational decisions were made, such as how orders were accepted and pricing policies determined within the joint venture.

Consequently, when negotiations for the dissolution of the joint venture began and immediately after the dissolution, the U.S. parent was totally confounded about the operations of the company. In Mr. A's words, the U.S. parent company had "questions on supporting data behind expense-account transactions, handling business that was entered as incoming orders on the basis of hopes rather than reality, and the detailed investigation of the estimated cost to finish jobs that were taken at unattractive prices by the previous administration of ANX Company."

Further complicating the lack of control by the U.S. parent company was the fact that most of the employees in the joint venture came from the Japanese parent company. Hence there was the problem of divided loyalty as exhibited in disagreements that became visible during the negotiations for dissolution, and as evidenced by the fact that after the dissolution most of the employees of ANX Company chose to return to the Japanese parent company. Only a few decided to join the U.S. parent company, and even these received a guarantee from the Japanese partner that after a two-year trial period they could return to the Japanese parent company.

In Mr. A's opinion, the joint venture "forever existed as an appendage to the entire XYZ Company." This was understandable to some extent because many of the people who worked for the joint venture still viewed themselves as employees of XYZ Company. Consequently, although the U.S. partner offered marketing ideas and suggestions, these were largely ignored by the Japanese partner because its interests lay elsewhere; the employees simply acted accordingly.

Because of divided loyalties, a clear distinction was often made between the Japanese from ABC Corporation and those from XYZ Company. As noted previously, in 1977 ABC established a wholly owned subsidiary in Japan that hired some Japanese on its own whose basic loyalties were to ABC Corporation. For some reason the latter never got on well with the Japanese from XYZ and ANX. In Mr. A's words, the Japanese managers from ABC's wholly owned subsidiary and a number of the operational people at XYZ "had some moments together that weren't as nice as we would like."

There had always been personality differences between the two groups of Japanese, and one of the Japanese associated with the original joint venture left to join ABC's wholly owned subsidiary. Throughout the years the relationship among the three key Japanese involved in the operation of the joint venture (two from ANX and the one who left ANX to join ABC's wholly owned subsidiary) were far from cordial. In Mr. A's words, "For whatever reason, each of them mistrusted the others."

Besides personality conflicts, one possible reason for such clashes could be that there is still a social stigma associated with Japanese who choose to work for a foreign firm, particularly individuals who leave a U.S.-Japanese joint venture to work for a U.S. firm. Hence relationships among the Japanese from the two parent companies were fairly tense at times. Consequently, the retired president of ABC was wise in keeping the Japanese manager of the wholly owned subsidiary out of the negotiations for the dissolution of the joint venture. His presence would certainly have exacerbated the conflicts. Conversely, it could be argued that given this Japanese manager's aggressiveness, his familiarity with the language and cultural innuendoes, and his "innate skepticism" about XYZ Company, had he been introduced into the negotiations, he might have discovered problems with the operations earlier in the negotiating process, which could in turn have affected the course of action adopted by ABC. The problems of the joint venture, however, may have been so deep-rooted and well concealed that no one could discern the real extent of the difficulties until later, when they surfaced. Mr. A indicated that there is "some evidence that even our partner and the joint venture arrangement might not have known about some of the more serious difficulties much earlier than we did."

Form of Ownership

As Maurer of Merck & Co. pointed out, it is important that a company decide on a mode of market entry with which it is comfortable. Some companies can share ownership and control with other entities; others may be uncomfortable with the process of making decisions jointly with other companies, particularly foreign concerns. In general, companies that are run as family-held concerns (that is, where top management is concentrated in the hands of family members) tend to experience greater difficulties in operating joint ventures. In this case all of ABC's operations, except for the three joint ventures in Asia, are on a wholly owned basis. Mr. A indicated that his company did not like to enter into joint-venture agreements and would avoid them where possible. Asked to explain the reasons for this, he indicated that there were often tremendous difficulties concerning management control. Furthermore: "We find that in all joint ventures we were involved in, we ended up having to provide the technology. We also had to provide the general management directions. The other side would provide the physical facilities and people. We felt that since we were really doing all the work, we should then be able to have complete control over the situation."

Thus from ABC's standpoint, a joint venture represents a dilution of control over technological know-how. Furthermore, Mr. A went on to explain that there are always problems of divided loyalty in a joint venture: "People had their loyalties elsewhere, and we were not going to get their complete loyalty." This leads to a dilution of managerial control.

The company's traditional dislike for joint ventures, coupled with its lack of actual involvement in the administration and management of ANX, compounded this problem of lack of control. Although the Japanese partner's opinion on this was not surveyed, it could be surmised that, given that, first, the company was run primarily as a family-held concern with top management concentrated in the hands of the family of the founding father, and second, XYZ had not entered into joint ventures with other concerns (other than the one with ABC that which has now been dissolved), the Japanese partner might be equally uncomfortable with joint-venture arrangements. As Mr. A indicated earlier, the joint-venture company was always treated "as an appendage" of the Japanese parent. It was staffed and run pretty much as a wholly owned subsidiary rather than as a joint venture with a U.S. partner. Hence it might be unwilling to share responsibilities or accommodate the needs of its partner.

Given these preferences by both partners, it is not surprising that a joint-venture arrangement involving joint decision making, control, and collaborative activities in practically all aspects of the firm's operations did not fit in with either company's philosophy, and consequently alienated the partners from each other.

Cultural Differences

Mr. A conceded that there was a "myriad of problems" caused by cultural differences. Although he refused specifically to spell out the details of these problems, he indicated that cultural differences posed a "very major problem in our relations with our own Japanese employees" and the customers. As noted in chapters 1 and 2, the relationships a Japanese company has with its employees and customers are very different from those in a U.S. setting. The customer is generally accorded a higher priority in a typical U.S. company, whereas the employees are paramount in a Japanese organization. Further-more, there are certain mutual obligations in these relationships; a foreign firm may sometimes have difficulty working within this system.

Although Mr. A felt that cultural differences did not significantly im-pede the progress or the outcome of the negotiations, he acknowledged that they did have a bearing on the situation: "I can't say that at the end of the negotiations I really knew who was in charge." He believed that most of the basic decisions were made by the group vice-president at XYZ, although the latter occasionally had to caucus with top mangement. In general, however, given the differences in styles of decision making and negotiating practices of Japanese firms, Mr. A was not able to read the situation as well as he would have in a U.S. or even a European context.

Differences in Perceptions

As Kapoor (1975) notes, either partner's perceptions of the other could significantly influence the progress and outcome of a negotiating situation. In this case the misperceptions the U.S. partner had of the Japanese may have affected the joint-venture relationship. As noted earlier, Mr. A had always thought that the joint venture was considered prestigious by XYZ. Thus the U.S. partner assumed that XYZ would do everything to nurture this venture, accommodate the interests of its U.S. partner, and make the operation successful. This may explain in part why ABC was willing to leave the management and administration of the joint venture entirely in the hands of the Japanese partner.

This perception, however, turned out to be inaccurate. Although the Japanese wanted access to ABC's products, they were not overenthusiastic about the joint venture, and in fact were quick to express their misgivings. Furthermore, the Japanese first raised the issue of dissolution, given the un-profitability of the venture and the lack of fit between the partners.

Negotiating Tactics

Mr. A was asked to comment on any perceived difference in negotiating tac-tics between the Japanese and the Americans. He indicated that although there were not many, he did notice a few, one of them the practice of "huddling among themselves" where possible. This could be related to the consensus decision-making process. A second difference was that the Japanese would "throw something out and if we come back hard, they would have a chance to retreat to their inner circles and decide how they should do it." This is consistent with the remarks made by a number of U.S. firms that although the Japanese tend to be persistent in their demands, they are also vague so that they can easily withdraw from a position without a loss of face.

A third difference is that since the U.S. partner generally relied on the executive from XYZ to serve as the interpreter, the Japanese had a tendency to discuss matters among themselves in their native tongue when ABC's Japanese employees were absent so that the Americans would not know what was being said.

Although the negotiations lasted more than a year, Mr. A felt that the time factor was not used as a negotiating ploy here. He indicated that the Americans were prepared to wait until all the issues were resolved to their satisfaction before signing the final agreement.

Operations of a Wholly Owned Subsidiary

Now that the joint venture has been dissolved and merged with ABC Corporation's wholly owned Japanese subsidiary, Mr. A was asked to comment on whether his company anticipates any difficulties in operating a wholly owned subsidiary in Japan. Mr. A indicated that although there are major problems for foreign companies in operating in Japan, which stem from both cultural differences and nontariff barriers: "I don't think they relate to whether you are 100- or 50-percent owned. We do not see that as making any major difference." Mr. A believed that "the difference between a joint venture and a wholly owned subsidiary in Japan is not that meaningful because there are problems in operating either one."

A major difficulty in running a wholly owned subsidiary would be the problem of recruiting competent Japanese to work for the foreign firm. This was the reason that the joint venture was staffed primarily by personnel from its Japanese parent company. Now that the joint venture has been dissolved, its former Japanese parent company is still lending some of its staff to help the U.S. partner run the day-to-day operations of the company. Eventually ABC plans to hire its own staff, but the company realizes that this will be very difficult.

Mr. A indicated that the company had so far been lucky to hire a young salesman "with some entrepreneurial flair" from a large trading company because this individual was dissatisfied with the slower rates of promotion typical of Japanese companies. Furthermore, they were able to attract a few talented managers from the joint venture to work for the wholly owned subsidiary; but, as noted earlier, two of the key executives have since resigned.

Mr. A was asked whether, given the nationalistic sentiments of the Japanese, those people who chose to work for ABC would be regarded negatively by their fellow Japanese. Mr. A acknowledged that in general those Japanese who choose to work for foreign companies are "looked down on by many of their compatriots." He was further asked whether the dissolution of the joint venture would be negatively perceived by the Japanese employees, given their attitude toward loyalty and commitment to one's employer. He indicated that this could be a potential problem because many of the employees were shaken up by the dissolution and greatly concerned about their future with the company. Many chose to revert back to the Japanese parent because of the guarantee of lifetime employment. Furthermore, those who chose to join the U.S. firm were promised an opportunity to return to the Japanese parent firm after a two-year trial period. Given the Japanese employees' concern with job security, the U.S. company had to provide assurances that all of them would be provided for in some way after the dissolution.

Mr. A recounted the difficulties his company had had in trying to recruit competent Japanese. In the past ABC had used the services of a U.S. management-search firm (which had a Japanese operation) to hire a managing director for one of their operations in another part of Asia and an administrative manager for the Japanese operation. Under normal circumstances it should be fairly easy to fill the position of administrative manager because the qualified candidate does not have to know much about the company's products, but simply has to be competent in accounting and finance. On the other hand, it should be more difficult to fill the position of managing director.

To Mr. A's surprise, however, the management-recruitment agency had little difficulty in locating five highly qualified candidates for the managing-director position. Furthermore, the individual who was selected for the position "turned out to be excellent." Contrary to expectations, however, ABC was unable to find a "respectable candidate" for the administrative-manager position in Japan for over a year. There were several applicants, but ABC found that many of them had serious health problems. In Mr. A's words: "It was literally getting the deaf, dumb, and the lame. We can take a chance, in the States—say a brilliant individual who had a long-term health problem whom we had a chance at. We couldn't do that in a small company. If the guy isn't able to work, you really lose a lot. We searched for over a year and really had great difficulty. Finally we got a man on our own. From that you get the feeling that unless you are lucky, you really have trouble getting people."

This ties in with the comment made by Maurer of Merck & Co. that in all his years of operation in Japan, he had never made a single personnel decision because he knew that Murphy's Law would always operate. The attributes that make a good manager in the United States and Europe are very different from those in Japan. Mr. A indicated that an alternative would be to send over a U.S. expatriate; but given the vast cultural differences between the two countries, the American might never "quite fit in the cultural milieu." In a comparative study of U.S., European, and Japanese multinationals, the failure rate was highest for U.S. expatriates (Tung 1982d). Furthermore, the study showed that the two principal reasons for a U.S. expatriate's inability to perform effectively in a foreign country were lack of human-relations skills and inability of the expatriate's family to adjust to a foreign cultural environment.

In Mr. A's opinion, the other major problem in operating in Japan pertains to nontariff barriers; but he believed that these are the same regardless of whether the operation is wholly or 50-percent owned. Although some nontariff barriers to foreign products remain, an influential Japanese partner who has access to the local market and is knowledgeable about local market conditions may help minimize these barriers to entry and facilitate operation in Japan. In the case of Merck & Co., for instance, it was noted that where influential members of the Japanese business and academic communities were called on to serve as members of the executive advisory committee in the joint venture, they could often provide invaluable advice to the company about penetrating the formidable Japanese market.

Mr. A does not anticipate any problems from the Japanese government with respect to the operation of a wholly owned subsidiary. The government was not involved in the dissolution proceedings in any way, except for granting routine approvals. He indicated that the involvement of the government should be "no more now that we are wholly owned than when we were a joint venture." Even in industries that are designated as strategic, such as computers, it was noted in the Sperry Univac case that the Japanese government never actively interfered in the operations of the company.

Mr. A was asked whether the dissolution of the joint venture could negatively affect his company's future operations in Japan. He noted that this would be an interesting development to watch. On the positive side, through the dissolution of the joint venture, the U.S. parent has acquired total control over the management and marketing of the operation and is consequently able to steer the company in those directions in which it feels it has a competitive edge. On the negative side, in Mr. A's opinion: "Anytime you liquidate a venture, that reflects negatively in some way. We lose some support of our partner. They were able to give us some help that we won't be able to get now. I think this had to happen. It has its pluses and minuses. It just had to happen for our business development."

A difficulty with the dissolution of some joint ventures relates to the fact that the former partner may be a dangerous competitor in the local market. Mr. A did not perceive this as a major problem for two reasons. First, if the two companies had enough common elements, the venture would not have been dissolved. Hence the products manufactured and sold by both companies should not be competitive. Second, since ABC Corporation already has so many competitors in the Japanese market, "It really does not make much difference to have one more."

Advice

After this sobering experience, Mr. A was asked to offer some advice to other foreign firms faced with a similar situation; in other words, if ABC had the opportunity to relive the entire joint venture over again, what would it do differently? Mr. A indicated that he did not have much advice on the actual negotiations "other than the usual thing that all the *i*s are dotted and the *t*s are crossed" because once the two partners have irreconcilable differences, there is nothing to do except salvage as much as possible from the operation and make sure that the separation is as clean-cut as it can be. Mr. A noted that although "it was a tough, sobering experience, the negotiations weren't all that bad." This is perhaps the value of the contractual agreement. If details are clearly spelled out in the original document, then disputes over the terms of separation will be minimal.

Mr. A indicated that ABC learned a lot about the operation and management of a company from this incident—for example, "knowing what's really going on, and trying to control any operation." Much of what it learned may not pertain to the "specific difficulties of doing business in Japan," but rather to the problems of management in general. One important lesson was "to dig more deeply into the details of the operations of a company. Our reasons are several. First, in a joint venture not all the management have your complete interest at heart or have their future tied up with your company. They may be more willing to gloss over things and do other suboptimal activities than someone who is an unquestioned employee of your firm. Also, with the Japanese tendency to avoid conflict, it is easier for problems to be hidden until too late. Also we have learned that a business with a long-term quotation/delivery period needs much tighter control than an over-the-counter business, which is typical of the rest of our operations."

A mistake commonly made by U.S. firms is to believe that equal partnership will automatically translate into parity of control, which may not necessarily be true. To maintain control, the U.S. firm has to keep in constant touch with the company, rather than rely on the Japanese partner to relate difficulties or problems every quarter. Because of differences in perceptions and ways of doing business, if the U.S. partner depends solely on the Japanese partner for information, it may already be too late to salvage a relationship when the situation reaches a crisis. What is needed is an early-warning system that will keep the U.S. partner appraised of any problems. Furthermore, in this instance ABC was definitely more comfortable with the operation of wholly owned subsidiaries, which apparently was also the case with its Japanese partner. Given these preferences, both partners have significant difficulties in collaborative teamwork, which is paramount to the successful operation of a joint venture.

Concluding Remarks

This case provided some interesting insights into the reasons behind the dissolution of a joint venture operation in Japan, and the negotiations for the dissolution. Although this may be an isolated incident, many of the factors responsible for the breakdown in the relationships could apply to other situations and should serve as a guide to other foreign companies that hope to cooperate successfully with a Japanese entity.

9 The Dos and Don'ts of Business Negotiations with the Japanese

For a variety of reasons, the number of joint cooperative agreements between U.S. and Japanese entities has mushroomed in the past decade and is expected to increase in the years ahead. One reason is the desire to share in the fruits of the Japanese economic miracle. Japan is one of the fastest growing economies in the world and has the second-highest gross national product in the noncommunist world. Consequently, there appear to be ample opportunities for U.S. firms that seek to expand their worldwide operations. Second, although Japan has liberalized its inward capital investment considerably over the past two decades, there are still barriers to penetrating the Japanese market, as discussed in chapters 1 and 2. Thus a joint-venture arrangement with a Japanese partner may appear to be the most viable route of entry into the country. Third, Japan has made rapid strides in technology; in some areas it has surpassed the United States. Consequently, the attitude of an increasing number of U.S. firms is "if you can't beat them, join them," and generate synergy rather than wasting resources trying to compete against them. Fourth, joint venturing allows the U.S. partner to exercise greater control than does licensing. Many U.S. multinationals view licensing as a least preferred mode of entry because of lack of control over technology and management. Fifth, because of the rising tide of protectionism on the part of the United States, many Japanese view joint ventures with U.S. partners in the United States as a means of circumventing any restrictions that may be imposed in the future (*Wall Street Journal,* 10 May 1983, p. 37).

The prospects for joint cooperation between U.S. and Japanese enterprises abound in the decades ahead. These opportunities, however, are usually fraught with challenges and frustrations. From the foregoing chapters it appears that although there is no single form of collaborative agreement or set formula for conducting business negotiations that can ensure successful penetration into the Japanese market, there are indeed common denominators to smooth operations in virtually all instances. These factors will be summarized and discussed in this chapter. This advice is offered by business people who have engaged in negotiations with the Japanese, including the six case studies presented earlier. The absence of such factors may lead to the disintegration and eventual demise of such collaborative efforts. The chapter will also examine some of the common themes perceived by U.S. negotiators pertaining to conducting business negotiations and implementing cooperative agreements with the Japanese.

Patience

Most Americans who have negotiated with the Japanese will readily acknowledge that the experience is unique. Although the negotiations can generally be characterized as cordial, they can also tax one's patience. An American doing business in Japan has to abandon his usual time frame and allow matters to proceed at their own pace, which is characteristically unhurried.

A number of factors have contributed to the general slowness in the progress of negotiations. First, as noted in chapter 2, human relations are fundamental to any kind of transaction, including business agreements, in Japan. These are usually developed over years of personal association. The Japanese need time to observe a prospective partner because a business agreement, like a marriage, once entered into is generally viewed as inviolate, and not to be easily discontinued according to the whims of the partners.

Second, although some top-level decisions are made through the mechanism described as one screech of the crane, approximately 90 percent of decisions at the middle- and lower-management levels are made through consensus. Even in the former instances, it is rare that a Japanese will unilaterally adopt a decision that may alienate the rest of the organizational members. In the case of Inoue, who entered into the joint venture with W.R. Grace, even though he was the owner/entrepreneur and did not have to consult with others in the organization to make important decisions, he felt it was his moral obligation and responsibility to explain and justify to his people why he undertook a certain course of action. In a slightly different vein, in the case of Fujisawa Pharmaceutical Co., Ltd., since Snable did not speak Japanese, he was not able to participate in all the important decisions. He noted, however, that his Japanese colleagues would never simply override him on a decision if they knew he felt strongly. Any difference in opinion is meticulously worked out among the individuals concerned until some form of consensus is reached. These procedures are often time-consuming.

Third, the Japanese generally have a longer-term orientation in planning; they look at what will happen ten or twenty years in the future. Hence delays of a few months or sometimes even years may appear inconsequential from their perspective. It is important to allow things to occur naturally in Japan, even though it may take time.

Fourth, since language barriers generally exist between U.S. and Japanese negotiators, interpreters are often used. This means that the negotiations may take twice as long with all the translations to and from a given language. Even where interpreters are not used and the discussions are conducted in English, the Americans may need to repeat information several times and exercise caution to ensure that their Japanese counterparts accurately understand the issues. In the case of SmithKline, for instance, in a session that lasted for four hours, the Japanese punctuated each sentence with the phrase, "Do you understand?" believing it meant "Do you agree?" The U.S. partner responded in the affirmative, meaning not that consensus had been reached but only that they "understood." These language barriers tend to prolong the negotiations.

For all these reasons, matters generally do not progress as rapidly as many Americans would like or expect. Americans who fly to Japan and expect to conclude an agreement within three to four weeks will be disappointed because things simply do not happen that way in Japan. Tales of such misadventures fill the air in the pub at the Hotel Okura, a favorite haunt of U.S. businessmen. In the words of W.F. Corkran, vice-president of international operations, Preformed Line Products Company (a manufacturer of a proprietary line of fitting for transmission and distribution lines used in communication and power industries), "There is a very hectic pressure in our society to come back with success immediately."

Throughout the cases, it can be observed that the negotiations for the formation (including dissolution) of the joint agreements often took years. In the words of Stanley Epstein, president of Anglo American Aviation Company, who had experiences with a number of Japanese general trading companies, it is important for Americans not only to understand this different time frame of reference in the Japanese context, but also to impress on their Japanese counterparts that "regardless of the length of time, they will stay in there to continue the negotiations until there is a clear understanding that everybody is working from a standpoint of advantage. If you can keep these in your mind during the negotiations, then you will be successful, at least from my experience. It is frustrating, exasperating, and time-consuming; but they have always turned out to be satisfactory."

Mutual Trust

Given the Japanese emphasis on human relations and the traditional dislike for law and litigation, business transactions are generally based on mutual trust and respect. Each partner must demonstrate a genuine willingness to understand and respect the interests and desires of the other party. Furthermore, because of the belief that a contractual agreement is an organic document that must change with evolving conditions, the continuation of a mutually beneficial relationship between the partners cannot depend solely on the written contract. Rather, there must be an implicit trust between the partners that whatever courses of action may be adopted in the future, it will be in the best interest of the venture as a whole. This points to the need, first, to develop long-term working relationships in Japan, and second, to try to have an intermediary (usually a mutual friend of both partners) who can in a sense vouch for the conduct or behavior of either party.

To promote mutual trust between the parties, there should be continuity in the relationships. Given the shorter-term orientation of most U.S. multinationals, there tends to be fairly rapid rotation of U.S. staff. The average duration of an overseas assignment for an American is typically two to three years, compared with five years for most Japanese expatriates. This policy of rapid turnover has led the Japanese to complain that it is difficult to befriend a U.S. staff member because by the time they begin to know the American, he is transferred elsewhere. In the case of business negotiations that may extend over several years, the members of the U.S. team may have changed completely in the interim, while those on the Japanese side may be largely the same. This lack of continuity in the composition of negotiating team members may often place the Americans at a disadvantage because of their inability to recall incidents that may have transpired before, and may limit their overall perspective on the situation.

Respect for Cultural Differences

The tremendous differences in social and cultural systems between the United States and Japan are reflected in the variations in principles of industrial management in the two countries. These differences, discussed in some detail in chapter 2, pose problems of adjustment for American firms. For decades, the Japanese have been assiduous students of U.S. styles of management and are knowledgeable about U.S. cultural values and traditions. Even today, when Japanese multinationals send people on overseas assignments, they prepare the expatriates through intensive language-training programs and study of the cultural norms of the host country, including several months of sharing the same dormitory with Americans and other Caucasians so that the Japanese trainees can be steeped in foreign practices (Tung 1984).

Americans, on the other hand, have generally adopted an ethnocentric approach to management and in most instances expect the foreign partner to make all the necessary accommodations. This attitude is not well received in Japan. Even when U.S. firms recognize the need to give their expatriates a nodding familiarity with the country of assignment, this may not be sufficient because mere knowledge of such differences does not necessarily imply the ability to cope with them.

In the words of Corkran: "there are differences in the culture—face saving, cult of obligation, patience, group thinking, and so on. To try to keep all this in your head when you are negotiating, when you are brought up in a completely different culture with very different views, is kind of difficult, as one is unconsciously motivated by what one thinks and what one has been used to in one's culture. It is very difficult to sit down and be thinking about a completely different modus operandi. You may be saying something to a Japanese, but he may not hear it the same way."

Similarly, even a Japanese well versed in the English language may not understand the message conveyed, at least not in the way intended by the U.S. speaker. For this reason, Corkran recommended engaging the services of a bilingual member who can not only perform literal translations, but also present issues in a manner palatable to the Japanese audience. In his opinion, "This sort of interpreting is a real art."

Maurer, of Merck, Sharp and Dohme International, discusses the issues with his Japanese staff before each negotiating session. The latter then convey these messages in the way he feels would be most appropriate. Maurer himself can remain silent during the negotiations beyond the exchange of formalities at the beginning and end of each session. A bilingual member of one's negotiating team can provide an accurate reading of the situation and give advice on how to stay away from certain sensitive issues.

In short, to compete effectively in the Japanese market, the U.S. firm must understand the variations in cultural and industrial systems between the two countries and, more important, accommodate such differences. This often requires tremendous adjustments.

Need to Study the Market and Work within the System

The Japanese market is unique. Its systems of marketing and distribution are very different from those of the United States. Some Americans, confusing modernization with Westernization, assume that since Japan is highly industrialized and modernized, the American and Japanese markets are similar, and hence that what sells in the United States will also find a niche in the Japanese market. This erroneous assumption could cost a firm millions of dollars on an aborted project.

There are substantial differences between the life-styles and buying behavior of U.S. and Japanese consumers. Given the highly developed Japanese economy, unoriginal products do not sell well in the country. A U.S. firm has to research the Japanese market thoroughly to determine whether there is a demand for its products and, if so, what types of modifications need to be made. For example, large refrigerators, which are the norm in the United States, do not suit Japanese needs because of the smaller size of the houses and the shopping patterns of families.

In the case of Merck & Co., for instance, when 'Blocadren' was marketed in the United States and Europe, the results of the control study indicating that the product can reduce the incidence of a second, fatal heart attack were highlighted. This was appropriate because of the high incidences of cardiovascular disease in these countries. Since such occurrences are minimal in Japan, however, the sales pitch there has to emphasize the remedial properties of the drug for hypertension, which *is* a problem in the country. These examples point up the need for foreign manufacturers to research the Japanese market thoroughly in order to determine the right product to sell and how to market it.

Since the system of distribution and the relationship between suppliers and customers in Japan are steeped in traditions that date back several centuries, it may be difficult for foreign firms to change them. Rather, they should understand such differences and work within them. For example, given the limited storage space and facilities of most Japanese firms, inventory deliveries have to be made more frequently than in the United States.

Another difference is in the terms of credit extended to one's customers. In the case of Epstein of Anglo American Aviation Company, his firm had once tried to establish an independent operation in Japan but failed—hence the decision to market through a Japanese general trading company. The independent operation turned out to be a disaster primarily because its customers, which were sub- or prime contractors in the Japanese aerospace industry, "did not have the facilities to pay their bills promptly. They required a massive amount of local credit, which we might have been able to acquire from U.S. banks domiciled in Japan on a common ledger sheet. In the final analysis, however, the amount of leverage acceptable in Japan is not acceptable in the United States. So there was just no way to go forward and compete in the Japanese market providing the credits that would normally be expected by the customer." These credit facilities stem from the supplier-customer relationship and the high debt/equity ratios prevalent in Japanese corporations. To compete effectively with Japanese manufacturers, the U.S. firm has to extend the same services and facilities, which may be difficult or impossible at times because of the different criteria used in performance evaluation by many U.S. firms. For this reason, Kinch of W.R. Grace had to convince top management in corporate headquarters to adjust their criterion on return on investment in their Japanese operation.

The neophyte U.S. firm that tries to penetrate the Japanese market is advised to seek assistance from U.S. and Japanese entities familiar with local market conditions, and to learn from the positive and negative experiences of other foreign companies in Japan. Furthermore, U.S. firms should not be shy about soliciting the assistance of knowledgeable and influential members of the Japanese academic and business communities to provide information on market needs and characteristics, just as the Japanese have benefited from such associations when they operate in the United States.

Type of Industry

Given the extremely competitive Japanese market, in order to be successful, the products and services marketed by foreign manufacturers have to be unique. Furthermore, they have to fit in with overall national objectives. Although the Japanese economy is not centrally planned, the government exercises considerable influence over the operations of the industrial sector through the principle of administrative guidance; and businesses operate within the broad framework of the country's industrial policy, as discussed in chapters 1 and 2. Because of the practice of industrial targeting, foreign firms operating in areas designated as growth sectors will either receive very favorable treatment, as in the case of Boeing Commercial Airplane Company, where the Japanese participants have been overly accommodating to U.S. terms, or be placed at a significant competitive disadvantage because of the protections and incentives provided by the Japanese government to indigenous enterprises. Furthermore, except for luxury consumer items, there is a distinct preference among local manufacturers to adopt a buy-Japanese policy. The U.S. firm has to examine how its product lines or services fit in with national objectives, and study the nature of competition in a given industry.

Compatibility of Objectives and
Complementarity of Needs

To ensure the continuation of a relationship between the U.S. and Japanese entities, the objectives of the partners have to be compatible. In chapter 8 it was noted that the diverging interests between the two partners were primarily responsible for the breakup of the joint venture. Given the differences in perspectives between U.S. and Japanese entities, the corporate objectives of the companies may often be in conflict. For example, many U.S. firms are concerned with immediate or short-term profitability, whereas Japanese firms typically appear to be obsessed with growth and market share, which often take time to develop and may involve operating losses for several years. This perceived difference in objective, for instance, was responsible for the one-year delay in the progress of the negotiations between SmithKline Beckman Corporation and Fujisawa Pharmaceutical Co., Ltd., for the formation of the second joint venture in the United States. This divergence in objectives was responsible for the dissolution of the joint venture presented in chapter 8. Ironically, in the latter situation it was the Japanese partner that apparently had the shorter-term orientation.

Besides compatibility of goals, a Japanese firm will seldom enter into a collaborative arrangement with a foreign enterprise unless the latter can contribute resources that other Japanese entities cannot provide. Conversely, many U.S. multinationals would not choose a joint venture with a Japanese firm unless there are clear advantages to be had from the relationship, such as circumvention of certain nontariff barriers to trade, provision of Japanese personnel for the operation, access to the market, and so on. In many instances the U.S. partner is responsible for technological inputs, and the relationship will continue as long as the joint venture depends on the parent company for expertise in this area. Consequently, it is important for the parent company to maintain a technological edge over its joint-venture subsidiary. If they are on a par or the latter supersedes the former, then the motivation that originally brought the two partners together dissipates; hence there may be no incentive to continue the relationship.

The importance of both compatibility of objectives and complementarity of needs to the successful formation and operation of a collaborative agreement points to the need to select one's partner carefully. A U.S. firm should research thoroughly the capabilities of prospective candidates for contractual agreements in Japan. Again, intermediaries can provide valuable assistance. They can help locate prospective candidates whose objectives and capabilities match and complement those of the U.S. firm and, if there is interest on either side, serve as go-betweens.

Equity Share

With the various rounds of liberalization of inward capital investment since the mid-1960s, most industries in Japan are now open to 100-percent foreign-equity ownership. Although there are virtually no legal restrictions on the percentage of equity ownership by U.S. firms, the issue of equity is still sensitive. In the case of SmithKline·Fujisawa K.K., for instance, the Japanese partner originally wanted a licensing agreement. Only after several years of hard persuasion and convincing did Fujisawa Pharmaceutical Co., Ltd., finally concede to a 50-50 joint-venture arrangement. In the case of W.R. Grace, the U.S. partner's desire to have majority control, primarily to consolidate worldwide profits, posed a major stumbling block; it took some time before the Japanese partner could be swayed.

The latter two were joint ventures entered into in the early 1980s. In the 1960s and 1970s, when Japan was just beginning to liberalize its inward capital investment, the issue of percentage of equity ownership was even more problematic. In the words of Corkran, vice-president of Preformed Line Products Company, which entered into a 51-49 joint venture with Fujikura Cable Works in the 1960s, with the latter as majority partner: "In the early years, for all practical purposes, it was not possible to get a majority equity, unless you have a product that the Japanese really want, and hence you could exercise a real lever. There are some of those, but not many."

This may explain why in the case of Nippon Univac Kaisha, where computer technology was urgently needed in the country, Mitsui Trading Company was willing to reduce its original equity position from 70 to 34.7 percent in 1972 when the company went public, and increase Sperry Corporation's share commensurately, from 30 percent in 1958 to 34.7 percent in 1972.

In the case of Merck & Co., because tuberculosis was a major problem in postwar Japan and the U.S. parent company was the manufacturer of streptomycin, the Japanese partner was willing to accept a minority position in a 50.5-49.5 joint-venture agreement. In the case of Boeing Commercial Airplane Company, the Japanese partner initially wanted a larger participation in the joint program for the production of Boeing 767s, but conceded to a smaller share because it was bargaining from a position of weakness. Japan is technologically behind the United States in the area of aircrafts; since the aerospace industry has been designated as one of the growth sectors in the 1980s, the Japanese were willing to make concessions in order to gain access to this much needed technology.

To continue Corkran's comments on the subject, he indicated that the Japanese are often very subtle in their objections to any request for a majority-equity position by the foreign partner. "The U.S. firm would say, 'We want control.' The Japanese would *not* say, 'No,' but the negotiations drag on [emphasis added]. All kinds of problems develop. But as soon as you agree to equal or minority partnership, all of a sudden the problems disappear. This is quite common in negotiations in Japan." Even in the 1980s majority ownership by a U.S. partner is a sensitive issue, as evidenced in the cases of W.R. Grace and SmithKline Beckman Corporation.

Use of Japanese to Manage

Given the tremendous cultural differences between the United States and Japan, which are reflected in the systems of industrial management in the two countries, it may be difficult for an American to manage Japanese employees effectively and relate to local clients. Hence there is a need to use Japanese to manage the day-to-day operations of the joint-venture company.

Problems may develop, however. One is the difficulty of recruiting capable Japanese to work for the company. When the joint-venture company is first established, it often has to rely on the Japanese parent company temporarily to lend its staff to the subsidiary. This may lead to problems of divided loyalty, as was obvious in some of the cases presented in the book. Consequently, as soon as the operation is well established, the joint venture should try to recruit its own Japanese whose commitment would be to the joint-venture company, not to either of the parent companies.

Second, although Japanese managerial staff may be effective in relating to local customers and managing their fellow countrymen, they may have problems of communication with the U.S. parent headquarters. This may not stem from language barriers but from a lack of understanding of the broader goals and objectives of corporate headquarters in the United States. Consequently, the use of a U.S. expatriate or two as liaison between the Japanese joint-venture subsidiary and U.S. headquarters may be necessary.

Need to Maintain Dialogue

Given the differences in culture and industrial practices between the two countries and the Japanese emphasis on human relations, both partners to a venture must maintain constant dialogue to cement the friendly ties between them and avoid misunderstanding. In the cases of Nippon Univac Kaisha and Nippon Merck Banyu, there was constant communication between the two partners and between the parent companies and the joint-venture subsidiary, in the form of personnel exchanges, regularly scheduled meetings, and almost day-to-day contact to keep both sides fully briefed about all aspects of the company's operation. These were supplemented by socializing, which is a common practice in the Japanese context. Other mechanisms for promoting and maintaining relationships between the parties were discussed in chapter 2.

Conversely, in chapter 8, which examines the dissolution of a joint venture, a reason for failure could be attributed to the hands-off approach to management adopted by the U.S. parent company. When contacts between the partners were largely limited to quarterly review sessions plus occasional visits by senior U.S. executives, problems were shielded from the U.S. parent company until they had deteriorated to a point beyond conciliation and compromise.

Although there are few exceptions, it appears that the factors discussed here are crucial to the success of negotiating and collaborating in joint cooperative agreements with the Japanese. Conversely, the absence of such factors may strain the relations between the partners and lead to the eventual collapse of any talks for cooperation. The experiences of the 114 U.S. firms, summarized in the survey findings in chapter 3, and the in-depth interviews with a select sample of firms in the subsequent chapters in the book, provide some insights into how certain U.S. firms have approached the Japanese successfully. Even though the experiences of these firms differ in many respects, the factors that account for the success of these ventures and the advice offered by those individuals who were active participants in the negotiations are basically the same. These were summarized and presented in this chapter.

In conclusion, although the road to success in the Japanese market may be rough at times, the rewards are indeed great. Many U.S. investors have demonstrated that through the correct mix of attributes, these difficulties can be surmounted, with impressive balance sheets to show for one's efforts.

References

Abegglen, J.C. "Narrow Self-Interest: Japan's Ultimate Vulnerability?" In
D. Tasca, ed., *U.S.-Japanese Economic Relations.* New York: Pergamon Press, 1981, pp. 21-31.

Abegglen, J.C.; Kato, T.; Mulkern, L.J.; Kawata, K.; Hoadley, W.E.; and
Narusawa, K., eds., *U.S.-Japan Economic Relations: A Symposium on
Critical Issues.* Berkeley: University of California Press, 1980.

Bacher, T.J. "The Economics of the Civil Aircraft Industry." Paper presented at Conference on the Role of Southeast Asia in World Airline
and Aerospace Development, Singapore, 24-25 September 1981.

Bartholomew, J. "Cultural Values in Japan." In B.M. Richardson and T.
Ueda, eds., *Business and Society in Japan.* New York: Praeger, 1981,
pp. 244-280. (a)

———. "The Impact of Modernization in Japan." In B.M. Richardson
and T. Ueda, eds., *Business and Society in Japan.* New York: Praeger,
1981, pp. 325-332. (b)

Boeing. *Annual Report,* 1981.

"Boeing Earnings Plummeted 49% in 2nd Quarter." *Wall Street Journal,*
3 August 1982, p. 7.

Cole, R.E. "Labor in Japan." In B.M. Richardson and T. Ueda, eds.,
Business and Society in Japan. New York: Praeger, 1981, pp. 29-36.

Corkran, W.F., vice-president, international operations, Preformed Line
Products Company. Interview, 18 May 1982.

Doing Business in Japan. Tokyo: Japan External Trade Organization, 1982.

Epstein, S., president, Anglo American Aviation Company. Interview, 12
May 1982.

Foreign Companies in Japan. Tokyo: Japan External Trade Organization,
1982.

Fujisawa Pharmaceutical Co., Ltd. *Prospectus,* 1981.

Grace Report. *Annual Report,* 1981.

Graham, J.L. "A Hidden Cause of America's Trade Deficit with Japan."
Columbia Journal of World Business, Fall 1981, pp. 5-14.

Gubbins, J.H. *The Progress of Japan: 1853-1871.* Oxford: Clarendon Press,
1911.

Hahn, E.J. "Negotiating with the Japanese." *California Lawyer* 2(1982):
21-59.

Hall, E.T. *The Silent Language.* New York: Anchor Press/Doubleday, 1973.

Haitani, K. *The Japanese Economic System.* Lexington, Mass.: Lexington
Books, D.C. Heath and Company, 1976.

Hughey, A., and Kanabayashi, M. "More U.S. and Japanese Companies Decide to Operate Joint Ventures." *Wall Street Journal,* 10 May 1983, p. 37.

"IBM Discusses Possible Venture with Japanese Firm." *Wall Street Journal,* 17 February 1983, p. 2.

Ishikawa, K. "The Regulation of the Employer-Employee Relationship: Japanese Labor-Relations Law." In A.T. von Mehren, ed., *Law in Japan: The Legal Order in a Changing Society.* Cambridge, Mass.: Harvard University Press, 1963, pp. 439-473.

Jaffe, T. "A Stitch in Time." *Forbes,* 22 November 1982, pp. 114-118.

Japan as an Export Market. Tokyo: Japan External Trade Organization, 1980.

"Japanese Approve Bill Easing Requirements for Range of Imports." *Wall Street Journal,* 19 May 1983, p. 38.

Japanese Consumer. Tokyo: Japan External Trade Organization, 1980.

Japanese Corporate Decision Making. Tokyo: Japan External Trade Organization, 1982.

Japanese Corporate Personnel Management. Tokyo: Japan External Trade Organization, 1982.

"Japan's Jobless Rate Tops 2.7%, a 30-Year High." *Wall Street Journal,* 9 March 1983, p. 32.

"Japan Will Sign Memorandum with Boeing on Plane Project." *Japan Economic Journal,* 25 January 1983.

Johnson, C. *MITI and the Japanese Miracle.* Stanford, Calif.: Stanford University Press, 1982.

Kanabayashi, M. "Japanese Aerospace Industry Takes Off as Government Defense Spending Grows." *Wall Street Journal,* 18 May 1982, p. 35.

_____ . "Japan's Economy Expected to Stay Weak in 1983, with Some Recovery Late in Year." *Wall Street Journal,* 1 February 1983, p. 38.

_____ . "As Japan's Auto Parts Firms Look to Start U.S. Plants, Joint Efforts Seen Most Viable." *Wall Street Journal,* 9 March 1983, p. 34.

Kapoor, A. *Planning for International Business Negotiations.* Cambridge, Mass.: Ballinger, 1975.

Kawashima, T. "Dispute Resolution in Contemporary Japan." In A.T. von Mehren, ed., *Law in Japan: The Legal Order in a Changing Society.* Cambridge, Mass.: Harvard University Press, 1963, pp. 41-72.

Keys to Success in Japan's Industrial Goods Market. Tokyo: Japan External Trade Organization, 1981.

Keys to Success in the Japanese Market. Tokyo: Japan External Trade Organization, 1980.

Kojima, A. "Avoiding a U.S.-Japanese Collision." In D. Tasca, ed., *U.S.-Japanese Economic Relations.* New York: Pergamon Press, 1980.

Koten, J. "How Toyota Stands to Gain from the GM Deal." *Wall Street Journal,* 16 February 1983, p. 28.

Krause, L.B., and Sekiguichi, S. "Japan and the World Economy." In H.

Patrick and H. Rosovsky, eds., *Asia's New Giant.* Washington, D.C.: Brookings Institution, 1976, pp. 385-458.

Lehner, U.C. "U.S. Lawyers Allege Tokyo Barriers." *Wall Street Journal,* 20 April 1982, p. 35.

———. "The Japanese Market, Once Hostile to U.S., Is Opening to Imports." *Wall Street Journal,* 12 May 1982, p. 1.

———. " 'Crying Wolf' on the Japanese Economy Is a Prelude to Ruling-Party Elections." *Wall Street Journal,* 15 September 1982, p. 34.

———. "How Japan Tries to Shut Out Foreign Goods." *Wall Street Journal,* 30 September 1982, p. 30.

———. "U.S.-Japan Talks Covering Trade Face Difficulties." *Wall Street Journal,* 3 December 1982, p. 36.

———. "U.S. News Is Big News in Japan, but the Angle Always Seems the Same." *Wall Street Journal,* 9 December 1982, p. 1.

———. "Nakasone Seeks to Increase Ties of Japan to West." *Wall Street Journal,* 7 January 1983, p. 20.

———. "Japan to Share Technology on Arms with U.S." *Wall Street Journal,* 17 January 1983, p. 26.

———. "U.S. Battle to Sell Baseball Bats in Japan Illustrates Difficulty of Opening Market." *Wall Street Journal,* 19 January 1983, p. 34.

———. "Brock Faces Tough Sledding in Japan." *Wall Street Journal,* 8 February 1983, p. 37.

———. "U.S. Firms' Market Penetration in Japan Is Much Deeper Than Thought, Study Says." *Wall Street Journal,* 16 February 1983, p. 35.

———. "Japan Standards for Its Imports Will Be Relaxed." *Wall Street Journal,* 25 March 1983, p. 26.

———. "Reluctance to Sue Attributed to Japanese Is Part Myth, Partly Due to Legal System." *Wall Street Journal,* 14 April 1983, p. 32.

———. "Is Nakasone Too Hawkish? June 26 Vote Offers Chance for Japanese to Speak Out." *Wall Street Journal,* 23 June 1983, p. 24.

Lehner, U.C., and Kanabayashi, M. "Japan Working on Another Pact to Open Market." *Wall Street Journal,* 12 January 1983, p. 33.

Levine, S.B. "Labor in Japan." In B.M. Richardson and T. Ueda, eds., *Business and Society in Japan.* New York: Praeger, 1981.

Lincoln, E.J. "A Review of U.S.-Japan Economic Relations." *Pacific Basin Economic Review.* Washington, D.C.: Wharton Econometric Forecasting Associates, Fall 1982, pp. 28-33.

"The Man from MITI Speaks His Mind." *Fortune,* 4 October 1982, pp. 91-96.

Marcom, J., Jr. "Reporter's Notebook: Japanese Coup; U.S. Waiters; $85-a-Night Student Digs." *Wall Street Journal,* 8 March 1983, p. 40.

"Matsushita Electric to Make Computers Developed by IBM." *Wall Street Journal,* 16 March 1983, p. 8.

Merck & Co., Inc. *Annual Report,* 1981.

Musashi, M. *The Book of Five Rings.* Trans. and commentary by Nihon Services Corporation. New York: Bantam Books, 1982.

Naitoh, M. "American and Japanese Industrial Structures: A Sectoral Comparison." In D. Tasca, ed., *U.S.-Japanese Economic Relations.* New York: Pergamon Press, 1980, pp. 61-75.

Nakane, C. *Japanese Society.* Berkeley: University of California Press, 1970.

"New Super Computer Units from Nippon Univac Firm." *Asahi Evening News,* 15 July 1982, p. 4.

Nierenberg, G.I. *Fundamentals of Negotiating.* New York: Hawthorne Press, 1973.

Nippon: The Land and Its People. Tokyo: Nippon Steel Corporation, 1982.

Nippon Univac Kaisha, Ltd. *Report to Shareholders,* 1 April 1981-31 March 1982.

Nukazawa, K. "The U.S.-Japanese Collision Course." In D. Tasca, ed., *U.S.-Japanese Economic Relations.* New York: Pergamon Press, 1980, pp. 39-57.

Ouchi, W.G. *Theory Z.* Reading, Mass.: Addison-Wesley, 1981.

Ozaki, R.S. *The Control of Imports and Foreign Capital in Japan.* New York: Praeger, 1972.

Pine, A. "Japan Nears a Choice of Easing Trade Curbs or Facing West's Ire." *Wall Street Journal,* 26 January 1982, p. 1.

Pine, A., and Lehner, U.C. "Protectionist Feelings against Japan Increase in the U.S. and Europe." *Wall Street Journal,* 14 January 1983, p. 1.

Planning for Distribution in Japan. Tokyo: Japan External Trade Organization, 1982.

Plimpton, J. "West Meets East in Japan." In *City Guide.* Tokyo: Airport Transport Service Company, Ltd., 1 July 1982, pp. 3-6.

Pollack, A. "The Far-Flung Wars of Mighty IBM." *The New York Times,* 19 September 1982.

Productivity and Quality Control. Tokyo: Japan External Trade Organization, 1981.

Rapp, W.V. "Japan's Industrial Policy." In I. Frank, ed., *The Japanese Economy in International Perspective.* Baltimore, Md.: Johns Hopkins University Press, 1975, pp. 37-66.

Ratcliffe, C.T. "Approaches to Distribution in Japan." In I. Frank, ed., *The Japanese Economy in International Perspective.* Baltimore, Md.: Johns Hopkins University Press, 1975.

Richardson, B.M., and Ueda, T., eds. *Business and Society in Japan.* New York: Praeger, 1981.

Roberts, J.G. *Mitsui: Three Centuries of Japanese Business.* New York: John Weatherhill, 1973.

Robinson, R.D. *International Business Management,* 2nd ed. Hinsdale, Ill.: Dryden Press, 1978.

Robock, S.H., and Simmonds, K. *International Business and Multinational Enterprises,* 3rd ed. Homewood, Ill.: Richard D. Irwin, 1983.

Role of Trading Companies in International Commerce. Tokyo: Japan External Trade Organization, 1982.

Sadler, A.L. *A Short History of Japan.* Sydney, Australia: Angus and Robertson, 1963.

Sales Promotion in the Japanese Market. Tokyo: Japan External Trade Organization, 1981.

Schoenberger, K. "Alien Law Draws Fire in Japan." *Philadelphia Inquirer,* 20 February 1983, p. 6-D.

Shaffer, R.C. "Japanese Now Target Communications Gear as a Growth Industry." *Wall Street Journal,* 13 January 1983, p. 1.

Seib, G.F. "Japan Resists U.S. Pleas for Quick Action on Trade but Pledges More Cooperation." *Wall Street Journal,* 19 January 1983, p. 3.

———. "Reagan Says U.S.-Japan Trade Disputes Are Easing as Talks with Nakasone End." *Wall Street Journal,* 20 January 1983, p. 3.

SmithKline Corporation. *Annual Report,* 1981.

Sperry Corporation. *Annual Report,* 1981.

Stevens, C. "Japanese Law and the Japanese Legal System." *Business Law* 27(July 1972):1259-1272.

Treece, J.B. "Last Year's Drop in Japan Exports Is First since 1952." *Wall Street Journal,* 20 January 1983, p. 29.

Tsurumi, Y. "Japanese Business Organizations." In B.M. Richardson and T. Ueda, eds., *Business and Society in Japan.* New York: Praeger, 1981, pp. 1-13. (a)

———. "Realities of the Japanese Consumer Imports Market." In B.M. Richardson and T. Ueda, eds., *Business and Society in Japan.* New York: Praeger, 1981, pp. 283-301. (b)

———. "Social Relations and Business Practices." In B.M. Richardson and T. Ueda, eds., *Business and Society in Japan.* New York: Praeger, 1981, pp. 305-322. (c)

Tung, R.L. "Selection and Training of Personnel for Overseas Assignments." *Columbia Journal of World Business,* Spring 1981, pp. 68-78.

———. *U.S.-China Trade Negotiations.* New York: Pergamon Press, 1982. (a)

———. "The Rise and Rise of the Japanese Automotive Industry?" *Proceedings of the Academy of International Business,* Honolulu, 1982, pp. 668-679. (b)

———. "Pacific Rim Countries: Problems and Prospects for the 1980s." Paper presented at the National Meetings of the Academy of International Business, Washington, D.C., 27-30 October 1982. (c)

_____ . "Selection and Training Procedures of U.S., European, and Japanese Multinationals." *California Management Review* 25, no. 1(Fall 1982):57-71. (d)

_____ . *The Key to Japan's Economic Strength: Human Power.* Lexington, Mass.: Lexington Books, D.C. Heath and Company, 1984.

Ulman, N., and Lehner, U.C. "Japan's Rearmament Is Too Slow for U.S., Too Scary for Others." *Wall Street Journal,* 22 November 1982, p. 1.

_____ . "Japan's Arms Industry Is Expanding Briskly, with Much U.S. Help." *Wall Street Journal,* 26 November 1982, p. 1.

Unique World of the Sogo Shosha. Tokyo: Marubeni Corporation, 1978.

Upham, F.K. "Litigation." In B.M. Richardson and T. Ueda, eds., *Business and Society in Japan.* New York: Praeger, 1981, pp. 149-155.

"U.S. and Japan Begin Talks on New Bid to Open Japanese Market to Imports." *Wall Street Journal,* 3 August 1982, p. 36.

"U.S. Gains Accords with Japan on Trade in High Technology." *Wall Street Journal,* 11 February 1983, p. 6.

"U.S. Is Disappointed with Japan's Increase in Defense Spending." *Wall Street Journal,* 31 December 1982, p. 9.

Van Zandt, H.F. "How to Negotiate in Japan?" *Harvard Business Review,* November-December 1970, pp. 45-56.

_____ . "Learning to Do Business with Japan Inc." *Harvard Business Review,* July-August 1972, pp. 83-92.

Wakamatsu, S. "Foreign Firms Vie for Local Talent in Japan." *Wall Street Journal,* 25 April 1983, p. 30.

Wallace, J. "The Festering Irritation with Japan." *U.S. News and World Report,* 23 August 1982, pp. 39-40.

White Paper on International Trade, Japan, Japan External Trade Organization, 1972-1981.

Williams, J.D. "Seven U.S., European, Japanese Firms Set to Sign Accord This Week for Jet Engine. *Wall Street Journal,* 9 March 1983, p. 6.

Yoshino, M.Y. "Japan as Host to the International Corporation." In I. Frank, ed., *The Japanese Economy in International Perspective.* Baltimore, Md.: Johns Hopkins University Press, 1975.

Appendix
Questionnaire Survey of United States-Japan Business-Negotiation Practices, Procedures, and Outcomes

1. Please indicate in space below the type of industry your company is engaged in (e.g., textiles, shipbuilding, etc.). _____

2. What are the 1980 assets of your company? Please check one of the following:
   ( ) Below $99 million.
   ( ) Between $100 and $499 million.
   ( ) Between $500 million and $1 billion.
   ( ) Over $1 billion.

3. Describe the nature of your present trade/contractual agreements with Japan. Please check one or more of the following:
   ( ) Joint-venture agreements of various types.
   ( ) Equity ownership *with* manufacturing facilities established within Japan.
        Write in percentage of equity owned by your company. _____%
   ( ) Equity ownership with *no* manufacturing facilities within Japan.
        Write in percentage of equity owned by your company. _____%
   ( ) Consortia.
   ( ) Import.
   ( ) Export.
   ( ) Franchising.
   ( ) Licensing (includes licensing for production processes, for use of a trade name, or for the distribution of imported products).
   ( ) Lease.
   ( ) Management contract (an arrangement whereby the management company manages all or some functions of another company's operations for a fee and/or a share of the profits).
   ( ) Provide technical assistance (includes contracts for engineering, architectural services, feasibility analysis, know-how, "show-how," and consulting generally).
   ( ) Turnkey (commitment to design and build a working plant).

( ) Turnkey-plus (commitment to design and build a working plant, *plus* train the operators from skilled workers to top management).

( ) Other (specify) _____

4. How important are trade/contractual agreements with Japan to the *overall profitability* of your company? Please indicate your response by circling one of the points on the following five-point scale:

Not important   Very important
  at all

```
  ├──────┼──────┼──────┼──────┤
  1      2      3      4      5
```

5. How many Japanese enterprises/partners is your company at present involved with for trade and other forms of economic cooperation? Please check one of the following:
( ) 1 Japanese partner/enterprise.
( ) 2 to 4 Japanese partners/enterprises.
( ) 5 to 7 Japanese parnters/enterprises.
( ) 8 to 10 Japanese partners/enterprises.
( ) More than 10 Japanese partners/enterprises.

6. Please indicate the number of times your company has entered into negotiations with the Japanese for trade/contractual agreements over the past ten years. Please check one of the following:
( ) 0 times.
( ) 1 to 3 times.
( ) 4 to 6 times.
( ) 7 to 9 times.
( ) 10 times.
( ) over 10 times.

7. What was the nature of these negotiations? Please check one of the following:
( ) Primarily for the establishment of joint ventures. These include the establishment of joint operations in a third country—i.e., a country other than the United States and Japan.
( ) Primarily for the establishment of manufacturing facilities in Japan.
( ) Primarily for the establishment of manufacturing facilities in the United States.
( ) Primarily exports *to* Japan.

( ) Primarily exports *from* Japan.
( ) Other (specify) _____

8. On average, how often were these negotiations conducted in Japan? Please check one of the following:
( ) Less than 20%.
( ) Between 20% and 39%.
( ) Between 40% and 59%.
( ) Between 60% and 79%.
( ) 80% or more.

9. On average, how often were these negotiations conducted in the United States? Please check one of the following:
( ) Less than 20%
( ) Between 20% and 39%.
( ) Between 40% and 59%.
( ) Between 60% and 79%.
( ) 80% or more.

10. Which side took the initiative in contacting the other party to establish trade/contractual agreements between the two parties? Please check one of the following:
( ) American side.
( ) Japanese side.
( ) Both sides.
( ) Other (specify) _____
( ) None of the above.

11. In establishing trade/contractual agreements with the Japanese, did your company deal with any of the following agencies? Please check one of the following:
( ) JETRO.
( ) MITI.
( ) Japanese government.
( ) Other (specify) _____
( ) None of the above.

12. If your company dealt with the aforementioned agencies, were any of these agencies active participants in the negotiations? Please identify.
( ) JETRO.
( ) MITI.
( ) Japanese government.
( ) Other (specify) _____

13. What were the criteria used by your company in selecting a Japanese enterprise/agency as a partner in trade/economic cooperation? Please check one or more of the following:
( ) Technological expertise.
( ) Access to Japanese market.
( ) Connections with Japanese government.
( ) Access to Southeast Asian market.
( ) Capital contribution.
( ) Other (specify) _____

14. On the whole, how would you characterize the quality of your past negotiations with the Japanese? Please indicate your response by circling one of the points on the following five-point scale:

Very dissatisfied   Very satisfied

1   2   3   4   5

15. If you were "dissatisfied" or "very dissatisfied" with the quality of your past negotiations with the Japanese, what were the major reasons/sources of discontent or dissatisfaction? Please check one or more of the following:
( ) Insincerity on the part of the Japanese negotiating team.
( ) Poor negotiating skills of the Japanese.
( ) Differences in negotiating styles between the two countries.
( ) Cultural differences.
( ) Delays in decision making.
( ) Lack of authority on the part of the Japanese negotiating team to make major decisions.
( ) Lack of control over *pace* of negotiation sessions.
( ) Lack of control over *content* of negotiation sessions.
( ) Inquiries not fully answered.
( ) Inquiries not promptly answered.
( ) Language barrier.
( ) Other (specify) _____

16. With respect to business negotiations with the Japanese, what are the areas in which you *hope* to see major improvements? Please check one or more of the following:
( ) Ability to make more rapid decisions.
( ) Greater trust between the two parties.
( ) More control over *content* of negotiation sessions.
( ) More control over *pace* of negotiation sessions.

( ) Improved communication between the parties.
( ) Inquiries answered more fully.
( ) Inquiries answered more promptly.
( ) Other (specify) _____

17. How would you characterize the decision-making styles of the Japanese negotiating team? Please check one or more of the following characteristics:
( ) None of the members in the Japanese negotiating team appears to have the authority to make the decision.
( ) There appears to be no single key decision maker. Every member in the team seems to have an equal say in the final decision.
( ) Slowness in arriving at decisions.
( ) Other (specify) _____

18. Overall, do you perceive any major differences between the negotiating styles of the Japanese and the negotiating styles of the Americans?
( ) Yes.
( ) No.

19. If "yes," how would you characterize such differences in negotiating styles? Please check one or more of the following:
( ) Time horizon of the negotiators. The Japanese negotiators seemed to be more concerned with establishing long-term associations.
( ) Flexibility versus rigidity. The Americans are more flexible.
( ) Speed. The Japanese take a longer time to make major decisions.
( ) Direct versus indirect. The Japanese like to avoid direct confrontation on issues.
( ) The Japanese place heavy emphasis on the concept of face-saving.
( ) Other (specify) _____

20. In the negotiations, what are the principal areas of conflict/differences between the two parties? Please check one or more of the following:
( ) Differences over percentage of equity ownership.
( ) Differences over extent of management control.
( ) Differences over contribution (e.g., technological know-how, machinery, etc.) by either party.
( ) Differences over remuneration policies for Japanese and U.S. personnel.

( ) Differences in opinion about the rights and responsibilities of management and those of labor.
( ) Other (specify) _____

21. In case of conflict, what methods have your company (or a company you know of) found useful in resolving the issues? Please check one or more of the following:
( ) Friendly discussion.
( ) Compromise.
( ) Open confrontation.
( ) Use of a third party.
( ) Arbitration.
( ) Other (specify) _____

22. Overall, how would you assess the importance of *each* of the following factors as they contribute to the *success* of the negotiations? For each of the factors, please circle one of the points on the five-point scale ranging from "1 = Not important at all" to "5 = Very important":

		Not Important at all				Very Important
(a)	Preparedness on the part of the U.S. team	1	2	3	4	5
(b)	Patience of the U.S. negotiating team	1	2	3	4	5
(c)	Sincerity, good faith, and honesty demonstrated by U.S. negotiators	1	2	3	4	5
(d)	Sincerity, good faith, and honesty demonstrated by Japanese negotiators	1	2	3	4	5
(e)	Uniqueness of product/service that U.S. firm could offer	1	2	3	4	5
(f)	Uniqueness of product/service that Japanese firm could offer	1	2	3	4	5
(g)	Personal relationships built up over a number of years	1	2	3	4	5
(h)	Familiarity with Japanese business practices	1	2	3	4	5
(i)	Familiarity with Japanese customs	1	2	3	4	5
(j)	Technical expertise provided by your company to the Japanese in the past	1	2	3	4	5
(k)	Other (specify) _____	1	2	3	4	5

23. Please evaluate the extent to which *each* of the following factors is responsible for the *failure* of business negotiations that you know of (this may not necessarily refer to your company). For each of the factors, please circle "0 = Not relevant" or one of the points on the five-point scale ranging from "1 = To a very little extent" to "5 = To a very great extent":

		Not Relevant	To a Very Little Extent				To a Very Great Extent
(a)	Lack of sincerity on the part of the Japanese	0	1	2	3	4	5
(b)	Communication breakdown	0	1	2	3	4	5
(c)	Insurmountable cultural differences	0	1	2	3	4	5
(d)	Differences in negotiating styles	0	1	2	3	4	5
(e)	Differences in business practices	0	1	2	3	4	5
(f)	Differences in social customs	0	1	2	3	4	5
(g)	Japanese did not need products/services offered by U.S. firm	0	1	2	3	4	5
(h)	There were too many competitors all offering the same products/services that U.S. company supply	0	1	2	3	4	5
(i)	Other (specify) _____	0	1	2	3	4	5

24. In preparing for business negotiations with the Japanese, did your company use any of the following techniques? Please check one or more of the following:
   ( ) Simulated negotiations in which members of one's own company are assigned to represent the other side in as vigorous a fashion as possible.
   ( ) Hire experts and/or consultants to train negotiators.
   ( ) Read books on Japanese business practices, social customs, etc.
   ( ) None of the above.
   ( ) Other (specify) _____

25. If your company used any of these formal preparatory procedures, how would you evaluate the importance of each of these procedures to

improving the quality of the negotiations? For *each* of the procedures/
techniques used, please circle one of the points on a five-point scale
ranging from "1 = Not important at all" to "5 = Very important":

	Not Important at all		Very Important		
(a) Simulated negotiations	1	2	3	4	5
(b) Experts and/or consultants	1	2	3	4	5
(c) Books on Japan	1	2	3	4	5
(d) Other (specify) _____					

26. If your company did not adopt any formal preparatory procedure,
what were the reasons for omitting such preparations? Please check one
or more of the following:
( ) Lack time.
( ) Lack resources.
( ) Previous experience in negotiating with the Japanese.
( ) Doubt effectiveness of such procedures.
( ) Consider these negotiations relatively unimportant to the
overall profitability of the company.
( ) Other (specify)_____

27. In going through your past experiences, please indicate the frequency
with which your company was able to obtain what you went in for; i.e.,
indicate the success rate of such negotiations. Please check one of the
following:
( ) 100% success rate.
( ) 80–99% success rate.
( ) 60–79% success rate.
( ) 40–59% success rate.
( ) 20–39% success rate.
( ) Less than 20% success rate.
( ) 0% success rate.

28. In doing business with the Japanese, did your company engage the ser-
vices of a third party or agent?
( ) Yes.
( ) No.

29. If "yes," who was the third party or agent? Please check one or more
of the following:

( ) An attorney.
( ) A consulting firm.
( ) An export-management company.
( ) A trading company.
( ) Other (specify) _____

30. Will your company *continue* to use the services of a third party or agent?
( ) Yes.
( ) No.

31. If your company plans to discontinue the services of a third party or agent, what are the reasons for so doing? Please check one or more of the following:
( ) Company plans to expand its trade relations with the Japanese.
( ) Lack of control over the third party or agent.
( ) Exorbitant rates/commission charged by the third party or agent.
( ) Dissatisfied with the services of the third party or agent.
( ) Other (specify) _____

32. In general, how many members (negotiators) were there on a Japanese negotiating team?
( ) Fewer than 2.
( ) Between 2 and 4.
( ) Between 5 and 7.
( ) More than 7. Write in number. _____

33. In general, how many members (negotiators) were there on your negotiation team?
( ) Fewer than 2.
( ) Between 2 and 4.
( ) Between 5 and 7.
( ) More than 7. Write in number. _____

34. Do you feel that you should have a larger negotiating team than you currently have? Please check one of the following:
( ) Yes, negotiating team should be larger.
( ) No, size of negotiating team should remain as it is.
( ) No, negotiating team should be smaller.

35. Briefly describe the composition of your negotiating team. Please check one or more of the following:

( ) Technical specialists. How many? (Write in number). _____
( ) Attorney.
( ) Owner/CEO of your organization.
( ) Accountant.
( ) U.S. industry representative.
( ) U.S. government representative.
( ) Other (specify) _____

36. Briefly describe the composition of the Japanese negotiating team. Please check one or more of the following:
( ) Technical specialists. How many? (Write in number). _____
( ) Attorney.
( ) Owner/CEO of the Japanese firm.
( ) Accountant.
( ) Japanese industry representative.
( ) Japanese government representative.
( ) Other (specify) _____

37. Was there any member in your negotiating team who was bilingual (i.e., had a working knowledge of both Japanese and English languages)?
( ) Yes.
( ) No.

38. If "yes," did he/she *actively* take part in the negotiations? Please check one of the following:
( ) Yes, made important decisions.
( ) Yes, but role was primarily that of an interpreter.
( ) No, did not actively take part in the negotiations.

39. If a member of your negotiating team had been bilingual, do you feel that his/her presence in the negotiation improved the *quality* of the negotiations?
( ) Yes.
( ) No.

40. If a member of your negotiating team had been bilingual, do you feel that his/her presence in the negotiation improved the *speed* of the negotiations?
( ) Yes.
( ) No.

41. If nobody in your negotiating team was bilingual, do you think the quality of the negotiations would have beem improved if your company brought along its own interpreter?
( ) Yes.
( ) No.

42. If "yes," do you intend to bring your own interpreter to future negotiation sessions?
( ) Yes.
( ) No.

43. Did the Japanese neogiating team furnish interpreters?
( ) Yes.
( ) No.

44. Were you satisfied with the translation services of the interpreters provided by the Japanese? Please indicate your response by circling one of the points on the following five-point scale:

Very dissatisfied   Very satisfied

```
├───┼───┼───┼───┤
1    2    3    4    5
```

45. If you were "dissatisfied" or "very dissatisfied" with the services of the interpreters provided by the Japanese, what were the major reasons/ sources of discontent or dissatisfaction? Please check one or more of the following:
( ) Lack of command of the English language.
( ) Unwillingness to present your points of view.
( ) Other (specify) _____

46. Would you or your company agree to let the present researcher do a more detailed study—a case study—of your business negotiations with the Japanese, which will be written up and published in a book. The name of the company could of course be disguised, depending on the company's preferences.
( ) Yes.
( ) No.

47. If "yes," please indicate in space below the name of the individual and the company the researcher should contact. Please include phone number.

Name: _____ Title: _____

Address: _____

_____

Telephone: _____

48. Please indicate date when it would be most appropriate to conduct this more detailed research:

_____

Name of firm (optional): _____

THANK YOU VERY MUCH FOR YOUR COOPERATION

Index

About the Author

Rosalie L. Tung received the Ph.D. from the University of British Columbia. She is an associate professor of management at The Wharton School, University of Pennsylvania. She was formerly on the faculty of the University of Oregon and has taught at the University of California, Los Angeles, and the University of Manchester (England) Institute of Science and Technology. She was invited as the first foreign expert to teach management at the Foreign Investment Commission (now known as the Ministry of Foreign Economic Relations and Trade), the highest agency under the Chinese State Council that approves all joint ventures and other major forms of foreign investment. She has been included in *The International Who's Who of Intellectuals, Who's Who in the Frontier of Science and Technology, The World's Who's Who of Women, Who's Who of American Women,* and elsewhere for outstanding contributions in her field.

Dr. Tung is the author of four other books: *Management Practices in China,* in China-International Business Series (1980); *U.S.-China Trade Negotiations* (1982); *Chinese Industrial Society after Mao* (Lexington Books, 1982); and *Key to Japan's Economic Strength: Human Power* (Lexington Books, 1984). She has also published widely on the subjects of international management and organizational theory in leading journals such as the *Columbia Journal of World Business, Journal of International Business Studies, California Management Review, Academy of Management Journal, Academy of Management Review, Journal of Vocational Behavior, Journal of Applied Psychology, Pacific Basin Economic Review, The Business Graduate*, and *Multilingua.*

Dr. Tung is a reviewer of peer proposals for the National Science Foundation and the U.S. Department of Education. She is a member of the Academy of International Business, Academy of Management, American Management Association, American Economic Association, American Psychological Association, and International Association of Applied Psychology.